Islamic Fundamentalism since 1945

Featuring a brand new examination of Islamic fundamentalism in the wake of the Arab Spring, this fully revised and updated second edition of *Islamic Fundamentalism since 1945* analyses the roots and emergence of Islamic movements in the modern world and the main thinkers that inspired them. Providing a much-needed historical overview of a fast-changing socio-political landscape, the main facets of Islamic fundamentalism are put in a global context, with a thematic debate of issues such as:

- the effects of colonialism on Islam
- secularism and the Islamic reaction
- Islam and violence in the 9/11 era
- globalisation and transnational Islamist movements
- Islam in the wake of the Arab Awakening.

Islamic Fundamentalism since 1945 provides an authoritative account of the causes and diversity of Islamic fundamentalism, a modern phenomenon which has grabbed the headlines as a grave threat to the West and a potentially revolutionary trend in the Middle East. It is a valuable resource for students and those interested in the history, effects and consequences of these Islamic movements.

Beverley Milton-Edwards is a Professor in the School of Politics, International Studies and Philosophy at Queen's University, Belfast. She is the author of *Contemporary Politics in the Middle East* (2011), *The Israeli–Palestinian Conflict* (Routledge, 2008) and with Peter Hinchcliffe, *Conflicts in the Middle East since 1945* (Routledge, 2007).

The Making of the Contemporary World
Edited by Eric J. Evans and Ruth Henig

The Making of the Contemporary World series provides challenging interpretations of contemporary issues and debates within strongly defined historical frameworks. The range of the series is global, with each volume drawing together material from a range of disciplines – including economics, politics and sociology. The books in this series present compact, indispensable introductions for students studying the modern world.

Islamic Fundamentalism since 1945

Second edition

Beverley Milton-Edwards

LONDON AND NEW YORK

First published 2014
by Routledge
2 Park Square, Milton Park, Abingdon, Oxon OX14 4RN

Simultaneously published in the USA and Canada
by Routledge
711 Third Avenue, New York, NY 10017

Routledge is an imprint of the Taylor & Francis Group, an informa business

First edition published by Routledge 2005

British Library Cataloguing in Publication Data
A catalogue record for this book is available from the British Library

Library of Congress Cataloging in Publication Data
Milton-Edwards, Beverley.
Islamic fundamentalism since 1945 / Beverley Milton-Edwards. – 2nd ed.
p. cm. – (The making of the contemporary world)
Includes bibliographical references.
1. Islamic fundamentalism. 2. Religious awakening–Islam.
3. Violence–Religious aspects–Islam. 4. Islam–21st century. I. Title.
BP166.14.F85M55 2013
297.09'045–dc23
2013004089

ISBN: 978-0-415-63988-0 (hbk)
ISBN: 978-0-415-63989-7 (pbk)
ISBN: 978-0-203-79848-5 (ebk)

MIX
Paper from
responsible sources
FSC
www.fsc.org   FSC® C013056

Printed and bound in Great Britain by
TJ International Ltd, Padstow, Cornwall

Contents

Acknowledgements

The first edition of *Islamic Fundamentalism since 1945* was published in 2005 and in it I developed a series of ideas about Islamic fundamentalism as a contemporary historical phenomenon. This second revised, updated and expanded edition of the book is a response to the ways in which Islamic fundamentalism in, particularly, its political dimensions has changed and been challenged since that time. Many people, in the past and present, have helped me with this book. The book would not have been possible without their support, feedback and advice. I would like to express my gratitude to my editors Laura Mothersole and Emma Hudson for their exceptional patience and input into the book. Dialogue with a number of people, including Amlendu Misra, Richard English, Mark Perry, Bobby Muller, Shlomo Avineri, Dominic Bryan, Alastair Crooke, Clive Jones, Steve Farrell, Reem Makhoul, Nuha Musleh and Katy Radford, played a part in influencing, for better or worse, how this book was written and then prepared for its second edition. I would also like to express special appreciation to my students in Queen's University Belfast, including the past assistance of Christian Nilsson for his research assistance, but not excluding my Ph.D. students, MA and undergraduate students undertaking modules in Islamic Politics, Violence, Terrorism and Security, as well as Middle Eastern Politics and the Politics of Deeply Divided Societies, who through their developing passion and interest are an inspiration. My final appreciation and deepest thanks go to those in my life who demonstrate constant love and support, including the awesome Cara Lily Mary Serenity Milton-Edwards and Joshua Norman Milton-Edwards, Johnny, Lynne and Nick, Trudy and Paul and Mark.

While every effort has been made to trace and acknowledge ownership of copyright material used in this volume, the publishers will be glad to make suitable arrangements with any copyright holders whom it has not been possible to contact.

The views expressed in this book are those of the author and do not represent the views of any institution or other individual.

Beverley Milton-Edwards
Belfast, February 2013.

Chronology

570	Mohammed is born in Mecca. He comes from a merchant family.
610	According to Muslim belief, at the age of 40, Mohammed is visited by the angel Gabriel where the first revelations of the Qur'an are given.
622	Mohammed and his followers migrate from Mecca to Medina – known as the *hijra*. In Medina the Prophet establishes a city-state and constitution.
630	Mohammed and his followers return to Mecca.
633	Mohammed dies and his Muslim followers elect his father-in-law and close associate, Abu Bakr, as Caliph, or successor.
661	Imam Ali is killed, bringing to an end the rule of the four 'righteous caliphs': Abu Bakr, Omar, Othman, and Ali. This also marks the beginning of the Umayyad rule. This is the root of the schism between *Sunni* and *Shi'a* in Islam.
1919	Afghanistan achieves independence from Britain.
1922	Caliphate is abolished.
1928	Muslim Brotherhood founded in Egypt by Hassan al-Banna.
1941	Lebanese independence proclaimed. Muwlana Mawdudi and others found Jama'at al-Islami Party in Lahore.
1944	Full independence achieved in Lebanon.
1945	End of Second World War. (August) Indonesia, most populous country in the Muslim world, gains independence.
1947	(August) Pakistan gains independence.
1948	(May) The State of Israel is established; Palestinian refugees flee their homes; the first Arab–Israeli war.

1951	(July) King Abdullah of Jordan assassinated in Jerusalem at the al-Aqsa mosque.
1952	Free Officers stage a coup in Egypt.
1953	(November) King Abdul Aziz of Saudi Arabia dies. He is succeeded by his son Saud.
1957	(August) Malaysia gains independence.
1958	(July) Monarchy in Iraq deposed, following a coup.
1962	(July) Algeria gains independence.
1964	Prince Faisal replaces Saud as King of Saudi Arabia.
1966	(August) Egyptian fundamentalist Sayyid Qutb executed.
1967	(June) Israeli victory in the Six Day War. Israel annexes East Jerusalem, including the Haram al-Sharif (third most holy site in Islam). Administration of the religious site remains in the hands of the Jordanian waqf (religious endowment) authorities.
1969	(September) Mu'ammar Gaddafi takes power in Libya. (October) Organisation of the Islamic Conference (OIC) founded at first summit of Islamic leaders representing 24 states, held in Rabat, Morocco.
1970	(September) President Nasser of Egypt dies and Anwar Sadat succeeds him.
1971	(April) Bangladesh achieves independence following secession from Pakistan. (August) Bahrain achieves independence from Great Britain. Qatar also becomes independent.
1973	(October) Ramadan War brings Arab Muslim states into war against Israel.
1975	(March) King Faisal of Saudi Arabia is murdered. Khalid succeeds him but his half-brother Prince Fahd maintains the reins of power. (April) Civil war breaks out in Lebanon.
1979	(January) Revolution in Iran. (September) Muwlana Mawdudi dies. (November) Uprising in Mecca, Saudi Arabia. (December) Soviet troops invade Afghanistan.
1980	(September) Outbreak of the Iran–Iraq War.
1981	(October) President Sadat of Egypt assassinated by Islamic fundamentalists.
1982	(June) Israeli forces invade and occupy Lebanon. (June) King Khalid of Saudi Arabia dies. He is succeeded by Fahd.

1983   (October) Car bomb attack on American forces in
            Lebanon carried out by radical Islamists, 241 US Marines
            are killed.
1984   Sultanate of Brunei achieves full independence from
            Great Britain.
1987   (December) Palestinian Uprising 'Intifada' breaks out
            against Israel's occupation of the West Bank, the Gaza
            Strip and East Jerusalem.
1988   (January) Palestinian Islamic movement Hamas is
            founded. Iran–Iraq War comes to an end.
            (August) President Zia-ul-Haq of Pakistan dies and is
            succeeded by Pakistan's first female prime minister
            Benazir Bhutto.
1989   (February) Front Islamique du Salut (FIS) (Islamic
            Salvation Front Party) founded in Algeria.
            (February) Soviet troops withdraw from Afghanistan.
            (June) The National Islamic Front (NIF) stages a military
            coup and takes control of the Sudan. Islamic governance
            established in Sudan, headed by Hassan al-Turabi.
            (June) Ayatollah Khomeini of the Islamic Republic of
            Iran dies.
            (October) Saudi-brokered Taif accord brings an end to
            civil conflict in Lebanon.
1990   (August) Iraq invades Kuwait.
1991   (March) Shi'ite uprising in Iraq.
            (August) Former Soviet Muslim states of Azerbaijan,
            Uzbekistan, and Kyrgyz Republic declare independence.
            (September) Tajikistan achieves independence.
            (October) Dzhokhar Dudayev elected president of
            newly independent state of Chechnya. Russian president
            Boris Yeltsin refuses to recognise independence and sends
            Russian troops. Turkmenistan declares independence.
            (December) Kazakhstan declares independence.
1992   (January) Elections in Algeria cancelled after first round
            deliver victory for Islamist Party FIS.
1993   (February) Attack on the World Trade Center, New York.
            Oslo Accords signed between Israel and the Palestinians.
            Sudan placed on US State Department list of state-
            sponsored terrorism.
1994   (November) Afghanistan starts to fall to the Taliban.
            Saudi government revokes citizenship of Osama Bin
            Laden.

1995	(August) Osama Bin Laden calls for American troops to be ousted from Saudi Arabia. Russian troops occupy Chechen capital of Grozny.
1996	(February) Palestinian Islamists embark on wave of suicide attacks on Israel.
	(May) Osama Bin Laden leaves Sudan for Afghanistan.
	(June) Islamist bomb attack in Saudi Arabia destroys the US military residence in Dhahran called Khobar Towers, killing 19 service personnel.
	(August) Ladenese Epistle issued by Osama Bin Laden outlining demands of his movement.
1997	(May) Pakistan joins Saudi Arabia and the United Arab Emirates in recognising the rule of the Taliban regime in Afghanistan.
1998	(February) Osama Bin Laden issues a joint declaration with the Islamic Group, Al Jihad, the Jihad Movement in Bangladesh and the Jamaat ul Ulema e Pakistan under the banner of the World Islamic Front, stating that Muslims should kill Americans – including civilians – anywhere in the world. US bombing of Sudan and Afghanistan.
	(August) Al-Qaeda bomb attacks on US Embassies in Kenya and Tanzania.
1999	(February) King Hussein of Jordan dies, succeeded by his son Abdullah.
	(March) Sheikh Isa bin Salman al-Khalifa, Emir of Bahrain, dies and is succeeded by his son, Sheikh Hamad bin Isa al-Khalifa.
	(July) King Hassan II of Morocco dies, succeeded by his son Sidi Mohammed.
2000	(June) Hafez al-Assad, president of Syria, dies and is succeeded by his son Bashar.
	(September) Outbreak of the second Palestinian uprising.
	(October) Bomb attack on *USS Cole* anchored off the coast of Yemen.
	(December) New constitution approved in Bahrain with provision for partially elected legislature and maintenance of constitutional monarchy.
2001	(September) Al-Qaeda attack on the United States of America.
	(October) Allied forces launch air strikes on Afghanistan.
	(November) Kabul and the Taliban fall in Afghanistan.

	(December) Interim administration led by Hamid Karzai formed in Afghanistan.
2002	(October) Islamic terror attack in Bali.
2003	(March) Allied forces invade and occupy Iraq.
	(April) Saddam Hussein is toppled from power.
	(November) Islamic terror attacks in Turkey.
2004	(January) The spiritual leader of Egypt's Muslim Brotherhood, Maamoun al-Hodeiby, dies and is replaced by Mohammed Mahdi Akef.
	(March) Islamic terror attack on Spanish capital, Madrid. Hamas spiritual leader and founder Sheikh Ahmed Yassin assassinated by Israel.
	(April) Hamas leader Dr Abdel Aziz al-Rantissi assassinated by Israel.
	(June) Al-Qaeda attacks in Saudi Arabia leading to kidnaps, attacks on housing compounds and the beheading of a US contractor. In Iraq, Islamist insurgents continue their attacks.
2005	(July) London series of suicide bomb attacks on public transport, fifty-six people and four bombers killed in the incidents.
	(September) Danish newspaper cartoon controversy. *Jyllands-Posten* publishes cartoons depicting the Prophet Mohammed with a bomb for his turban-like headdress. Wave of protests grows and is prolonged for a number of years against such publication.
2006	(January) Hamas win majority in Palestinian legislative elections against secular rivals in the PLO's Fatah faction.
	(August) British foil al-Qaeda planned attacks to take liquid bombs on aeroplanes.
2007	(June) Hamas assume complete control of the Gaza Strip after Fatah ousted in takeover.
	(August) Osama Bin Laden releases first video for three years and makes threats of attacks.
2008	(June) Al-Qaeda car bomb attack against the Danish Embassy in Pakistan in protest over cartoons controversy.
2009	(December 25) A man who admitted to being an al-Qaeda supporter tries to blow up a Northwest Airlines plane as it prepares to land in Detroit.
2010	Egyptian Muslim Brotherhood leader Mohammed Mahdi Akef replaced by Mohammed Badie.

(June) Al-Qaeda's number three, Sheikh Sa'id al-Yazid, is believed killed by a US Predator drone strike.

(December) Popular protest breaks out in Tunisia following the self-immolation of a vegetable vendor.

2011 (January) Tunisians oust President Zine el-Abidine Ben Ali in Jasmine Revolution. Protests in Jordan, Lebanon, Oman, Yemen, Morocco, Algeria, Egypt and Syria.

(February) President Hosni Mubarak ousted from power as Arab Spring protests break out in Egypt and elsewhere across the Arab world.

(March) Uprisings break out in Bahrain involving nascent Islamist elements.

(May) Osama bin Laden, head of al-Qaeda, is killed when CIA paramilitaries and a US Navy SEAL team attack his hideout in Abbottabad, Pakistan.

(October) President Mu'ammar Gaddafi of Libya injured in NATO airstrike and subsequently killed.

(October) Tunisians head to the polls and Islamist party Ennahda wins.

(November) Egyptians participate in free parliamentary elections. Islamist salafi and Muslim Brotherhood candidates win a majority of seats.

2012 (February) Ali Abdullah Saleh officially resigns, and then transfers his powers to his vice president, Abd Rabbuh Mansur Al-Hadi.

(June) Muslim Brotherhood candidate Mohammed Morsi declared winner in Egypt's first freely conducted presidential elections.

(September) Thousands of Muslims from across the globe protest at a film with alleged anti-Islamic sentiments.

(December) Egyptians support a new Constitution.

2013 (January) Al-Qaeda Islamic Maghreb (AQIM) offshoot cell led by Mokhtar Belmokhtar attack an Algerian gas production plant, kidnapping and killing Algerian and foreign workers.

(January) Elections in the Hashemite Kingdom of Jordan are boycotted by the Muslim Brotherhood's Islamic Action Front.

Introduction

In June 2012 Islamists around the globe heralded Muslim Brotherhood candidate Mohammed Morsi's election as Egypt's first freely chosen president as a triumph for their cause. This historic event was widely perceived as having far-reaching consequences for the fate of Islamic fundamentalism in its contemporary guise. The election victory emphasised once again that in the first two decades of the twenty-first century the phenomenon of Islamic fundamentalism remains one of the most significant issues in global politics, discourse and international relations. Contemporary accounts of the phenomenon, however, often overlook and pay little attention to the political history of Islamic fundamentalism. Such accounts are concerned with the 'here and now' threat that Islamic fundamentalists are understood as posing to particular conceptions of political and economic order. There is a concern to equip policy-makers with the ways and means to combat Islamic fundamentalists and their supporters. Much analysis simply contends that to look at the historical contexts in which this phenomenon is manifest is a diversion and irrelevance in terms of determining a response to the terrorism that the Islamic fundamentalists have wrought against modern Western societies. Yet contemporary history is important to an understanding of this very modern phenomenon. It is important because it alerts us to the changes and upheavals apparent in so many of the societies that Muslims inhabit, and it should alert us to the powerful myths that leaders construct around these experiences as a way of mobilising for change; to break with the past and take control of the future. This book sets out to address this debate by examining a number of issues that account for and explain the present-day phenomenon of Islamic fundamentalism.

Rather than being geographically specific and focusing on the regional heartland of Islam – the Middle East – the focus of this book is the whole of the Muslim world, or rather those countries where the majority of the population are Muslim. Suffice to say that since the Second World War citizens in the majority of these countries have been subject to a range of forces: foreign rule and occupation, movements for independence, rising nationalism and secularism, growing Islamist movements, reform, revolution, post-revolution repression and revolt.

The analytical perspective guiding the study centres on Islam as a political experience. This is not to say that the religious/spiritual dimension of Islam is ignored but instead it is to say that in this book I will concentrate on the political manifestation of Islam in the late twentieth and early twenty-first centuries. Moreover, Islam for the purposes of this book is defined as a fundamentalist phenomenon. Although this implies a singular unitary entity, as the historical account that unfolds in these pages reveals, the reality is rich in diversity, context and response. This definition also emphasises the exogenous development of Islam as fundamentalist doctrinal debate and discourse.[1] It should also be acknowledged that this embrace of fundamentalism as reflected in Muslim movements, and from Muslim thinkers and activists, is modern but draws on historical interpretation of Islam's past.[2] Suffice to say, then, the term Islamic fundamentalism is employed in this book as a form of generalisation to encompass a variety of impulses, movements, ideas, thinkers and groups. What such elements have in common, as distinct from other forms of Islamic fundamentalism, is the political prism of analysis. In one respect, the term is employed this way because there is in fact little agreement of what fundamentalism strictly constitutes. Scholars can agree to nothing more than the assertion that the term refers to 'family resemblances' between a variety of monotheistic faiths and includes characteristics such as: religious idealism, cosmic struggle, demonising the opponent, reactionary thinking, and envy of modernist hegemony and the revolutionary overthrow of power.[3] Moreover, it is important to note that in the context of this book it is acknowledged that Islamic fundamentalism is not gender-neutral but is largely represented as a specifically male business. Fundamentalism is also interchangeable with the term Islamism – this underlines the political emphasis that is attached to expressions of Muslim religiosity in specific contexts.[4]

A route to fundamentalism

The explanatory framework of this book, therefore, centres on a deeply contested concept as a tool of analysis. For fundamentalism in relation to Islam is subject to debate and controversy, in particular because of the way in which Islam has been objectified as fundamentalist by the West.[5] Fundamentalism is understood as something that relates to the nucleus of modern faith systems. Fundamentalism is understood as exclusive to religion. It is signified in relation to faith and the process of signification is powerfully negative rather than positive.[6] In relation to Islam, it is important to recognise that the term fundamentalism (*usil-iyyah*) is not self-descriptive but has been applied by others in their attempts to describe and understand contemporary Islamic history and politics.[7]

Islamic fundamentalists include state and non-state actors, historic societies and associations, factions, vanguards, thinkers, philosophers, authors, clerics, individuals across the globe. Islamic fundamentalists are not ethnically or geographically homogeneous – although there are some who would try and ascribe particular primordial ethnic markers to Muslims in this way. Those who are labelled as *Sunni* and *Shi'a* as well as its minor sects and schismatic tendencies are often accused of fermenting political disorder, revolution and violence. The reference point of Islam through fundamentalism consists of a never-ending catalogue of instability in the political sphere. Fundamentalism is defined as indicating a certain 'intellectual stance that claims to derive political principles from a timeless divine text ... three separate movements are identified ... revivalism, reformism and radicalism'.[8]

Fundamentalism was identified as a key characteristic of late twentieth-century religious revivalism across the globe. Islamic fundamentalism was recognised alongside the manifestation of Hindu, Christian, and Jewish variations. In principle, fundamentalism, therefore, is equated with a rejection of modernity and its secular variant in both democratic and non-democratic societies. In reality, however, fundamentalism has been recognised as a central, if not the defining, feature of historic and contemporary Islamism. Moreover, as the Cold War ended and communism was perceived as vanquished by the forces of modern democratic capitalism, writers grew concerned that a new enemy had appeared on the horizon. That enemy took the guise of Islamic fundamentalism: 'a spectre is haunting Europe – and the world in general: the spectre of Islamic fundamentalism. All the world powers have entered into a holy alliance to exorcise this spectre'.[9]

In the West, Islamic fundamentalism has often been used as the primary analytical tool for the study of contemporary Islam and politics. Fundamentalism is the primary reference point of Islam in the majority of works of academics, journalists, and other writers who seek to relate, describe and analyse manifestations of Islam from Beirut to Birmingham, Lahore to London, Dacca to Detroit. This visioning of Islam draws on a deep historic antipathy that grew between Islam and the West in the Middle Ages in the Crusades. Islam's victory over the Crusaders was written into Western history as an episode that should never be forgotten or allowed to be repeated. Some dimensions of Islamic fundamentalist discourse have also represented contemporary relations with the West as a neo-crusader alliance. It also emphasises the extent to which it is no longer possible or realistic to present Islamism as relatively benign or misunderstood. With respect to Islam and the West, there is an element of the past and present colliding in the formation of opposing positions founded on mutual fear and distrust, 'this centuries-old military interaction between the West and Islam is unlikely to decline', contended one author, 'it could become more violent'.[10] In the case of Islam, literatures and accounts emerged providing a narrow conception of Muslim identity and politics in the twentieth and early twenty-first century. This identity was portrayed as constricted, anti-modern, anti-secular, anti-democratic, anti-globalisation, anti-Semitic, anti-emancipation, anti-feminist, anti-plural, and consisting of followers enthralled by the promise of revolution that would put Islam in charge of the state again. This desire for power, independence and control has meant that post-1945 Islamic fundamentalism has frequently been conceptualised as on a crash course with secularism. This conceptualisation has failed to understand that Islamism and Islamic fundamentalism are very much a modern phenomenon, 'no cliché is more stupefying than that which describes al-Qaeda as a throwback to medieval times', and the insistence that Islamism is anti-modern fails to grasp the primary motive for Muslim political action in the contemporary age.[11] From the perspective of the secularists, Islamists make false claims on modernity. Islamists are also accused of 'cherry-picking' at the modernity project – using science and technology but not the values that appear to go with them – in order to achieve their political goal of new state forms based on a throwback to the past. The religious and more specifically Christian values inherent to Western secularist discourse are ignored in the construction of a case against Islam and its fundamentalist majority. As one author avers:

> The underlying assumption has always been that Islam – as a culture and not only a religious creed – was primitive, underdeveloped, retrograde, at best stuck in the memory hole of a medieval splendour out of which it could not disentangle itself without a radical transformation; and this could only be based on Western, 'rational', 'progressive' values. Ex Occiendente lux.[12]

Ancient foe

Islam is not welcomed with open arms in the debates about modern society. Islamic fundamentalists have agitated against what they believe to be the deleterious effects not only of the activities of the West in their own countries whether as a legacy of colonialism, a by-product of superpower rivalry during the Cold War, or economic manoeuvring to secure energy resources in Muslim countries, but also of Western ideas and political thought on the absorption of the process of modernisation that has affected their nations. As one of the most prominent radical Islamist thinkers, Sayyid Qutb, has contended:

> a second step, or a second battle, began in the form of a final offensive which is actually taking place now in all the countries which used to be Islamic … It is an effort to exterminate this religion [Islam] as even a basic creed, and to replace it with secular organisations. These conceptions were expected to fill the vacuum of faith with faithless dogma.[13]

In short, Islamic fundamentalists have declared to their fellow Muslims and the rest of the world that they no longer wish to be held up in comparison to the West and be found wanting. Instead they propose that Muslims reassert control over their own political structures, institutions, ideas and political destiny. Their emancipation is posited through the prism of modern Islam.

Multitude of meanings

In this book I will demonstrate how Islamic fundamentalism is manifest in many ways. Islam has been involved in politics since 1945 in a variety of ways; some Islamic movements have been allowed a modicum of political power at a popular level, some have succeeded in controlling the state. Along the way many Islamists and their movements have failed, been repressed by the state or other forces on a trajectory that has, however, seen Islam weave itself back into the public domain.

First, the many dimensions of Islam as a faith experience are outlined for the reader by way of an introduction to the deep historical resonance that shapes Muslim experience in the late twentieth and early twenty-first centuries. From its roots in seventh-century Arabia to the present day it is contended that Islam has always been connected with politics. Through history many have claimed to rule in the name of Islam and employed its principles in the governance of subject peoples and the institutions of the state. Great empires, wars and people have rallied around the banner of Islam and advocated its principles in doctrines on law, government, politics, economy, culture and the arts. Over the centuries Muslim rule has found expression in monarchs, sultans, soldiers, mullahs, ayatollahs, men and women who have embraced principles of Islam in the service of their governance.

Chapter 1 goes some way in explaining this historical diversity. Moreover, this chapter highlights the disruption of the political socio-economic foundations of many Muslim societies wrought as a result of the imposition of foreign non-Muslim rule. In Indonesia, for example, which is the largest Muslim state in the world, the indigenous population was made subject to over 350 years of foreign European control over their resources and people. In Central Asia the Muslim populations of ancient cities and provinces such as Uzbekistan were subject to Soviet Communist control for more than 70 years. During this time all religious rights were denied to them. Their mosques and seminaries crumbled through neglect. In Africa, European rule over Muslim countries such as Egypt and Algeria resulted in the apparent total transformation of these societies for their Muslim inhabitants.

By the middle of the twentieth century Muslim leaders had come to the fore in movements for independence and the embrace of modernist thinking. A number of thinkers had emerged to challenge the traditional clerical elites and augment the burgeoning movements for independence that had sprung up across the globe. In this respect many Islamic fundamentalists were little different in their desires for reform, autonomy, independence and liberty than others elsewhere across the colonised world, who also recognised that the modern age offered the potential for greater individual rights. Where they did differ was in their desire for what would come after independence.

As we shall see, the desire of the fundamentalists to establish political regimes that not only ruled in the name of Islam but were Islamic in terms of all aspects of governance, led to fissures and tensions throughout the 1950s and 1960s in countries as varied as Afghanistan and Egypt. The fundamentalists were driven to the margins of public life by zealous nationalist secularists who contended that modernisation left little room for them. Indeed, the presence of the Islamists was construed as inimical to the many dimensions of the modernisation process being pursued in Muslim countries. Islam, in its political form, was seen as a hindrance to the high modernity project imposed by new state elites on the popular masses. Islam appeared only to have its use as an empty symbol for newly independent nations. In many respects

Islam was made apolitical or only political in service of the state and the legitimation of particular rulers. Political autonomy was undermined.

By the late 1960s and 1970s, however, a sense of revivalism, prompted by a series of political, cultural and economic crises across the globe was apparent in many Muslim domains. Revivalism took place at many levels of Islam, including the political. Revivalism should, I contend, be viewed as an inherent feature in Islam as a dynamic rather than static phenomenon. In this way the revolution in Iran in 1979 should not be understood as a 'bolt out of the blue' but as part of the seamless history of renewal and revival of Islam in contest with, in the twentieth century, an unjust and repressive state. The key to analysing the fundamentalist phenomenon outlined in this book, then, lies in recognising a sense of historic depth and continuity in relation to politics. This is not the same, however, as asserting that fundamentalist movements are stuck in the past and only look to the past as a guide to the future.

Structure of the book

In respect of the arguments above, the book has been laid out to follow the ebbs and flows of political Islam. In Chapter 1, the important historical outline of Islam from its founding to the twentieth century is outlined. This should reinforce the working assumption that Islam has always maintained a political profile. In Chapter 2, I examine the advent of national independence and secular rule in a variety of Muslim countries and the impact of this on the place of Islam in the public sphere and the role of the Islamists in helping to shape political discourses in the modern age. Moreover, we discover a series of systematic state-enforced campaigns against Islam and Islamists leading to the virtual suppression of such movements in many areas. The repression of such movements left many Muslim countries subject to secular dictatorship and freedom and democracy were denied to the popular masses. In Chapter 3, I address the fallout of this campaign and the stirrings of revivalism and fundamentalist thinking in the late 1960s and early 1970s. In Chapter 4, the examination focuses on the extent to which the fundamentalist project assumed a militant character in its confrontation with the state. There is also a focus on the emergence of new challenges and issues altering and affecting dimensions and struggles for power in Muslim countries. This analysis is deepened in Chapter 5 when I appraise the emergence of new global political orders and their impact on Islamism. The changing structure of world order and the balance of power compelled Islamists to rethink the political project and their responses to it. This included a new focus on the West and the growing impression that American global strength would be translated as new cultural and imperial hegemony over Muslim countries. In Chapter 6 the devastating consequences of such assumptions are examined in the wake of the al-Qaeda attacks on America. I will in turn also focus on the tension apparent in what appears in the twenty-first century to be two mutually exclusive phenomena: Islam and secularism, and the struggle that currently ensues between the two. In the final chapter the Islamist dimension of the Arab Awakening will be examined. Though many of the protest groups and activist elements movements associated with the Arab Awakening appeared to be largely non-Islamist in nature, Islamic fundamentalist elements have not only been winning electoral power in the wake of newly ousted regimes and leaders, but have been able to rely on regional networks of support to reinvigorate their agendas. This has caused unease both within the Middle East and beyond its borders and it is coupled with the post Bin Laden contraction of al-Qaeda.

Islamic Fundamentalism since 1945 places the phenomenon of modern Islamism in context and discusses the power of Islam as a new global force in the twenty-first century. By looking at examples of Muslim countries, Muslim thinkers, movements, trends and organisations, the diversity of this phenomenon will be displayed. Finally, the issues generated by Islamic fundamentalism and the conflict with a global order dominated by Western secular thinking will be assessed. The challenge here is to increase our comprehension of the historical impulses and changing realities that shape and make the modern Islamist experience.

Notes

1 Y. Choueiri, *Islamic Fundamentalism: The Story of Islamist Movements*, London: Continuum, 2010.
2 J. Esposito, *The Future of Islam*, New York: Oxford University Press, 2010.
3 Y. Choueiri, *Islamic Fundamentalism: The Story of Islamist Movements*, London: Continuum, 2010.
4 F. Volpi (ed.) *Political Islam: A Critical Reader*, London: Routledge, 2011.
5 B. Tibi, *Islam's Predicament with Modernity, Religious Reform and Cultural Change*, London: Routledge, 2009.
6 E. Laclau, *Emancipation(s)*, London: Verso, 1996.
7 K. Armstrong, *The Battle for God: Fundamentalism in Judaism, Christianity and Islam*, London: HarperCollins, 2001.
8 Y. Choueiri, *Islamic Fundamentalism*, London: Pinter, 1990, p. 9.
9 S. Avineri, 'The return to Islam', in W. Spencer (ed.) *Global Studies: The Middle East*, Guildford, CT: Dushkin, 1993 (3rd edn), p. 167.

10 S. Huntington, 'The clash of civilizations?', *Foreign Affairs*, 72:3, 1993, p. 31.
11 J. Gray, *Al-Qaeda and What It Means To Be Modern*, London: Faber and Faber, 2003, p. 1.
12 S. Avineri, 'The return to Islam', p. 67.
13 S. Qutb, *Islam: The Religion of the Future*, Kuwait: IIFSO, 1971, p. 8.

1 A diverse tradition from past to present

> Appeals to the past are among the commonest of strategies in interpretations of the present.
>
> (Edward W. Said)

From the rich historical tradition of Islam, a spectre has ascended to trouble the world. That spirit is defined more specifically as Islamic fundamentalism. The *Concise Oxford Dictionary of Current English* describes *fundamentalism* as the 'strict maintenance of ancient or fundamental doctrines of any religion, especially Islam'. In the twenty-first century, Islam and fundamentalism are perceived by some as a significant if not the greatest threat to global security. Fundamentalism in its Islamic guise has led to the execution of hundreds in suicide bombing attacks across the world, including the attacks of 11 September 2001 when over 3,000 people perished in the al-Qaeda attacks ordered by Osama Bin Laden.

Fundamentalism is a major threat not just in terms of global security but as a manifestation of extreme attachment to faith and religious revivalism at a fanatical level. The militant dimensions of Islam are apparent in the anti-Western rhetoric of some Muslim preachers, the revolutionary fervour of Muslim protesters and the rigid ideology of many Islamist groups, movements and organisations. In media images, Islamic fundamentalists have rarely been portrayed as peacefully protesting or organising support for dialogue with the opposition or engaged in conflict resolution efforts. The bearded clerics, gun-wielding and masked supporters of Islam, the arms dealers and secret world of covert operations and international terrorism, all serve to strengthen the ideology of fundamentalist thinkers and clerics who advocate a totalitarian vision of Islamic governance.

There have been scholarly attempts to highlight Islam's diverse character in respect of this phenomenon, although it is barely possible to address the rich manifestation of Islam when the fear of the fundamentalist has been so powerfully played on the Western popular imagination. Even when fundamentalist activists speak of, or address, the commonalities between Islam and the West, they are drowned out by a hail of bullets or the explosion of the suicide bomb. It appears difficult to reconcile Islam's claim to peace when its leaders are accused of acquiring the technology of destruction. Jihad, not *Salam* (peace) is the word mostly commonly associated with Islam.

The spectre has undermined and encompasses the whole of Islam and today Islam is classified principally as fundamentalist. Talk of 'moderate or radical fundamentalism' is often dismissed as an exercise in apologetics. The pejorative and emotive use of the word, synonymous with terrorism, has largely been ignored as armies have been despatched to wage a war against the enemy. Fundamentalist Islam is easy to classify if the common motif of anti-Westernism or terrorism is perceived as the single thread that ties this group of believers together. Fundamentalism then becomes a formidable challenge and the political, social and economic context of politics ceases to matter when Muslims are portrayed as united in a hatred of the West and their own violent and anti-democratic traditions. The pursuit of power is seen as the primary motivation for Muslim political culture and its acquisition is expressed in a despotic, totalitarian form with no accommodation or plural vision. In the contemporary era Muslim fundamentalists are seen as the vanguard force of the faithful and the embodiment of the project to restore power to Muslim hands.

In this scenario Islam becomes the solution to the travails of modern society, under which so many millions of Muslims labour. The universal characteristics of Islam are promoted by many fundamentalist leaders as a blueprint for peace and tranquillity governed by Islamic law, Muslim rulers and a Muslim society. The separation of mosque and state is abhorred, along with the secularist ideologies promoted by the West. The ideal of Muslim governance transcends the geographic, economic, social and developmental barriers of the modern world and strikes a chord in the hearts of so many Muslim populations. Since 1945, Islamic fundamentalism has grown and demonstrated a dynamic and diverse capacity for renewal and relevancy. And although the terrorists may appear to signify this trend, the real explanation lies in the conditions under which the majority of Muslims live and the historic processes and legacies that account for the parlous state of so many Muslim countries in the present age.

It is contended that since 1945 the ideological clash epitomised by the Cold War between communist East and capitalist West has now been eclipsed by a new ideological war between the Islamic fundamentalists and the democratic West. The Islamic fundamentalists are, it appears, prepared to advocate revolution and jihad in their quest to take power from the hands of corrupt elites and tyrants they condemn as infidels controlled by *kufr* Western elements. Through revolution Islamists could control the state and enjoy the monopoly of power. In this way Islamic fundamentalism, as a modern ideology, appears to challenge and rival all ideological comers.

Our past, their present

Muslims currently constitute over one billion people worldwide and their faith system is the second largest in the world. Although the roots of Islam lie in the monotheistic traditions of Judaism and Christianity, acknowledgement of the theological commonality between these faiths is sometimes obscured by the manifestation of what appear to be greater differences. The rise and expansion of Islam were a formidable challenge to the prevailing Judaeo-Christian orders over many centuries and the apparent universal appeal within Islam allowed little room for accommodation of power cradled in the Christian realm. The battle appeared to be initially lost to Christianity from the seventh century onwards and throughout the medieval period. The Enlightenment (and the eclipse of faith as politics) led to the regeneration and flourishing of secular and industrialised European domains at the expense of many Muslim territories. By the late twentieth century it is contended by some that Muslims have resurrected a battle cry against the West and a struggle has ensued. This struggle has been epitomised by the veiled demonstrators of Tehran who shouted 'Death to America' in their thousands and the war of terror and terrorism that has unfolded between what appears at first glance to be a rigid faith system and its robotic followers and the defenders of the 'free world'. The origins and history of Islam, however, demonstrate a more subtle and varied picture.

The religion of Islam was founded by the Prophet Mohammed in the seventh century CE among the desert communities and tribes of Mecca and Medina in Arabia. Islam is a monotheistic faith founded on the acceptance of one god (*Allah*) and owes much to the earlier expressions of monotheism common in Judaism and Christianity. As the faith system took root, and then grew, its leaders and followers challenged the status quo of the rule of the Byzantine and Sassanid empires. Islam has always been described as a universal religion in the sense that Islam dominates all dimensions of the human existence. With respect to the political realm, Islam is labelled and understood as enjoying an intimate or symbiotic link to the political realm and the generation of a particular political culture.

This challenge took the form of both peaceful and contested conquest that led by the eighth century to the eclipse of Byzantine, Sassanid and other forms of rule in the Middle East, North Africa, Asia and Europe, including Spain and as far north as Tours in France. Through trade, military conquest, geographic proximity and the continual flux of global politics over the centuries, the expansion of Muslim rule continued into other areas of the globe. In the modern day, there are as many as 60 nations across the globe where Muslims comprise the majority of the population.

This process did not unfold in a uniform manner, and nor did the nature of Islamic or Muslim rule. In this respect, Muslim politics was always a diverse spectrum of expressions of rule, governance, economy, social orders and military norms. As the faith grew through inter-connected networks of religion, trade, politics and travel, Muslim polities reflected the synthesis of local or indigenous customs that in turn shaped Islam and made it relevant across large sections of the globe. Few unitary factors were identifiable. But the few unitary factors were important in giving the faith its unique character and pace. The five fundamental characteristics of Islam are commonly referred to as the pillars of the faith and they include the obligation incumbent upon Muslim believers to do the following:

- *Shahada*: To bear witness that there is none worthy of worship save Allah and that Muhammad is the Messenger of Allah;
- *Salat*: To observe prayer;
- *Zakat*: To give alms;
- *Hajj*: To perform the pilgrimage;
- *Sawm*: To observe fasting during the holy month of Ramadan.

There is some debate within and outside the Muslim community as to the extent to which jihad (striving) should be considered a sixth pillar of the faith. This discussion with respect to jihad is a modern one that has reflected the concern at the apparent attachment to jihad as a mechanism of faith protection and propagation in the late twentieth and early twenty-first centuries. Particular fundamentalist thinkers have claimed that jihad considered to be a defence of Islam is obligatory for all Muslims. This is not generally accepted and is seen in the context of modern conflicts and tensions. By and large, and over the centuries, Muslims in different areas of the world have created for themselves a wide array of cultural traditions that reflected their attachment to the faith of Islam and their own local or indigenous identities as well. In Islamic Spain, for example, Muslim society developed a rich tradition in arts and sciences that endures to the present-day in the architectural heritage of sites such as Granada. Throughout the medieval period, the work of Muslim scholars, poets, artists and scientists contributed to a great flourishing of state, arts, culture, science, medicine and trade throughout Muslim domains. Moreover, other societies, including those in Europe, unconsciously adopted the new customs and advances of Muslim society as their own. Through the generation of carefully calibrated relationships between trading Muslim and non-Muslim states, a variety of cultures and world-views were intertwined.

Deeply divided society

With such diversity, even from the earliest foundations of Islam, it should come as no surprise that within the Muslim fold there are various communities. Under the crescent of Islam there are major divisions, exemplified by that between the majority *Sunni* and minority *Shi'a*, as well as minor schisms or sects such as the Ismailis, Druze and Sufi Muslims. The major schism between *Sunni* and *Shi'a* Muslims derives from a succession dispute that arose after the death of the Prophet Mohammed in the seventh century. The dispute centred on the figure of Ali, who was the son-in-law of the Prophet Mohammed and whom *Shi'a* followers believe should have been the rightful successor (caliph) after the death of the Prophet. After the death of the Prophet Mohammed in 632 CE, tensions grew as Ali was sidelined in favour of other rulers including Abu Bakr, Umar and Uthman. Ali did become caliph after Uthman but his rule was opposed by Aisha, the second wife of the Prophet Mohammed. In an ensuing battle Aisha was defeated by Ali. Opposition remained in other quarters, and at the battle of Siffin Ali came up against an array of forces against him. The term *Shi'a* was applied to those who joined Ali in battle during this period of civil conflict in the house of Islam. Ali was assassinated in 661 CE by the Kharijites, who themselves were dissidents who contended that all Muslims should adhere to Islam in its purest form. They attacked those they considered to be promoting deviance from the primary sources and spirit of Islam. In this respect they can be classified as the original fundamentalists of the faith system. Orthodox elements from within Islam, however, see the Kharijites as dangerous heretics and they were historically ostracised. Ali's son Hussein was regarded as martyred in battle against *Sunni* forces in the battle of Karbala (in present-day Iraq) in 680 CE. Even today, the martyrdom of Hussein is commemorated by *Shi'a* through mourning ceremonies and rites. This, despite the many common tenets of faith, has marked relations between *Sunni* and *Shi'a* Islam and signifies the dangerous potential for civil dispute within the faith. *Shi'a* Muslims are found in Iran, Iraq, Pakistan, Lebanon and Bahrain. Along with the other minorities within Islam, they have experienced hostility from offcial *Sunni* sources and historical tension still lingers. *Shi'a* followers of Islam believe that leadership and political guidance from within Islam should remain within what is referred to as the House of the Prophet – the blood succession line of the Prophet's descendants. This bestowed a particular religious or spiritual status on the caliphate that divorced it from succession preferences as expressed within orthodox *Sunni* circles. The *Sunni* preference remained dominant and the caliphate endured as a means of governance until the end of the Ottoman Empire in 1918. A ruler was not required to be a spiritual leader or cleric of Islam but he was supposed to frame his rule according to the laws of Islam. This generated a form of authority and legitimacy for those who claimed to rule in the name of Islam that endures to the present day. It also meant that the manifestation of Muslim rule could be erratic, imperial, fair and just, despotic and tyrannical, dynastic or individual. Muslim rulers were obliged to institute Islamic law (*shari'a*) over the territories of their authority, which in turn ensured that all aspects of life, from birth, taxes and death, were accounted for.

Jews and Christians also had their place in the new Muslim states and domains. This position would be coloured by their minority status and Islamic norms and theological positions around it. The early respect that grew between Islam on the one hand and Jewish and Christian communities on the other later dissipated. However easy and close relations between Muslims, Jews and Christians might be, there remained a gulf of ignorance and prejudice between them. They worshipped separately and had their own high places of worship and local shrines of saints.[1]

Sufism is an expression of what may be referred to as mystical Islam. Here the spiritual dimension of attachment to the faith is the primary emphasis and purpose of the believer. There is a focus in the Sufi tradition on the direct linkage to God through personal meditation, prayer and even dance. Sufi practices can be seen in a wide variety of populist Muslim practices across the globe and Sufi brotherhoods (*tariqa*) have established strong communal links in both urban and rural locations. Throughout the centuries and particularly in the nineteenth and early twentieth century, the mass appeal of Sufi doctrines and brotherhoods was regarded as a threat to the official expression of Islam and by a new generation of Muslim thinkers and preachers who regarded Sufi practices as folkish and against the fundamental tenets of the faith.

Age of empire

From this foundation, Islam expanded at a remarkable rate. By the eighth century the empire of Islam and its rulers had established their power across the globe. The previously disparate and unruly tribes of Arabia had gathered together under the banner of Islam and advanced the cause of their faith into the known world and through the unitary mechanism of the faith. The global system would never be the same again. The Byzantine and Sassanid empires declined as the unitary force of Islam became apparent.

> In this sense, the conquests were truly an Islamic movement. For it was Islam – the set of religious beliefs preached by Mohammed, with its social and political ramifications – that ultimately sparked the whole integration process and hence was the ultimate cause of the conquests' success.[2]

Yet integration was by no means a uniform process:

> In fact, the means used by the state to integrate the tribal population of Arabia to itself during the conquests were highly varied, and some tended to be more effective than others in binding particular individuals or groups to the state. They ranged in character from the purely ideological or idealistic to the crassly venal, and it is no doubt the very breadth of this spectrum of inducements to loyalty, all tied up in one way or another with the Islamic regime, that made the integration process so successful.[3]

In this variety of experience, Muslim rule was accommodated and incorporated in a host of settings. A religious force was deemed capable of achieving great power and conquest in a variety of domains. The appeal of Islam was widespread and Muslim politics proved enduring. Arab state-building and empire expansion were chiefly accredited to Islam and its power to unite those who had previously been regarded as divided in dispute and violent warfare. Now obedience to God transcended the primordial pattern of loyalty to the tribal chief or head of clan. Under the banner of Islam, the new warriors of the faith became part of a wider movement for change that, through an attachment to faith, allowed them to transcend the mundane and achieve great power. Power was expressed in conquest, rule, governance, economy, society, arts and sciences, in the architecture of great Muslim cities such as Samarkand, Baghdad and Cairo. Muslim states arose throughout Asia and Africa alongside the greater Muslim empires that had their genesis in the Middle East. For these reasons Islam was considered a threat to the principal powers of Europe, and Christianity in particular.

The expansion of Islam, through war and economy, appeared to put the new faith and the older and powerful faith of Christianity on a collision course, that was epitomised by the historic epic of the Crusades throughout the eleventh to thirteenth centuries. The memorialising of the Crusades, the extent to which the Crusades shape contemporary understandings of modern Muslim polities and their inevitable encounters with the West, are powerful and enduring. Much myth and folklore now colours the ways in which both Muslims and Westerners reflect on this encounter from 1,000 years ago. The Crusades are commonly depicted as an epic struggle of the Cross over the Crescent that culminated in the deliverance of Holy Jerusalem from bloody Muslim hands into Christian custodianship. The memory of the Muslim victory over the imperial might of the Crusader knights of Europe, however, is the tale most often related in the history books of the Muslim and Arab worlds. The memory of such ambitions, and its portent in terms of delivering ordinary Muslims from the rapacious appetite of Christianity, militantly hostile to Islam and its believers, are kept alive in countless tracts and accounts related by radical Islamist groups and organisations in the present day. Islamist preachers, activists, ideologues and supporters parrot the myth of the 'Crusader West' against the faithful armies of Islam. In a transparent attempt to sow a seamless thread between past and present, figures like Osama Bin Laden repeated a mantra where people like former President Bush of America was epitomised as the modern-day manifestation of the imperial and militant fundamentalist face of Christianity that seeks only to deliver the Middle East from the atavistic grip of the Muslim peoples. In a declaration in 1998 Bin Laden linked the presence of US forces stationed in Saudi Arabia to the Crusades of the past in the following way:

> The Arab Peninsula has never – since Allah made it flat, created its desert, and encircled it with seas – been stormed by any forces like the Crusader armies spreading on it like locusts, eating its riches and wiping out its plantations. All this is happening at a time in which nations are attacking Muslims like people fighting over a plate of food.[4]

This highlights an enduring source of tension rooted in the past but kept alive in the modern era by parties in opposition to each other, who are prepared to use the emblems of faith as a means of conflict and enmity. For modern-day Islamists, the victory of Saladin over the Crusader 'occupiers' of Jerusalem in 1187 reversed the fortunes of Islam after a series of short-lived but bitter wars that had engulfed many Muslim domains for over a century. By the thirteenth century Islam was ascendant again and its military leaders had liberated much Middle East territory from the Crusaders; and in 1453, Constantinople fell into Muslim hands. The new seat of the Ottoman Empire was sited in the same place as the old Christian throne, 'it absorbed what was left of the Byzantine Empire and took Constantinople as its new capital, Istanbul ... The Ottoman Empire was now the principal military and naval power in the eastern Mediterranean, and also in the Red Sea'.[5]

Such immense power challenged a variety of European forces. While some scholars acknowledge that Ottoman influence was intimately felt in ways throughout Europe that endure to the present, by and large, the Ottoman Turks were viewed as a counterweight to the rising forces of new Europeanism, whether in terms of Enlightenment thinking, the Reformation, imperial expansionism or military adventure. The extent of the Ottoman Empire was felt in many quarters of Europe and throughout other domains in Asia, North Africa and the Middle East. The Ottoman state machine was highly sophisticated; a neat bureaucracy presided over by Sultans of great power. The first epoch of Ottoman rule from 1300 to 1481 was characterised by territorial expansionism as a result of conflict and coalition. The first Sultan and his successors established a territorial presence in Europe by the middle of the fourteenth century with ties subsequently established in the Balkan region. The Ottoman armies were able to pursue conquest in both East and West and were the envy of other European states and powers (characterised as it was by the janissary corps attached to the ruler). In the sixteenth century further battles against the Mamluks resulted in the expansion of the empire. Many have described this period as the golden age of the Ottoman era. From the end of the century, however, the power of the Ottomans went into decline as successive rulers oversaw the corrosion of state authority and other actors took advantage of its increasing vulnerability. Reforms from within did come, but too late to halt the deterioration of the ruling elite and its associated classes. By the early eighteenth century, the rising nation-states of Europe had stepped beyond their new boundaries with the express ambition of territorial conquest, control and economic betterment. The Ottoman Empire began to unravel, not only at the fringes but also at the seams. In the nineteenth century local opposition to the central authority of the Sultan in Istanbul was rife throughout the empire and, despite the modernisation embodied in the *tanzimat* reform efforts by Mahmud II and his sons, the death knell of empire was nigh. By the late 1870s, the authorities in Istanbul had granted a formal constitution – the first for a Muslim country. Such administrative, legal and political developments and reforms (*tanzimat*), however, were not enough to stave off the inexorable pressure to relinquish territory from the periphery of empire and for further reforms.

By the early 1880s, territorial control had been surrendered in Eastern European countries such as Serbia, Montenegro, Romania and Bulgaria. If the Ottoman rulers had hoped to preserve stability in the heart of the empire by letting go of other areas, the nationalist movement that culminated in the widespread revolts throughout the Middle East and the emergence of the Young Turks in 1908 dispelled such hopes. The revolt of the Young Turks 'weakened the position of the Sultan, the traditional focus of loyalty, and led ultimately to the seizure of power ... strengthening central control and laying emphasis on national unity', both as a bulwark against European pressures and as a means of challenging the status quo from within.[6] The dynamism and challenge that quickly evolved in such a context found expression, not just in new thinkers and movements associated with nationalism, but in Islamic circles as well. Much of the impetus in the new approaches was apparent in the demand to address contested identity, as the European-inspired imperial project affected more and more Muslim domains or countries. In Africa, Asia and the Middle East, the extension of European power as part of the imperial project disrupted political norms and cultures that embraced the expression of Muslim governance and identity, whether in India, Nigeria, Algeria, Egypt or Sudan. Moreover, as the Caliphate teetered on the brink of collapse after disastrously siding with Germany during the First World War, the prospect of the end of Muslim states ruled independently by Muslim rulers in the name of Islam galvanised a new generation of preachers, thinkers and activists to reclaim the Islamic project as a defence against change, as well as a vehicle to assist Muslims through the modernisation and transformation processes that gripped their societies.

End of empire

Hence, by the late nineteenth century, millions of Muslims found themselves living in societies where the norms, values and principles of governance derived from Islam were increasingly being disrupted by the alternative imperial project pursued by European nation-states. While it is true that Muslim rulers also had pursued ambitions for empire, the period of conquest was relatively short-lived and the subsequent embedding of Islam into local territories and cultures succeeded in mostly a naturalised phenomenon. The Muslim response to the imperial challenge was but one part of a wider intellectual movement manifest in colonised societies.

The manifestation of a fundamentalist trend had its roots in this period of transformation and in particular the prominence of a number of individual thinkers in both Asia and the Middle East. The fundamentalist trend gave rise to a multitude of ideas across the political spectrum. This resulted in thinking that sometimes advocated a radical embrace of the modernisation process, including the political dimension, while also embracing individuals who advocated the primacy of a strict interpretation of Islam and a renewal and renaissance that eschewed more liberal approaches. In one respect, however, there is evidence of a unity that transcended the internal division, and this was that the new phenomenon came as a reaction and response to Muslim emasculation in the spheres of politics, economics, culture and social order.

These early advocates of fundamentalism as a political, social and economic totem believed that Muslims could restore their identity and dignity and achieve independence, through adherence to and rediscovery of a faith system made relevant to the contemporary era. These advocates were a manifestation of a common problem, with common roots that gave rise to parallel patterns of expression across Muslim domains.

The fundamentalists are a modern phenomenon, an indication along with the nationalists, of a reaction to the crushing impact of the modernity project in colonised Muslim countries. In this sense, the historical development of these countries was characterised by a transition from a Muslim-governed mode of production (which was characterised by mostly agrarian economies) to industrialisation determined by European commercial and later political imperatives. The process of change wrought by the advent of new modes of production was experienced by Muslims in a variety of contexts. Change everywhere was highlighted by the emergence of new norms and values that cut Islam off and placed it at the margins of society. Relationships changed, the balance of power shifted from Muslim to non-Muslim hands and everything was transformed.

The speed of this transition from one way of life to another created a number of issues concerning the stability and durability of Muslim institutions. Moreover, traditional society was disrupted as a result of migration, urbanisation and development of consumerist trends, and the notion of family or tribe was increasingly eclipsed by the individual as the primary social unit. Social mores and values informed by Islam were also affected by processes of Westernisation that accompanied the imperial economic and political project. Laws replaced customs, and new frameworks for governance that were inspired by secular nation-building came into being.

The lives of millions of Muslims, therefore, were deeply affected by this period of transformation. A palpable tension between tradition and modernity grew to a point where it triggered a response. For some, the response had and maintains a dual nature: modernist and fundamentalist,[7] but I would contend that the modernist/reformists represent the first kernels of fundamentalist thinking and approach. The intelligentsia were thus engaged and compelled to develop a response to the crisis in their midst. The modernist/reformists are concerned to preserve and maintain the *fundamental* or essential elements of Islam while being careful to align the faith to the demands of the modernity project. Figures associated with the modernist/reformist school include Jamal ad-din al-Afghani (1838–97), Mohammed Abduh (1849–1905), Sayyid Ahmed Khan (1817–98), Mohammed Iqbal (1877–1938) and Rashid Rida (1865–1935). Among their number there developed what is referred to as a *salafi* adherence. For this group of thinkers, the basic principles of Islam were inviolate and the ways of the Prophet should be strictly adhered to. *Salafism* is now associated with the literal and fundamentalist dimensions of post-1945 Islam and its ideas and supporters can be found across the globe. Moreover, elements of the jihad movement are also referred to as *salafi-jihadi* as a means of distinguishing their agenda from other Islamist groups and movements.

Pre-fundamentalist thinkers and movements

One figure who predates the modern *salafists* and yet remains instrumental in formulating a fundamentalist doctrine within Islam is Mohammed Ibn Abd al-Wahhab (1703–92). Wahhab was an important Muslim scholar from the Hanbali school of Islam who, in turn, was said to be influenced by the fundamentalist thinker, Ibn Taymiyyah. Ibn Abd al-Wahhab preached against deviation within Islam and demanded that believers adhere only to the fundamental doctrines of the faith and practice outlined by the Prophet Mohammed. Ibn Abd al-Wahhab, in alliance with Arabian tribal forces from the al-Saud family, was able to establish a formidable new movement for reform of Islam and its purification. Only a literal approach to the faith was acceptable to Ibn Abd al-Wahhab and his followers. Evidence of this strict adherence is seen in the historic alliance between Ibn Abd al-Wahhab and the al-Saud in contemporary Saudi Arabia. When the Kingdom of Saudi Arabia declared its independence in 1932, the teachings of Ibn Abd al-Wahhab were recognised by the ruling al-Saud family as the religious foundation of this Islamic state.

Thus, the rise of a new group of thinkers and associated movement to meet the challenges posed by modernity and the manifestation of the European imperial project did not occur in a vacuum. It is important to remember that through the latter part of the nineteenth century there were instances of Muslim revolt against both local and foreign-imposed rule. The Libyan-based Sanusiya revolt and the Mahdi's campaign in Sudan demonstrated that popular sentiment could be powerfully harnessed.[8] Moreover, in West and South Asia, Muslim revivalism was prominent in the development of anti-colonial movements and modernist Islamic thought in areas such as India and Afghanistan.[9] The pre-fundamentalists were deeply interested in a project of Islamic renewal from within, as well as devising a means of meeting the threat posed by European ambitions for their territories. Their rejoinder resulted in a major effort to illuminate Islam in ways that met the demands of ordinary Muslims experiencing major upheaval. The demand was to maintain the centrality of Islam to the experience of ordinary Muslims, whether that was in the sphere of education, welfare, political or social issues. This implied that a major challenge would need to be mounted against the progressive and successful Westernisation of many Muslim societies. Sometimes this was manifest in movements and thinkers who challenged the status quo, and sometimes the strategy was to transform from within by applying pressure and legitimating new movements for Muslim statehood. Among the new movements such as the Muslim Brotherhood (*al-Ikhwan al-Muslimeen*) or the Islamic Movement (*Jama'at al-Islami*) would arise the leaders and supporters of fundamentalist Islam in all its modern guises.

Among the diverse voices of response in the pre-fundamentalist modernist spectrum were many deeply influential thinkers and their supporters, who contended that Islam needed to be remodelled if the decline of Muslim civilisation were to be reversed. These reformers demanded that the faith should be made relevant and responsive to modern demands through the operation of the principle of *ijtihad* (interpretation) of dogmatic religious sources alongside the discerning Islamisation of Western advances, most notably technology. Most historians of this period are agreed that a number of key figures symbolise this process, including Jamal ad-din al-Afghani (1838–97), Mohammed Abduh (1849–1905), Rashid Rida (1865–1935), Hassan al-Banna

(1906–49), Sayyid Ahmed Khan (1817–98) and Mohammed Iqbal (1877–1938). Their influence was to spread geographically across Asia and the Middle East and endures to the present day through the movements and ideological inheritors of the pre-fundamentalist trend.

The new Islamists

These new thinkers were also concerned to mount a challenge to their compatriots who were successively turning to nationalist and secularist ideas. Jamal ad-din al-Afghani is the figure credited as the 'catalyst' for reform. He spearheaded a group of thinkers, followers and movements that would promote pre-fundamentalist approaches.

Jamal ad-din al-Afghani is considered to be the founding father of Islamic modernism. Throughout his early life he travelled widely within the Muslim world, as well as Europe. He trained as a Muslim scholar and was exposed from an early age to the ideas of scholars such as the Indian Muslim modernist thinker Sayyid Ahmed Khan. By 1870 he was in Istanbul where he played a principal role in devising the *tanzimat* reforms of the Ottoman authorities. He later settled in Cairo, and it was here that many of his ideas were developed and disseminated to audiences drawn from the religious schools. Al-Afghani also started publishing a journal in collaboration with his student, Mohammed Abduh. He used this publication and other opportunities as a platform from which to launch attacks on the grip of Western European intellectualism in the Islamic world. Moreover, as his influence grew, he also became an outspoken critic of Muslim regimes. Muslim rulers first in Iran and then in Istanbul tried to co-opt al-Afghani for their own purposes. Yet al-Afghani's critical views fatally undermined such efforts. Al-Afghani was deported from Iran and later, despite agreement on the issue of Muslim unity, in Istanbul he was regarded with some mistrust by the Sultan.

Al-Afghani's work is symbolic of an attempt to find a middle path between Islam under the traditional clerics, and the West, as promoted through the imperial project. His main thesis was that Islam's embrace of modernity should not imply a wholesale acceptance of secular principles or norms. His political agenda centred on the notion of revived and restored Muslim unity (pan-Islamism) as a vehicle for anti-imperial struggle and liberation. The right of Muslim self-determination and independence was clearly an item on al-Afghani's agenda. Through public meetings, lectures and activism he stirred up intense debate. He was prepared to take on Western attacks and criticisms of Islam and counter such assertions. This was typified in the exchange in the early

1880s between al-Afghani and the French philosopher Ernest Renan. Such ideas were also reflected in the later activities of Muslim nationalists in India.

Al-Afghani's pre-fundamentalist credentials derive from his anti-materialist stance, his hostility to the political and economic oppression of Muslim peoples as a result of the European imperialism, and his desire to resurrect the superior Muslim civilisation in the modern age. He understood that for this project to be undertaken and achieved, Muslims had to engage in their own revival and return to the fundamentals of faith as central to all aspects of their daily experience.[10]

After his death, most of al-Afghani's work was carried on by his student, Mohammed Abduh. Abduh was an Egyptian religious scholar who trained at one of the most eminent religious universities in the world: al-Azhar in Cairo. His association with al-Afghani meant that Abduh always would find favour with the British-dominated Egyptian authorities. In 1882, after enjoying a government position, Abduh was exiled by the British, following his expression of anti-imperial opinion. When he eventually returned from exile in 1888, he rejoined the institutions of the state and in 1899 he was appointed Grand Mufti of Egypt. This appointment made Abduh the most senior Islamic official in all Egypt, with influence throughout Muslim domains. Abduh believed that by working within the system, reform could be achieved at a more significant rate than by simply advocating Muslim activism. Abduh argued for reform in the areas of law, education and personal status issues for women. He was successful in persuading others to support his agenda, though it should be noted that elements of the conservative *ulama* of Cairo saw him as a real threat. Moreover, at a popular level, his pre-fundamentalist concern with *salafi* doctrine, as opposed to the folkish practices of the day, were unfamiliar to the majority of illiterate Egyptian Muslims.

After his death, his follower Rashid Rida took up the cause of modernism. Rida's journal entitled *al-Manar* (the Lighthouse), outlined the tenets of the *salafi* movement and Rida himself was an avowed anti-imperialist. By this time the Muslim world had been drawn into the First World War, and the actions of Britain and France after the war only exacerbated anti-Western feeling in many Muslim countries. Moreover, Rida advocated the re-implementation of Islamic statehood. He argued against the dangers of a Muslim embrace of Western ideas of secularism and nationalism, contending that a return to Islam would deliver the Muslim people to their rightful position in the modern age. In this way he was more conservative than al-Afghani and Abduh. Rida's approach was dynamic and towards the end of his life, the modernist project demanded less of his attention. Indeed, his increasing antipathy to the West also strengthened his argument for the centrality of Islam to any Muslim revival. In this respect, his approach owed much to al-Wahhab, as it was predicated on strict adherence to the fundamental principles of the faith.

In nineteenth-century India the continuing domination of the British also accounts for the modernist approach symbolised by Sayyid Ahmed Khan (1817–98) and Mohammed Iqbal (1877–1938). By the mid-nineteenth century in India, Muslim power was at its nadir. The project to rescue Islam from obscurity fell on the shoulders of Sayyid Ahmed Khan, who advocated a modernist agenda for his faith. As a *salafi*, Khan believed that the process of *ijtihad* would protect Islam and contribute to its survival. Khan, however, also believed that it was in the best interests of Muslims in India to accept rather than resist the realities imposed by the political rule of the British, but at the same time to strive for a return and protection of the essential tenets of the faith. Khan confined his attentions to India and was not an advocate of the pan-Islamism spearheaded by al-Afghani or Abduh. His reinterpretation of Islam also led him to advocate major educational reforms in India. Yet he was also seen by other Islamists as a collaborator with Western imperialism and many traditional and conservative clerics distrusted him. But his modernist interpretation of Islamic doctrine played an important part in the pre-fundamentalist trend in India.

Mohammed Iqbal, the poet, was also a prominent scholar and politician. Iqbal was one of the first Indian Muslims to advocate Muslim self-determination in the early twentieth century. He advocated separate statehood for India's Muslims at a time when they perceived they might be marginalised. Much of his work focused on the recovery of Islamic identity. In this sense, Iqbal was a Muslim nationalist visionary who was able to realise his dreams and ambitions in the establishment of the Muslim state of Pakistan, following the partition of India in 1947. His pre-fundamentalist philosophy emphasises the exclusive nature of Islamic revivalism and a desire to seek communal disengagement with both the colonial overlord and representatives of the Hindu majority. Moreover, Iqbal maintained the fundamentalist adherence to the universal nature of Islam in all domains. As Jalal notes, 'Iqbal's philosophical reconstructions of Islamist thought made plain the gaping chasm between a view of Indian nationalism based on keeping religion out of politics and the normative Muslim conception of treating the spiritual and temporal domains in non-oppositional terms.'[11] By 1930 as the movement for nationalism grew in India, Iqbal argued that Islam offered the best route for Muslim independence. He emphasised the past glories of Islam and argued that through recovery and revival, Islam could be great again. He recognised the public rather than purely private role that Islam should play.

In his most famous speech to the All-India Muslim League in 1930, he declared:

> I, therefore, demand the formation of a consolidated Muslim state in the best interests of India and Islam. For India, it means security and peace resulting from an internal balance of power; for Islam, an opportunity to rid itself of the stamp that Arabian imperialism was forced to give it, to mobilize its laws, its education, its culture, and to bring them into closer contact with its own original spirit and with the spirit of modern times.[12]

Although Iqbal died before the establishment of the state of Pakistan, he is regarded as one of its chief inspirations. His vision was realised in some respects but Pakistan's contemporary history demonstrates the diffculties of marrying the ideal vision with the realities of Muslim state-building in the twentieth century. Today Pakistan is portrayed as a Muslim country ruled by a powerful marriage of fundamentalist and neo-fundamentalist forces and the military. It is a post-colonial Muslim state where the potentiality of modernist Muslim democracy that was articulated by Iqbal has never truly been achieved.

Men and movements

The manifestation of pre-fundamentalism in the inter-war period of the early twentieth century was evident in the rise of new Muslim figures such as Hassan al-Banna in Egypt and Muwlana Mawdudi in India. Both established major Islamic movements that remain active to the present day and account for a variety of activities associated with Islamic revivalism and Islamic fundamentalism as a political force. Both were key figures in articulating nascent fundamentalist political agendas that motivated millions to participate in processes that became the struggle in colonial Muslim domains for self-determination and independence.

Mawdudi was born in southern India under British colonial rule. He had a traditional upbringing and his early studies were conducted in Muslim seminaries in Delhi and Hyderabad where he later settled. Mawdudi, like Iqbal, was alarmed at the apparent decline of Islam in India. He believed that the true nature of Islam had been contaminated by alien practices and invented folkish traditions. He argued that Islam had to be purified to be revived and reclaimed as relevant to all domains of life, including the political. A return to the fundamental practices of the faith and the early example of the Medinan community was actively advocated by him. By 1941, Mawdudi was prepared to put his vision into practice and was one of the founders of the *Jama'at al-Islami*. Mawdudi believed that the party would be the vehicle or means by which to achieve Islamic independence and statehood. He contended that the means to the end could be revolutionary if it hastened the advance of Islamic governance for Muslims. He declared:

> Islam is a revolutionary doctrine and system that overturns governments. It seeks to overturn the whole universal social order ... and establish its structure anew ... Islam seeks the world. It is not satisfied by a piece of land but demands the whole universe ... jihad is at the same time offensive and defensive ... The Islamic party does not hesitate to utilize the means of war to implement its goal.[13]

Mawdudi also articulated a specific vision of statehood that would inspire many Muslims engaged in state-building projects. The proposed state would be majority Muslim, with a presidential government and a consultative legislature elected by Muslim mandate. He envisioned a separation of powers among institutions of the state, including an independent judicial system. The non-Muslim minority would not enjoy the same rights as the Muslim majority. His ambitions were universal in goal, pan-Islamic in articulation and his call to jihad would strike a potent chord, not just in Asia, but other Muslim countries as well. Jihad, for Mawdudi, was the means by which Islamic governance and statehood would be achieved. He declared that

> Islam wants to employ all forces and means that can be employed for bringing about a universal all-embracing revolution. It will spare no efforts for the achievement of this supreme objective. This far-reaching struggle that continuously exhausts all forces and this employment of all possible means are called jihad.[14]

One essential element of most revolutionary thinking is the vanguard, and this is particularly associated with Marxism and Leninism. Yet vanguardism was advocated by Mawdudi and can be identified as a core component of other fundamentalist groups such as the Palestinian Islamic Jihad and al-Qaeda and the works of other ideologues such as Qutb. The vanguard enjoys Qur'anic sanction and leads the revolution, or jihad, itself. This bypasses the wider community in terms of direct action but remains dependent on them for legitimacy and support.

Mawdudi was determined to ensure the religious content of political rule in whatever homeland Muslims carved from the partition project in India. This clashed with the largely secular vision of Muslim statehood articulated by the political class. Mawdudi advocated Islamic statehood based on the strictures of Islamic law, combined with a governing function for the Muslim clergy. The result of these conflicting visions was largely characterised by unrealistic compromises that made the state vulnerable to other forces, principally the military.

In sum, Mawdudi symbolises the transition from pre-fundamentalist to fundamentalist thinking. He is avowedly anti-Western, he advances a totalitarian political philosophy and undertook to provide strategies that recognised the predicament of Muslims in modern societies. He established an Islamic political ideology that was fundamentalist in content and strategy. He viewed Islam as a fundamental prescription for governance and life. Unity (*tawhid*) and exclusiveness in relation to the others (non-Muslim) were significant elements of his political agenda. This translates into a form of religious homogeneity that put the community (*umma*), rather than the individual, at the heart of any project. He was a purist who looked to a vision of Islam that was untainted by the West. The fusion of Islam with other faiths, civilisations and cultures was not part of Mawdudi's fundamentalist plan. His critics were drawn from both the secular fold and those within Islam in the clerical elite. He was accused of politicising the faith and marginalising the spiritual dimensions of Islam in favour of a political agenda.

Hassan al-Banna is in many respects the founding father of modern Islamic fundamentalism. Zubaida contends that the movement that al-Banna founded, the *al-Ikhwan al-Muslimeen* (Muslim Brotherhood) 'has been the most prominent fundamentalist current in *Sunni* Islam'.[15] Al-Banna, who was born in 1906, represents the transition from pre- to full-fundamentalist articulation of ideas within many Muslim realms. This transition coincides with the change, mostly characterised by conflict, that beset so many Muslim countries in the inter-war period. The flowering of full fundamentalism, however, would occur only as a result of internal contest in the wake of the break with the colonial past.

In the meantime, al-Banna, like so many of his modernist pre-fundamentalist contemporaries, grew up in a society in which the mantra of secular nationalism had been embraced by many local elites and intellectuals. Islam was largely deemed irrelevant to the nationalist project for self-determination. Islamic fundamentalists were regarded as 'old-fashioned'. But what the nationalists and the *Ikhwan* had in common was an antipathy and hostility to Western colonialism. In

1928, al-Banna formed the *Ikhwan al-Muslimeen*, to promote an Islamic response to the obligation to preach and spread the message of Islam through social, educational, welfare and political work. Al-Banna advocated a renaissance of Islam in the lives of ordinary people. The *Ikhwan* quickly established a programme of social, welfare and educational support based on Islamic principles among all sectors of society. Moreover, it was a matter of years before further branches of the organisation were founded outside of Egypt in neighbouring Muslim countries. The *Ikhwan* also represented formidable opposition to the ruling authorities. This was manifest in the social and political challenge they represented as well as a 'secret apparatus' (*al-jihaz al-sirri*) that was established within the movement in the early 1940s to undertake jihad. Through close links with the Egyptian military, *Ikhwan mujahideen* were trained and armaments acquired.[16] This was not a unique course of action. Indeed, political violence was part of the Egyptian landscape from all quarters and factions. The *Ikhwan*, however, also proved themselves capable of transcending local or national arenas to mobilise the Muslim masses around wider issues of concern, such as the situation in Palestine. It should have been no surprise, therefore, that the authorities took seriously the inherent threat they represented.

The writer Mitchell refers to the period from 1945 to 1949 as an 'apogee' for pre-fundamentalist Islamism as represented by al-Banna and the *Ikhwan*, but it also represents the transition that I referred to earlier. Many charges were levelled against the *Ikhwan* during this period. The organisation was considered a major security threat and the state used all available coercive measures to bring about its dissolution. And Mitchell as somewhat presciently claimed, 'For whatever the [*Ikhwan*] ... may be remembered in Egyptian history, its political role will probably remain dominant'.[17]

The association with violence, however, is also dominant and remains a primary label attached to the fundamentalist expression in the present day. This violence was endemic to the context and cultures of oppressive rule and localised revolt and rebellion at the time, whether in Asia, Africa or the Middle East. Yet, it is argued that the difference 'lay in the Islamic dimension which the [*Ikhwan*] claimed as their own, and which precipitated a variety of violence in both political and social life which was characterised primarily by rigid intolerance'.[18] The *Ikhwan* would remain on the landscape and re-form under more militant and fully fundamentalist terms.

Accounts of early fundamentalist thinking and the formation of new movements give rise to a set of patterns that have continued to characterise and play a part in accounting for the variety and nature of

Islamic fundamentalism since 1945. Pre-fundamentalist thinking was concerned with establishing a response to the inherent challenge posed by non-Muslim rule and subjugation without rights. Its proponents recognised that much of the responsibility for the parlous state of Islam lay with the faith system itself. If the faith had declined and atrophied, then at least this had been established and the pre-fundamentalist modernists and radicals set about constructing a new alternative. The alternative lay in a renaissance and revival of the faith. Moreover, Islam should be open to new interpretations, stripped of everything except its fundamental principles, and its adherents should be ready to reclaim the faith and the Muslim territories from the rule of unbelievers. The immediacy of the project varied from one location to another. Furthermore, the means also varied greatly. Mawdudi's revolutionary zeal was very different from al-Afghani's evolutionary modernist agenda. Confrontation was, however, inevitable and often unlikely alliances were forged for the common cause of liberation.

What these thinkers, followers, activists and supporters shared in common, and with other organisations of the time, was a desire to supplant existing rule with Muslim rulers and states. Islamic governance was a common aspiration. Yet governance was envisaged in a variety of ways and means. It did not necessarily imply the absence of constitutional governance or plurality in politics between Muslim and non-Muslim citizens. But it is fair to say that, in opposition to the secular nationalists of the time, the pre-fundamentalists prized Muslim unity (*tahwid*) above other attributes of statehood. This has been interpreted by some as reinforcing a Muslim predilection for totalitarianism, authoritarianism and violence. This makes much of an argument that rests on the assumption that Muslims are innately violent. The condemnation of violence by Muslims, by leaders, ideologues and clerics is regarded as nothing more than a ruse, a means to deceive and wage Islam's war by sleight of hand. The pursuit of violence against Muslim activists by the state and other actors is also left unexplained.

The pre-fundamentalists also alert us to the transnational nature of Islamic fundamentalism as a political expression and ideology. Al-Afghani, Abduh, Sayyid Khan, Rashid Rida and others also took advantage of the technological developments in communications, travel and culture to get their message across to a wider audience. Pan-Islamism – the ambition of Islamic governance that transcends imposed borders and frontiers on Muslim territories – is apparent in the global and transnational message of many contemporary fundamentalist movements. This combination of transnationalism in both theory and practice currently defines the element of fundamentalism that threatens the West. Osama Bin Laden's call to global jihad against the West is rooted in the pre-fundamentalist fear of foreign domination and the belief that the revival of Islam is a global project. In this way, global ideas are communicated to local contexts, particularly contexts that are characterised by pre-existing conflict. There is an aspiration that sectarian division will be transcended in the battle to recover Islamic territories from *kufr* or *jahilli* (pagan) rule. National identity is then subsumed under the banner of Islam. The strict *Sunni*, inspired *salafi* and Wahabbi character of full-blown fundamentalism since 1945 is also apparent in its predecessors. In the pre-fundamentalist stage, however, the manifestation of such tendencies was not always intimately linked to the political agenda.

An unyielding suspicion of the West, modernity, aspirations for Islamic statehood and governance, resistance and armed struggle, a transnational appearance and recognition that Muslims must make Islam relevant to all aspects of their lives were the features of the pre-fundamentalist Muslims. Such features would define and betray the ideals of movements, organisations, thinkers and activists in the turbulent decades of ending empire that have characterised so many Muslim countries in the post-1945 world order.

Notes

1 A. Hourani, *A History of the Arab Peoples*, London: Faber and Faber, 1991, p. 188.
2 F. Donner, *The Early Islamic Conquests*, Princeton, NJ: Princeton University Press, 1981, p. 269.
3 Ibid., p. 256.
4 Declaration of war by Osama Bin Laden, 1998. See: www.pbs.org/newshour/updates/military/jan-june98/fatwa_1998.html
5 A. Hourani, *A History of the Arab Peoples*, London: Faber and Faber, 1991, p. 215.
6 Ibid., p. 309.
7 See A.S. Moussalli, *Moderate and Radical Islamic Fundamentalism*, Gainesville, FL: University Press of Florida, 1999.
8 I. Lapidus, *A History of Islamic Societies*, Cambridge: Cambridge University Press, 1988.
9 A. Ahmad, *Islamic Modernism in India and Pakistan 1857–1964*, London: Oxford University Press, 1967, pp. 123–40.
10 For more on the pre-fundamentalists, see Hamid Enayat, *Modern Islamic Political Thought*, Austin, TX: University of Texas Press, 1982; H.A.R Gibb, *Modern Trends in Islam*, Chicago: University of Chicago Press, 1947; A. Hourani, *Arabic Thought in the Liberal Age, 1789–1939*, Cambridge: Cambridge University Press, 1982; Nikki Keddie, *Sayyid Jamal al-Din Afghani: A Political Biography*, Berkeley, CA: University of California Press, 1972.

11 A. Jalal, 'South Asia', in *Encyclopaedia of Nationalism*, www.tufts.edu/ajalal01/Articles/encyclopedia.nationalism.pdf, p. 19.
12 For details of quote and biography of Iqbal, see: www.jadoo4u.com/iqbal_islam_1.htm
13 See Y. Haddad, *Islamists and the Challenge of Pluralism*, Washington, DC: Center for Contemporary Arab Studies and Center for Muslim–Christian Understanding, Georgetown, 1995, p. 10.
14 See R. Peters, *Jihad in Classical and Modern Islam*, Princeton, NJ: Marcus Wiener Publishers, 1996, p. 128.
15 S. Zubaida, *Islam, the People and the State*, London: I.B. Tauris, 1993, p. 47.
16 See A. El-Awaisi, *The Muslim Brothers and the Palestine Question, 1928–1947*, London: I.B. Tauris, 1998, pp. 119–22.
17 R.P. Mitchell, *The Society of the Muslim Brothers*, New York: Oxford University Press, 1969, p. 306.
18 Ibid., p. 320.

2 The advance of secularism
The decline of Islam?

> An Islamic state must, in all respects, be founded upon the law laid down by God through His Prophet. The government which runs such a state will be entitled to obedience in its capacity as a political agency set up to enforce the laws of God and only in so far as it acts in that capacity. If it disregards the law revealed by God, its commands will not be binding on believers.
>
> (Muwlana Mawdudi)

The beginning of the end of colonial rule, mandate assistance, protectorates, Western-dominated alliances and the advent of self-determination and independence in many Muslim countries in the post-1945 era did not augur well for Islamic fundamentalists. The inter-war period had already seen the collapse of the last vestiges of the Ottoman state, the loss of Muslim territories in Asia to the revolutionary forces of the Soviet Union and the break-up of states with significant Muslim populations. While the immediate post-war era would give rise to movements for liberation and independence in which Muslims were prime movers and voices, the advent of independence in so many Muslim countries, whether in Africa, Asia or the Middle East, did not guarantee the hoped-for establishment of Islamic statehood.

The advent of independent states that inevitably followed the end of European empire and domination, appeared to consolidate the forces of secularism and the concurrent demise of Islam as a political feature of contemporary landscapes in Muslim countries. With few exceptions it appeared that the most that Islamic fundamentalists could hope for was that the leaders of newly independent states would acknowledge dimensions of Islam through courts, law and maintenance of state support for the mosque and its employees. As secular rule unfolded, however, it appeared that Islamic fundamentalists would not be treated benignly. The evolving and emerging relationship between Islamic fundamentalism and the state was subject to rupture and crisis, damaging the hopes that many had envisioned in the utopian aspirations for a modern political Islam in the twentieth century. The path to conflict rather than peace seemed to pull at the emergent aspirations of Muslim fundamentalists, while the nationalists practised the doctrine of secularism that would bring achievement, development and modernity to Muslim societies in the twentieth century.

The displacement of secular colonists by the secular nationalist elite that dominated the post-independent and revolutionary regimes of the Muslim world, was read as a declaration of war by many Islamic fundamentalists. Islamic principles of governance and rule, through consultation and jurisprudence, were abandoned by the new elites. Instead, they established power through coercion, often by coups d'état that relied heavily, once in power, on the strong arm of the military to quash local opposition and stifle democratic impulses irrespective of their origin. In the name of national populism they promoted cults of personality and ruled Muslim populations with an iron fist. Islam was seen by such figures as an impediment to progress and development. There was little room for the public dimension of faith tied to power in the slavishly interpreted Western models of modernisation, actualised in so many Muslim states during this period. Instead, the faith, its symbols, leaders and institutions, would be swallowed up by the state, leaving its citizens devoid of a voice that was not sanctioned by the 'regime'. Islam was employed to lend legitimacy and potent symbolism in the eyes of the popular mass to new tyrannical leaders and despots. Any independence of the religious establishment was severely weakened and undermined. Those who dared to oppose the state were thrown in prison, tortured and executed as traitors and enemies of the state. In this 'Brave New World' Islam's activists hid in the shadows, languished in jails without trial and were denounced as obstacles to progress.

Being modern and Muslim was viewed as an oxymoron and the secular project left no room for Islam. The Muslim past was repudiated and rejected while secular Muslim leaders appealed to their popular masses. In 1956 in Tunisia, after agreeing arrangements for independence from the French, the country's new prime minister, Habib Bourguiba, set about reforming the political, social and economic structure, leaving Islam out in the cold. This was apparent by 1959 when the legal system and constitution reflected the delegation of Islam as the ultimate authority within the legal framework. While the 1959 Constitution recognised Islam as the religion of the state, *shari'a* (Islamic law) courts were abolished. Personal status laws prohibited polygamy and *talaq* (extra-judicial divorce) and increased rights for women. It has been asserted that 'for Bourguiba, Islam was represented as a thing of the past; the West was Tunisia's only hope for a modern future'.[1] Moreover, the secularists of the new era denied Islam a role in the shaping of national curricula, running down religious institutions such as *Zaytouna* University which became part of the University of Tunis. Mosques and *waqf* (religiously endowed) properties including schools, clinics and Muslim charitable associations were made subject to the authority of the new state and its secular elites, and their independence was lost in the process. Imams and others became employees of the state, constrained by the new ideologies of secular Arab nationalism and state socialism.

The leaders of such regimes also undertook major cultural, educational and political campaigns to 'convert' the Muslim masses to the populist anthems of socialism, and secular nationalism. This worked on the assumption that Islam threatened the secularist ambition for modernisation in Muslim societies and should hence be limited in dimension to the new orders and states that were being shaped and built. Enlightenment thinking, with its emphasis on rationality, the separation of church and state, and democracy, left little room for the representatives of an ancient faith system increasingly regarded as old-fashioned and irrelevant. New national myths were consciously constructed on the belief that modernity demanded a rejection of the religious in Muslim societies, if they were to progress and make way in an international order shaped by modern Western ideologies – whether they were capitalism, communism or socialism. The task of reshaping society and rendering Islam to the borders of political, social and economic power was undertaken with a zeal that was almost religious!

The secularising projects of the post-independent states of the Muslim world, were not, however, a byword for liberal democracy, pluralism, freedom of speech and liberty. Moreover, the Islamic fundamentalists were initially back-footed as they struggled in an environment of repression to develop and articulate a reply to the monopolistic possession of modernity by the secularists. This process of exclusion ignored a rich history of Muslim societies characterised by a *de facto* separation of power between mosque and state.[2] Such societies also revealed evidence of an earlier Muslim acceptance of the doctrines of reason and scientific rationality that the single-minded secularists ignored. For most of these new leaders, unless the fundamentalists were going to support them and walk in their shadow, they were branded as an enemy from within; one that would hold back the progress that might be possible for modern Muslim societies in the post-war era.

The military not the mullahs

The imposition or advent of post-independent states ruled by newly configured elites such as the military led inevitably to the establishment of tensions and contests over power and the nature of the state in modern Muslim societies. By the 1950s and early 1960s, military elements had staged coups, coupled themselves to weak monarchs or leaders, headed revolutionary movements, and had seized control of the state in Muslim countries such as Egypt, Iraq, Indonesia and Turkey. In Iraq, for example, the coup of 1958 deposed the British-inspired monarchy and put the military in power. Later, in alliance with the secularist Ba'th party, Iraq would be dominated by such forces until the downfall of Saddam Hussein in 2003. In the 1950s, the new elites set about tearing down and doing away with the previous frameworks of governance and socio-economic alliances that had given the illusion of social, ethnic and religious stability in this invented state. The military-dominated populist autocrats of the new regime set about a programme of enforced modernisation and secularisation. New wealth that accrued to the state through nationalised oil revenues also promoted a sense of autonomy from traditional elements, such as the religious classes, in society. The benign patrimony of the aristocratic religious families of the *Sunni* elite of Iraq was no longer essential to the maintenance of national cohesion or the unity of state power. Furthermore, as early as the 1920s, the *Shi'a* clerical class had already been 'weakened and rendered apolitical by firm secular measures', undertaken by the British Mandate authorities as they embarked on the task of state construction in ancient Mesopotamia.[3] Things had started badly for the *Shi'a* and the British, for although the *Shi'a* were often persecuted under the *Sunni* Ottoman powers, upon the arrival of the British they rose to defend themselves as the symbol of Islamic power. The British, responded by executing and deporting their leaders. The *Shi'a* were hampered by the fact that they 'were very inexperienced when it came to government and power'.[4] Moreover, *Shi'as* began to realise that although, in principle, the Iraqi constitution guaranteed equal rights to all, in practice its secular framing principles favoured some more than others. The leaders of both *Sunni* and *Shi'a* communities experienced the rise of a state power where army officers, who espoused a Ba'athist doctrine that denied Islam a political voice, took ever increasing control of the state, society and the economy. Islam was no longer the organising or principal motif of state power. Ba'athism as an expression of Arab nationalist identity had little patience for a political discourse limited by an attachment to a single faith system. For the founders of

Ba'athism, the principles of secular, nationalist socialism would unite all Arabs irrespective of religion, nation or class. The banner of 'unity, liberation and socialism' held aloft by early Ba'athists was, however, soon torn down by the army officers who used such doctrines to coerce and repress millions of citizens in Iraq. Of course, the official state-sanctioned rhetoric and attachment to Ba'athism left the Islamic fundamentalists vulnerable. Aggressive secularisation undermined many of the autonomous powers previously enjoyed by clerical groups, classes or families in Iraq. Driven by centralising nationalist secularist tendencies, coercive expression of power and repression, the nationalist and Ba'athist regimes of Iraq implemented policies that formalised the separation of faith from politics. As a social grouping *Shi'a* elements took advantage of the opportunities for education and social mobility that the nationalist regimes of the 1950s offered to all Iraqi citizens. As one *Shi'a* figure asserts, 'There was a very gradual increase in *Shi'a* participation in society in Iraq but real power in the army, real power in the bureaucracy remained in the hands of the few ... and they weren't *Shi'a*'.[5] Those elements of the *Sunni* religious establishment that had already been co-opted into the state in the early 1920s remained co-opted. They formed the official religious establishment and provided functionaries for state-administered mosques and other foundations. Later these elements would be mercilessly exploited by Saddam Hussein to provide religious sanction for aggressive wars against Iran, Kuwait, and a jihad against the West. In the mid-1980s he established fundamentalist *Sunni* clerics as part of a 'faith campaign' to support his regime and mobilise popular support. He was depicted as 'faithful' to *Sunni* Islam, at prayer, celebrating Muslim festivals such as *Eid al-Fitr* and exhorting, in countless speeches, his fellow Muslims to aid him in his jihad.

For the *Shi'a*, the advent of secular, socialist nationalist rule in Iraq signalled the start of a state campaign to undermine their autonomy, limit their financial and community-based resources and the role that their clergy could play, independent of the official offices of the Iraqi state. Just as the Ottoman overlord Najib Pasha had issued orders to end *Shi'a* autonomy following the Karbala risings of 1843, so in the 1950s and early 1960s the army officers of Baghdad's new political elite would implement a series of measures designed to erode *Shi'a* influence and presence in Iraq.[6]

Secularism and Westernism

Contemporary thought on secularism outlines a series of approaches or models for governance, power and economy in many modern and

Western democracies. As the essence of modernity, secularism is seen through the framework of Western political thought: the departure from theocratic models of governance and the advent of popular sovereignty, plurality and liberalism. Yet, 'Western societies are governed by the belief that modernity is a single condition, everywhere the same and always benign, as societies became more modern ... they become better. Being modern means realising *our* values – the values of the Enlightenment'.[7] Under the increasingly autocratic rule of the army officers and despots, however, the Islamic fundamentalists of the Muslim world did not experience modernity in quite the same fashion.

Ultimately the inauthentic and artificial nature of secularism as a Western construct, import or, as fundamentalists are fond of referring to it, cancer, led to its dismissal in Islamist circles. For fundamentalists in Egypt and Gaza, the advent of secularist governance in the late 1950s led to the inception of state-orchestrated campaigns of repression against their kind. Hundreds and thousands of members or supporters of the Muslim Brotherhood found themselves subject to arrest without trial, lengthy imprisonment, torture or execution. Although the Egyptian Muslim Brotherhood had supported the aims of the Free Officer movement that led the 1952 revolution and deposed the Egyptian monarchy and ended British influence, the *Ikhwan* also made it clear that the new regime should rule according to Islamic principles. Moreover, though they were invited to sit in the cabinet of the revolutionary government formed by Gamal Abdel Nasser, the Muslim Brotherhood refused and took the possibly fatal step of actively distancing itself from the power-holders of the new regime. Along with other elements, the regime moved to counter popular support for the Muslim Brotherhood in Egypt and in Gaza. As one former member declared, 'It was a hard time for us and our ideas. The society turned against Islam, we were forced underground and then I was arrested and put in jail in Cairo alongside the other Brothers and the Communists.'[8] The Islamist pretenders were now viewed with suspicion and hostility, and were forced underground and into relative inaction. By 1954, some 18 months after the revolution, the nationalist government in Cairo outlawed membership of the Muslim Brotherhood, and from this point onwards tensions grew between mainstream elements of the society, as it struggled with its militant elements, and a regime bent on the destruction of this important counterforce in Egyptian society. It was a battle that ultimately would be lost when in June 2012 Egyptians voted Muslim Brotherhood candidate Mohammed Morsi into power as president. Violence carried out by Muslim Brothers against regime targets scarred future relations, yet it has been argued that it was 'in many respects a response to the situation in Egypt and had much in common with the violence of other Egyptians. The difference lay in the Islamic dimensions which the Brothers claimed as their own'.[9] The Islamic fundamentalists were compelled to go underground and rethink their responses to the process of modernisation, wrought in their societies as a result of their participation in liberation movements, that had delivered them from colonial rule into the hands of the secular nationalists. This was a bitter pill to swallow.

Developing Muslim society through the mechanism of modernisation steered by technocrats and army officers may well have led to initially successful and popular land reforms and the nationalisation of natural assets, but in the realm of developing democracy and political liberal-isation it became increasingly clear that there would be little by way of plurality of power that might give the Islamic fundamentalists a place in the political scheme. Secularism blossomed in Muslim domains but with a distinctly authoritarian bloom to its flower. In Iran, Shi'ism had been the state religion since the sixteenth century and over 80 per cent of the inhabitants of this multi-ethnic and multi-religious state are *Shi'a*. Historically the *Shi'a* clerical establishment of mullahs and ayatollahs had enjoyed a degree of autonomy from the structures of the Iranian state. The *Shi'a* religious establishment enjoyed wealth and resources independently of a weak and undeveloped state that were derived through land ownership, *Zakat* funds, and *waqf* endowments. The twentieth century, however, was to bring a reversal of this balance of power as the state's two successive Pahlavi leaders embarked on what has been referred to as a 'high modernist project' of accelerated secularism that threatened to erode the power of religious elements in Iranian society completely. The mullahs had played a part in early opposition movements such as the tobacco protests of 1891. In the early 1950s, following the CIA-backed coup that deposed the populist prime minister Mohammed Mossadeq and put Reza Shah Pahlavi back on the Peacock Throne, major constitutional measures were introduced by the Shah to limit all kinds of independent opposition, including the *Shi'a* clergy. As the Shah strengthened his power and control of the state, modernism and secularism were employed as his weapons of choice. In 1963, the Shah's reform programme, 'the White Revolution', put an effective end to *Shi'a* economic, legal and educational autonomy. The *waqf* system was put under state control and taken out of the hands of the mullahs, and the state-led secularisation programme led to a burgeoning of curricula and schools, universities and colleges that were under state, not religious, patronage. The mullahs were represented by the state as backward-looking and attached to medieval practices that, if allowed to flourish, would militate against the high modernist project. The political power of the mullahs was effectively limited by the Shah and his international backers in the West. Yet it has been highlighted that the mullahs' 'social and ideological power ... remained strong beneath the surface ... The faithful have continued to pay them *Zakat*, and it is generally believed that [they] receive more in religious taxes than the government does in secular ones'.[10] The mullahs and their supporters were prepared to bide their time, build on their support in exile and prepare to work with other elements in Iranian society to end the high modernist project as steered and shaped by the secularist-leaning Shah.

It was apparent that although moves to modernisation and secularism went hand-in-hand in Muslim societies during this period, they were allied to powers of different varieties. Although socialist secularism in Algeria was markedly different in style to capitalist secularism in Iran, the outcomes in terms of state power and relations with civil society bore startling similarities with respect to the Islamic fundamentalist movement. Local patterns of governance and historical dynamic appeared to unfold in a depressingly linear fashion when tied to the expression of religious identity in the political arena during this period. The legitimacy of the post-independent states was quickly called into question, as modernity projects began to fall apart and failed to deliver on the expectations that had been raised by their leaders in their speeches and broadcasts to the popular masses. Moreover, the advent of the secular coupling to the modernity project ensured that there was little hope that religion could ever be central to the political and public arena again. This was a powerfully frightening message to the millions of adherents to Islam and altered the ways in which they reflected on the modernisation processes at work in their own societies. Increasingly their leaders, activists and thinkers met in secret and courted the wrath of the state by taking the doctrine of secularism and its link to modernity as the starting point in a new discourse of refutation that was designed to reclaim modernity for Islam.

Devoid ideologies

The new discourses, authored by figures like Sayyid Qutb, controversially contended that secularism, as expressed through the powers that be in their own societies, brought with it anti-democratic autocrats and despots and that only a true Islam, active in the public sphere, would bring real peace, prosperity and fair governance. Qutb was an Egyptian member of the Muslim Brotherhood whose ideas and writings were progressively radicalised by his direct experiences of the West (including some time spent in the USA) as well as his imprisonment and subsequent execution at the hands of the Nasserist national authorities in the 1960s. His death is regarded by Islamist radicals as a martyrdom in the name of Islamic revivalism. His works reflecting on modernisation in the Muslim world are deeply influential. As Qutb stated:

> Look at this Capitalism with its monopolies, its usury and whatever else is unjust in it; at this individual freedom, devoid of human sympathy and responsibility for relatives except under the force of law; at this materialistic attitude which deadens the spirit; at this behaviour, like animals, which you call 'free mixing of the sexes'; at this vulgarity which you call emancipation of women; at these unfair cumbersome laws of marriage and divorce, which are contrary to the demands of practical life; and at this evil and fantastic racial discrimination. Then look at Islam … [11]

Such thinkers argued against attempts by the state to privatise Islam and deny it a place in public. They contended that it was clear that secularism would bring with it contest, conflict and state-based repression of the citizenry. And in this respect they spoke from bitter experience. They argued that the much-vaunted dimensions of secularism as liberty were entirely alien to their experience of it in practice. There was little in the concept for them that did not have connotations in practice with tyranny, fear, impoverishment and crisis for millions of Muslims across the globe. Secularism took on a very different meaning in these contexts.

Thus, while it may be true to assert that 'to "secularise" meant to make someone or something secular – converting from ecclesiastical to civil use or possession', what was contested by the Islamic fundamentalists was the very method and processes of possession employed.[12] The transition, viewed from the camp of the fundamentalists, was nasty, brutish and short: a deeply Hobbesian experience altogether. While in Europe the transition from ecclesiastic to secular rule was similarly punctuated by episodes of violence and conflict, the transition itself took place and unfolded over a number of centuries and was indigenous and integral to the dynamic of societies. This was simply not the case in the Muslim world. There was no slow unfolding struggle but what appeared to be an irreversible transformation, disruption and dislocation of Muslim societies almost overnight as resources that were traditionally the preserve of clerical class, groups and organisations were appropriated by the state. In the realms of law and education, where *qadis* (judges), mullahs and religious scholars had run schools, colleges and universities that were the symbols of Islam's role in the public sphere, secularisers now took control. The autonomous space of society carved out through the religious networks and structures of Islam would be corrosively eroded by the acid test of secularism. The modern secularists were driven to employ any means to modernise society according to a series of ideas, standards and doctrines garnered from cultures other than their own.

It was inevitable, then, that a contest or conflict would eventually erupt as secularists gained power and control of the state. In Muslim domains, secularism would come to be understood and signified not for its unique qualities but in distinction to Islam. The secularists would struggle to deny Islam a place in the public psyche and in many respects they failed to draw such distinctions at all. The traditional religious elites of Muslim societies were to be excluded and denied a role in shaping the modernisation process. To be tied to Islam appeared to be tied to a past that the secularists wanted to leave behind. They constantly struggled to exclude Islam and its historic dimension from the identities of the nations they sought to shape.

Empty Islam

Islam was progressively emptied of its power; only its symbols were employed by the state. Islamic fundamentalists were denied a place in the new political order, constrained by states that were only prepared to recognise them if they eschewed politics altogether. As a political force, the fundamentalists were regarded as a threat to the state. The birth of Pakistan in 1947, following the partition of India, did not herald the ascension of the fundamentalists to the portals of power. Although Pakistan was to be in essence a Muslim state, the mullahs were denied political control by the secularists. The architects of the state were determined to possess it as a secular product and to exclude the Islamists from the corridors of power. Similarly, in 1965 in Indonesia when the nationalist Suharto achieved power, he instituted a raft of policies and actions that were designed to exclude the Islamists from Indonesian politics. The pressure was on to remove elements such as the *Nahdatul Ulama* (Muslim Scholars League) from the formal political arena. Islam's role in struggle, revolution and post-independence politics was denied. The leaders of the state were determined to enforce the symbolic exile of the Islamists from power and deny them a say in governance, law and economic issues.

The secularists were hostile and suspicious of the Islamists. The Islamists appeared to represent biased, medieval, traditional philosophies whereas the secularists themselves failed to realise that they were already 'ruled by the myth that, as the rest of the world absorbs science and becomes modern, it is bound to become secular, enlightened and peaceful – as contrary to all evidence, they imagine[d] themselves to be'.[13] The Islamists did not see the secularists as neutral torch-bearers of a doctrine that would lead to peace and justice in their own societies; in fact, they believed quite the opposite would happen. Secularism was perceived as nothing more than Western colonialism in disguise. For the Islamists it became clear that there would be little to no opportunity to mediate the secularisation of society, to discuss its boundaries and the implications for Islam. The politics of secularisation led to the rapid expulsion of the Islamists from national narratives of liberation and independence, from the corridors of power and populist political movements. The politics of secularisation was laden with the subjectivity of those who acted as its interpreters; it was marked by violence not peace, oppression not liberty.

Despite protests to the contrary, the Islamic fundamentalists came to understand secularism not as a series of ideas with universal values at their core but as a Western construct around which the domination of other cultures and civilisations could be facilitated. Moreover, at this period the newly independent states were inexorably drawn into the great power politics of the Cold War. This resulted in a series of interdependencies that had less and less to do with Muslim community and solidarity transcending borders and more and more to do with client–patron relationships of dependency between either the Soviet East or the American West. Few Muslim states remained neutral or non-aligned during this period. The ideals and ambitions of the early Muslim modernisers for pan-Islamic solidarity were overshadowed by the realpolitik of inter-regional alliances in Asia, the Middle East and Africa of progressive secular regimes. At a time of great change and upheaval in Muslim societies, fundamentalists struggled to tell the difference in policy outcomes between the old European colonial overlords and the new secular socialists who now governed their countries.

Yet throughout this period there was very little realisation of the consequences of the disruption within and between Muslim societies wrought by secularisation by official decree. There was a hint of a backlash from the Islamists but it appeared that the regimes they rebelled against were quick to quell their political voice and pacify them through sheer force and repression. The voices of dissent were temporarily silent and that silence was mistakenly interpreted as Islamist acquiescence to the imposition of secularisation. In truth, as later chapters of this book highlight, resistance had merely been forced underground to explode a decade later in a conflict for the soul of modern Muslim societies.

The virtue of patience

Palestinian fundamentalist leaders, when reflecting on the enduring conflict with Israel in the late twentieth century, are fond of reminding their audience that they have a great sense of historic destiny and are prepared to wait for victory and bide their time against their opponents. In this respect, for these Islamic fundamentalists and many others, their sense of history is often condensed so that events that took place over a millennia ago are part of the narratives of activism today. They clung, and still cling to, versions of the past in their attempts to explain the nature of society in the present. Secularism was viewed as an attempt to sever the past from the present. Yet the past was symbolised, shaped and given depth and character by Islam. Secularism was viewed as a declaration of war against Islam, a religion that, unlike any other, shapes and influences the lives of Muslims, a religion whose values and principles are aimed at liberating mankind, establishing justice and equality, encouraging research and innovation and guaranteeing the freedoms of thought, expression and worship.[14]

The secularists believed in their mission to revolutionise and modernise Muslim societies, and their mission was crowned with the opening of nationalised factories, hydro-power dams, the advent of literacy programmes, the banning of the *hijab* (headscarf) and other forms of Islamic dress, the burgeoning of film industries, the arts and technological programmes. For a short while there were benefits that were to be enjoyed but a high price was exacted in terms of a decline in political freedoms. Internal enmity became an inevitable outcome and Islamists were often caught up in the growing opposition movement. Indeed, throughout this period it is difficult to find evidence of Islamists enjoying any formal political power or as significant players in other institutions of the state. If they were found to have a presence in, say, the army, they were purged out and denounced as traitors. Even in conservative Muslim states such as Jordan, although the Islamists were never formally prohibited from political life (unlike many other opposition elements that were proscribed by King Hussein in 1957), they enjoyed no influence in the corridors of power. In Saudi Arabia, although the ruling al-Saud family were close followers of the Wahabbi doctrines, the clerical elite did not have the power to exercise political influence in matters of state, governance, defence, economy or foreign affairs. King Faisal, the moderniser king of the early 1960s, trod a fine line in his attempts to institute change in the country while preserving its Islamic Wahabbi character. In the eyes of some of the fundamentalists, he failed.

Secularism was opposed by the Islamists for a number of reasons, and its meaning in the context of Muslim societies was contested. Furthermore, it is asserted that in relation to Islam there was a very clear assumption: 'Islam was assumed to have a spiritual authority, or a clergy, that hindered progress and prohibited the freedom of thought, and that should therefore be prevented from interfering in temporal matters.'[15] It was clear that the battle lines would be drawn around the working assumptions of Western-inspired secularism and Muslim interpretations. By coupling secularism to the national project during this delicate period of state-building in Muslim societies, disaffection with the project inevitably implied the same in respect of secularism. The perception that secularism implied the exclusion of Islam from the public domain established a deep fissure in society.

In Indonesia, the largest Muslim country in the world, the advent of independence after 350 years of Dutch rule might have been a portent for the flourishing of Islam. Instead, it signalled the rise of a secularist state where, although Islam was recognised as the predominant faith system, it was given no formal political power within the state's institutions. Islam, however, remained an important social force that would provide the bedrock for the emergence of a multi-faceted Islamic movement that would have both pro-secular and anti-secular elements. The advent of secularism did not lead to the diminishing appeal of Islam. The promulgation of a nation-state based on the doctrine of *pancasila* (nationalism, justice, democracy, faith and unity), however, did signal a temporary end to its political power. The traditionalists who had founded the *Nahdatul Ulama* (Muslim Scholars League) in 1926 and their reformist co-religionists in the *Muhammadiyah* movement, found themselves increasingly marginalised as tensions erupted in the late 1950s and early 1960s over their political activities. *Nahdatul Ulama* had even succeeded in forming an alliance with President Sukharno against radical leftist elements. By paying lip service to the *Pancasila* doctrine, such elements were able to survive but only as 'paper tigers'. *Pancasila* doctrine enshrined nationalism and secularism to the exclusion of Islam as a significant political force.

Muslim leaders had signed the 1949 Jakarta Charter enshrining *pancasila* republicanism on the understanding that Muslim citizens would be ruled in the independent state according to *shari'a* law. The new government reneged on its promise and in the early 1950s Muslim rebellion broke out. The public domain of Islam was subject to restriction and came into conflict with the elites of the new state: 'the nationalist imagining of Indonesia stresses the importance of cultural and social integration while shying away from religious tension and disintegration ... pancasila philosophy ... draws a distinction between politics and religion'.[16] In following decades that distinction would be tested to its limits by a new generation of Indonesian Muslims who embraced the revivalist philosophies of the 1970s and 1980s in their own contexts. The challenge for Indonesia's leaders would be to preserve the secular, plural character of the state and yet be democratic at the same time.

Throughout this period, government repression of Muslim identity can be identified as a significant feature of secularisation in the Muslim world. In many cases this repression – a denial of the democratic impulse supposedly inherent in secularism – served to radicalise Muslims and their religious leaders. Political liberalisation simply failed to materialise in the new Muslim regimes. Political parties were banned, political organisations were prohibited, the legislature was suspended, martial law was introduced, the army officers were called upon for support and Muslim leaders were blamed for fermenting a crisis against the state. All Muslim agitation was regarded as a threat to the regime.

The legitimate concerns of Muslim leaders were largely ignored by the state. Within Muslim communities, however, concern over such issues struck a sympathetic chord. In Egypt, for example, the leadership of the Muslim Brotherhood had raised grave concerns over the secularisation of the education system and the impact of such reforms on dimensions of religious-based education. The Brotherhood had organised campaigns to promote alternative curricula and look at ways in which secular and religious curricula could be merged. The Muslim Brotherhood leader, Hassan al-Banna, wary of the route to secularisation that was occurring in Turkey and Iran, argued that in Egypt, 'education should be neither purely Islamic nor purely secular (i.e. Western), but should harmoniously blend religious character and moral training with scientific training'.[17] The leaders of post-revolutionary Egypt, however, viewed the high modernity project somewhat differently. For nearly two decades (the 1950 to the 1970s) the Islamic fundamentalists were denied a place in the public arena. The prisons and underground cells became the locus of an increasingly radicalised Islamist force. Secularism was increasingly associated in the doctrine of Islamic fundamentalism with the extension of the Western project to impinge on and dominate Muslim countries.

Phantom of the Islamic state

In other contexts, secularism appeared as both the means to end colonial rule and commence the state-building project. In the case of Pakistan, the difficulty in the transition from Raj rule to independence lay in the key tension over whether Pakistani national identity would be shaped and defined by Islam or not. The adoption of Islam would mean that important ethnic and sectarian differences might be emphasised. Secularism, on the other hand, offered the prospect of transcending such core points of identity. In many respects the prospect of state formation offered both an opportunity and a defeat for India's Muslims in the late 1940s. It was a defeat that the end of empire might necessitate the break-up of the territories of India. The opportunity, however, for the architects of the new Muslim state lay in negotiating a vision for modern statehood and whether that vision would be shaped in terms of secular democracy or some kind of theocratic Islamic state structure. There were clear divisions of opinion when envisioning the future state. Modernisers such as Mohammed Ali Jinnah sought to establish a modern Muslim state that was both plural and open in outlook. In his addresses to the new nation in 1947, Jinnah outlined his vision clearly:

> We are starting in the days when there is no discrimination, no distinction between one community and another, no discrimination between caste and creed and another. We are starting with this fundamental principle that we are all citizens and equal citizens of one state.[18]

Jinnah espoused a vision of Muslim nationalism and nation that was based on precepts of plurality, equality of citizenship, openness and democracy. He was wary of the traditionalist mullahs who sought to tie state-creation and state-building to Islam by putting them in charge of the country. Mawdudi, who had supported the struggle for independence, however, opposed the elites that shaped Pakistan into a secular rather than Islamic Muslim nation. He was the torchbearer for the establishment of an Islamic state in Pakistan, and the *Jama'at al-Islami* Party was the institutional vehicle for this goal. The mullahs demanded that the constitution of the new state reflect Islamic principles at its core even if that meant that notions of equality among all citizens (whether Muslim or non-Muslim) were abandoned. Mawdudi contended that the full potential of Pakistan could never be realised until the state vanquished secular tendencies and was fully emblematic of the Islamic project. Mawdudi was deeply critical of the Muslim League and its leadership for failing to deliver statehood, Islamic-style. He contended that Muslims were obliged to struggle for statehood in order to establish the modern Islamic state rather than a political entity that was empty of meaning as a religious or faith-based structure.

Moreover, if the state and its institutions stood in the way of the goal, Mawdudi advocated more revolutionary tactics:

> Islam is a revolutionary doctrine and system that overturns governments. It seeks to overturn the whole universal social order ... and establish its structure anew ... Islam seeks the world. It is not satisfied by a piece of land but demands the whole universe ... Islamic Jihad is at the same time offensive and defensive ... The Islamic party does not hesitate to utilize the means of war to implement its goal.[19]

Islamisation of Pakistan resulted in decades of civil instability and political tension as the secularists and mullahs struggled over the nature of the state. Such tensions played out in the spheres of constitutional debate to include law, legislature and offices of government. In advocating the imposition of *shari'a* and specific limits on popular democracy and sovereignty, it was inevitable that the mullahs would clash with the Muslim secularists. By 1953 the crisis had exploded in the Punjab and martial law was declared by the government in the Pakistani capital, Lahore. In 1958, following yet another constitutional clash, martial law was imposed again. State repression of the Islamic fundamentalists was soon in evidence and any further attempt at Islamisation was put on hold. As with so many Muslim states, it would not be until the 1970s that the secular scheme would be undermined by the revival of the fundamentalist project, and its adoption, in the case of Pakistan, by the leaders of the state.

Interestingly, such developments in the debate about the nature of the state as Islamic or secular in Muslim societies also impacted on neighbouring Afghanistan. Secularist nationalists were able to successfully marginalise religious elements from the core of this ever-fragile state and its institutions. Post-1945, Afghanistan was initially characterised by a modernising monarchy and political elite that sought to develop the country according to the doctrines of the high modernity project. A semblance of political liberalisation, including relatively free elections to the Afghan legislature, were allowed by the ruling family. King Shah Mahmoud, however, like so many of his counterparts in other Muslim domains, understood the threat inherent in opposition movements – whether leftist or fundamentalist – and employed state power to effectively limit such activities.

The most vocal of these groups was the *Wikh-i-Zalmayan* (Awakened Youth), a movement comprised of diverse dissident elements founded in Qandahar in 1947. A newly formed student union not only provided a forum for political debate but also produced pieces of theatre critical of Islam and the monarchy. Newspapers criticised the government, and many groups began demanding a more open political system. By the late 1940s, opposition elements and groups had been rendered powerless following state orders to ban their activities, dissolve their groups and imprison their leaders. By the early 1950s political liberalisation was effectively halted by the regime and a sense of entrenchment was palpable in Kabul. Working against this manifestation of urban-based power were the multiple layers of tribal, leftists, religious and ethnic loyalties in the rest of the country. An iron fist did not necessarily imply complete state control of the country; internal fissures were apparent in the Afghan royal family, reflecting a struggle between the old guard and younger members of the regime. A victory of sorts for the modernists was apparent in the appointment of Mohammed Daoud, himself a member of the royal family, to the post of prime minister. Mohammed Daoud championed the high modernity project and the accompanying principles of secularisation in Afghanistan throughout the late 1950s and early 1960s. He was a reformist rather than a revolutionary, but he also demonstrated he was prepared to crack down on opposition to his changes coming from Afghanistan's clerical class. In the late 1950s he imprisoned clerics who protested at his policies of state-led secularism and emancipation. Throughout the early 1960s, Mohammed Daoud characterised his tenure by pursuing a series of policies that emphasised nationalism and, more specifically, Pashtun-nationalism in Afghanistan. Such policies contributed, in part, to a breakdown of relations with neighbouring Pakistan and a parallel deepening of ties with the Soviet Union. By 1963, Mohammed Daoud was compelled to resign (only to return some ten years later at the head of an Afghan coup that deposed the monarchy). The king appointed another modernist, Mohammad Yusuf, to lead the country and through him the secular scheme appeared to be secured through the new Afghan Constitution that was promulgated in 1964. The Constitution outlined the nature of the state as a unitary constitutional monarchy where all citizens, irrespective of Muslim or non-Muslim status, would enjoy the same rights and duties. The Constitution recognised Islam as 'the sacred religion' of the country but also noted that non-Muslims had the right to enjoy freedom of religion. The clerical class had not achieved the goal of establishing Afghanistan as an Islamic state. The judicial system would not be based on the *shari'a* although there was a provision within one article of the Constitution to ensure that all laws respected the principles of Islam. Moreover, to a certain extent, the provision of an independent judiciary undermined the monopoly of the clerical class. Subsequent elections in the 1960s confirmed the secular rather than religious nature of the legislature and the state. In most respects, tribal and ethnic differences accounted for the era of instability that ensued: 'the new constitution was seen as an attempt by Pashtuns to assert majoritarian hegemony ... ethnic division was key to state failure and, consequently to the continuation of civil war in Afghanistan'.[20] By 1973 the increasing political crisis, internal tensions and discord had created the right conditions for the coup led by Mohammed Daoud. By this point, however, the forces of fundamentalist revivalism were afoot in Afghanistan and the country itself remained vulnerable to the influences of other external Islamist and foreign elements. Following years of marginalisation, the religious dimension of ethnic politics in Afghanistan would reignite in the 1970s and 1980s.

During this time in some countries, the secularisation of Muslim society did occur to be succeeding with little in the way of resistance from the Islamists. In Turkey, the Attaturkist programme that had commenced at the beginning of the twentieth century had by the 1950s and 1960s given rise to a modern society where the public expression of Islamic identification had successfully been suppressed. Turkey's political leaders managed to successively disestablish Islam, but only by relying on power structures such as the military that underscored the undemocratic character of secularism in contemporary Muslim contexts. Turkish society and culture were transformed from a plural to a monolithic vision of national identity in which faith and ethnic identity were brutally subsumed. Although this policy was more successful in urban than rural areas, by the 1960s Islamic revivalism – spiritual, cultural and political – was in evidence in the formation of organisations and societies. It would take several more decades, however, until such forces could garner the strength to successfully penetrate the political arena. Only when the military was removed from the political arena could the Islamists begin to exploit the vacuum. In the 1960s, however, the complex social and political development of the country had undermined the centrality of Islamic issues in the political system. In a largely secularised and pluralistic society, Islam played the role of a private religion inherent in the national identity of the majority, but was only faintly able to lay claim to the control of public life.[21]

The deliberate exclusion of the fundamentalists inherent to secular doctrine affected the whole spectrum of Islam. Increasingly, secularism was given significance and meaning as the antithesis of Islam. This established the notion that the high modernity project could not accommodate the fusion of faith and politics so intrinsic to Islam.

Modernity in these societies was only given meaning when actively divorced from the traditional sources of faith that had previously shaped and governed politics, culture, economy and foreign relations. The project of secular constructionism as developed in states such as Tunisia, Egypt, Iran and Turkey during this period, with its emphasis on leftist doctrines, to the development of modern society through manipulation or top-down engineering of society, economy and culture, effectively narrowed the space in which Muslims could advocate an alternative agenda. The new national elites viewed both the Muslim establishment as well as opposition or reform groups with deep suspicion and as virtual saboteurs of their carefully constructed project to transform Muslim societies.

The phoenix

By the end of the 1960s, however, there was evidence that the great experiments in secular nation-building in Muslim societies across the developing world were beginning to fall apart. The task of exporting a 'universal' doctrine to Muslim domains would need to be rethought. At the time, however, nationalist regimes sought only to engage further repressive strategies against their citizens to maintain power and preserve their hold on the state. Popular support and legitimacy were no longer a necessary element in their strategies of regime maintenance and self-preservation. Islamic fundamentalism was seen by these state elites as a new threat in a modern era. For a while, Islamists were successfully portrayed by the state and secular intelligentsia as the impediment to progress, development and stability in modern Muslim societies. Islamists were denied a part in the modernity project and their pronouncements on the compatibility of Islam and the modern were regarded with deep scepticism. The secularists appeared to eschew the indigenous Muslim dimension of identity that was core to Muslim societies in favour of new doctrines devoid of Islamic cultural value. In the place of Islam, new myths of nation and past were carefully constructed by state-appointed historians, artists and poets. Secularists contended that Islam was incompatible with secular nationalism. The secularists failed to understand that despite the attempt to marginalise and exclude Islam from the formal structures of political power in Muslim societies, it remained the key characteristic in the formation of identity and cohesion in modern Muslim societies. More than that, however, the secularists of this period denied the democratic content of secularism to Muslim citizens at a time when they had clamoured for an end to authoritarian governance. The secularists did attempt to construct new identities around notions of a more pluralist nationalism – Pakistani, Egyptian, Indonesian, Tunisian and Iranian; 'nation' would replace 'faith' as the bonding mechanism of modern societies. National leaders, such as Gamal Abdel Nasser, would in turn be semi-deified by the state and held up as icons of modernism.

Secularism saw no mirror image in Islam; as one writer declares,

> Islam and nationalism are mutually exclusive terms. As a constructive loyalty to a territorially defined national group, nationalism has been incompatible with Islam ... Nationality among the majority of their populations is still overshadowed by the religious community; national frontiers are still measured by religion.[22]

Yet Islamic fundamentalists, as the following chapters highlight, would not be pacified or content to accept a secularism that was empty of the very values – liberty, stability, justice and democracy – that its advocates claimed to represent. As *Shi'a* leader Ayatollah Fadlallah opined, 'the West speaks of justice and freedom but when we demand justice ... we are denied'.[23] The tenacious grip on the state that the secularists had secured for themselves in the early years of independence, coup and revolution would be challenged by the fundamentalists. The Islamic phoenix was about to rise from the ashes.

Notes

1 J.L. Esposito, *The Islamic Threat: Myth or Reality?*, New York: Oxford University Press, 1992, p. 153.
2 See B. Milton-Edwards, *Islam and Politics in the Contemporary World*, Cambridge: Polity Press, 2004; and L. Carl Brown, *Religion and State: The Muslim Approach to Politics*, New York: Columbia University Press, 2000.
3 F. Abu-Jabar, *The Shi'ite Movement in Iraq*, London: Saqi, 2003, p. 65.
4 Interview with Dr Laith Kubba, London, December 2002.
5 Ibid.
6 J. Cole, *Sacred Space and Holy War: Politics, Culture and History of Shi'ite Islam*, London: I.B. Tauris, 2002, pp. 117–18.
7 J. Gray, *Al-Qaeda and What it Means to Be Modern*, London: Faber and Faber, 2003, p. 1.
8 Interview with Abu Shaban, Deir al-Balah, Gaza, September 1989.
9 R.P. Mitchell, *The Society of Muslim Brothers*, New York: Oxford University Press, 1969, p. 320.
10 F. Halliday, *Iran, Dictatorship and Development*, Harmondsworth: Penguin Books, 1979, p. 212.
11 S. Qutb, *Milestones*, Beirut: Holy Koran Publishing House, 1980, p. 28.
12 J. Keane, 'Secularism', in D. Marquand and R.L. Nettler (eds) *Religion and Democracy*, Oxford: Blackwell, 2000, p. 6.

13 J. Gray, *Al-Qaeda and What it Means to be Modern*, London: Faber and Faber, 2003, p. 118.
14 A. Tamimi, 'The origins of Arab secularism', www.sullivan-county.com/x/islam_sec.htm
15 Ibid.
16 I. Abu-Rabi, 'Christian–Muslim relations in Indonesia: the challenges of the twenty-first century', *Middle East Affairs Journal*, 4:1–2, Winter/Spring 1998, p. 24.
17 R.P. Mitchell, *The Society of Muslim Brothers*, New York: Oxford University Press, 1969, p. 285.
18 As quoted in A.S. Ahmed, *Jinnah, Pakistan and Islamic Identity: The Search for Saladin*, London: Routledge, 1997, p. 175.
19 As quoted in Y. Haddad, *Islamists and the Challenge of Pluralism*, Washington, DC: CCAS, 1995, p. 10.
20 A. Misra, *Afghanistan: The Labyrinth of Violence*, Cambridge: Polity Press, 2004, p. 44.
21 I.M. Lapidus, *A History of Islamic Societies*, New York: Cambridge University Press, 1988, p. 901.
22 P.J. Vatikiotis, *Islam and the State*, London: Routledge, 1987, pp. 42–44.
23 Sayyid Mohammed Husayn Fadlallah, interview with author, Beirut, May 2000.

3 Identity and revivalism

There is nothing in our book, the Koran, that teaches us to suffer peacefully. Our religion teaches us to be intelligent. Be peaceful, be courteous, obey the law, respect everyone; but if someone puts his hand on you, send him to the cemetery. That's a good religion.

(Malcolm X, Detroit, 1963)

Religious revivalism is common to the processes of faith and renewal the world over. For centuries faith systems have renewed and revived themselves in response to the challenges inherent in the historical dynamic. There has often been evidence of a connection between revivalism or resurgence of faith practice and its link to politics. It is no coincidence then that since the 1960s there has been evidence of a significant revivalist movement within Islam that has included politics. The 1960s, particularly the latter part of the decade, are characterised by protest movements, revolution and counterculture as orthodox notions of governance and society were challenged by a post-war generation.

Modernisation and the modernity project had offered opportunities to countless millions in the developing world, but the rising tide of social and economic expectation crashed in a crisis of identity when states failed to meet the demands of their citizens for more justice, power and liberty. Religious revivalism was but one dimension of the era of change that gripped the world during this period.

The experiment in religious renewal took an Islamic dimension, impacting on dimensions of the Muslim faith system. The agenda of Muslim renewal or revival centred on both a personal and political dimension to identity. Islamic revivalism was apparent not only in increased religious observance of rites such as Ramadan, mosque building, Muslim dress and customs and prayer, but was translated into political and social action around Muslim perspectives on governance, civil society, economic reform and law. What was remarkable was that one single faith system could account for the burgeoning and myriad manifestations of a revived Islamic form apparently varying limitlessly from one Muslim context to another. In part, this revivalism was a reaction to the sense that current political frameworks were failing. The mission of a more authentic, indigenous and relevant response to the demands of modernity became the compelling task of the new generation of interpreters and activists of Islam.

These new actors pushed at the complex boundaries of faith and politics in a variety of ways. Their political engagements took place in a dizzying array of activities and levels. In respect of the levels at which interaction and engagement took place, it became clear that the Islamists were prepared to work not just in the form of spheres of political life but to look at localised and informal dimensions of power and politics as well. Often it was at the bottom or grassroots where the effects of such interactions were most noticeable. In the formal realms of politics, particularly at the state level, secular elites themselves donned the cloak of religious respectability to meet the new Islamist opposition head-on. They announced new policies and ventures tied to the Islamisation of society but not necessarily politics. During this period of change, revivalism and politics were identifiable across the spectrum from liberal to reactionary. In other words, Islamic revivalism was not merely a byword for reactionary fundamentalism as is commonly assumed. New doctrines and ideological departures were apparent in the writings of ascendant figures and personalities who, although they had not emerged from the seminaries of Islam, claimed religious credentials. New social action agendas were detected in the activities of the revivalist movements. Everything was fluid and up for grabs in an intellectual and political context within Muslim domains. As translators of the new doctrines of Islamism, the new leaders, preachers and activists represented Islam to the popular masses in a simplified form that obviated the need for the traditional translators of faith doctrine from the seminaries of Islam. This implied an internal challenge to Islam, especially within *Sunni* circles where questions of religious interpretation (*ijtihad*) had been in stasis. A new tone of urgency was also suffused into Islamic revivalism. There was a sense that the decay of Islam had to be halted before an irreversible collapse took place. The revivalists were determined that Islam would be relevant again.

One issue that did become relevant, however, was the extent to which every expression of Islam and Muslim identity was labelled revivalist, and, therefore, fundamentalist. Yet, in the popular-based movements for Islamic revivalism led by increasingly charismatic and powerful figures, there was an indication that at the root of all their activities a fundamentalist agenda was being pursued. This fundamentalist agenda was characterised by simple populist slogans such as 'Islam is the Solution'. How could such an appeal fail when directed at the urban slum dwellers of Lahore? The fundamentalists determined that the revivalist project should incorporate a reassertion of a pure Islamic identity shaped at the level of the individual. This demanded that the accretion of un-Islamic ways were no longer to be tolerated in any way, shape or form. Immorality – alcohol, mixing between the sexes, non-Muslim dress styles and lifestyles – was to be conquered, even if it demanded force. As a tract distributed around the Islamic University of Gaza in the early 1980s declared, 'How can uncovered women and men with Beatle haircuts liberate our holy places?' In this slogan a direct link was apparent between social or Muslim custom and political action. Indeed, as we shall see in this chapter, the Islamists declared that Muslim defeat on the battlefield was directly linked to the abandonment of Islam. The recovery of political power, they argued, was inextricably linked to a return by society to 'the straight path' of Islam. Yet that recovery of the political often offered the glimmer of a more progressive – justice-based – vision of Islam in the modern context. The fundamentalist dimension to revivalism was rivalled by progressive dimensions in geographic contexts as diverse as Iran and the United States of America. Moreover, progressive technologies and techniques were also employed, consciously or otherwise, by the revivalists to disseminate their messages to as wide an audience as possible.

One issue that united the Muslim revivalists across the political spectrum, however, was secularism. They variously interpreted the impact of secularism on Muslim societies as a curse, establishing a condition of *jahilli* (pre-paganism) on all Muslims. The revivalists asserted that faith should be reunited with the political. This was a task that the revivalists addressed themselves to in constituting their movements and activities. As the influential thinker Sayyid Qutb asserted,

> the movement addresses human beings as they exist in actuality, and mobilizes the resources and means that are in accordance with practical conditions. Since this movement has to confront such *jahilli*, which prevails over ideas and beliefs on the basis of which a practical system of life is established duly backed by political and material authority, the Islamic movement, has, therefore, to produce parallel resources to countenance the *jahilli*.[1]

The recovery of that which was Muslim demanded that in Muslim countries the government and the law incorporate and reflect Islam.

The adoption or incorporation of secular forms of governance, moreover, was seen as nothing more than capitulation to Western ways. Inherent to revivalism, therefore, was a conscious rejection by Islamists of Western political constructs. If such demands for Islamisation could be accommodated by the state engaging in reform, then the majority of revivalists implied they would be content. There emerged, however, an increasingly militant and more radical dimension of the revivalist project that demanded nothing short of revolution to replace an existing *jahilli* Muslim state order with an authentic Islamic one. In the eyes of the state, such sentiments were understood as treason.

The revivalism incipient from the late 1960s, then, would have a very diverse character that would reflect the social and historical contexts from which it emerged. Islam would become more public once again – political and ideological – often putting it in conflict with others. This movement was classified as religious, reformist and radical in hue. In this way both the political and non-political dimensions of revivalism were incorporated. The latter two categories obviously interface with the political realm directly, but in very different ways. As I have already mentioned, the reformists were prepared to see the state change gradually in respect of the demand for more Islamic governance; the radicals, on the other hand, often advocated direct action and revolutionary methods.

The wretched of the earth

The story of Islamic resurgence is one of constant 'ebb and flow' so it is not possible to point to one date as the starting point of an episode of change. There are, however, historic episodes in the late 1960s and 1970s which have been described as a watershed or turning point, and they include the defeat of the Arab forces in the Six Day War against Israel in 1967. The rudiments of history also tell us that the core of the resurgence phenomenon took place in an urban setting among the poor – at least it is the poor who were the target of the leaders of the resurgence movement. The gap between the disempowered Muslim poor and the wealthy secular elites of the state was increasingly exposed and exploited during this period. Although it was true that economic development in Muslim majority countries had occurred since 1945, by the late 1970s and early 1980s many problems were apparent: 'population explosion, urban hypertrophy, lagging food production, low industrial productivity, inadequately trained labour force, huge defence expenditures, increasing inequality, political instability, and social fragmentation'.[2] The belief arose that the root of Muslim poverty lay in the abandonment of faith.

It was as if a chasm had emerged and Islam in revival bridged the gap. Revivalism then became implicitly, if not often explicitly, linked to populism and struck a chord with other social movements that arose in the developing world during this time. This approach recognised the socio-economic context in which Muslims were compelled to exist and found it wanting. Hence revivalism, as much as it was about the spiritual or cultural lineage of Islam, could also provide a new voice for the silent oppressed Muslim. As Sheikh Naim al-Qassam, deputy leader of Hizb Allah, proclaimed: 'We want to build society, to provide essential services and meet the prevailing challenges ... Putting our interests first, our principles first and meeting the needs of all confessions'.[3]

This populist perspective was apparent and increasingly common in Muslim movements such as the Muslim Brotherhood and epitomised by the *Shi'a* Lebanese cleric, Imam Musa al-Sadr. The politics of economy mattered to these Muslims and they used this as a platform from which to re-energise the Muslim community. For a generation of young people (a population explosion had gripped many Muslim domains) denied opportunities for an education, employment and shelter, the activist stance on such issues taken by the Islamists struck a popular chord.

> [The] root of the 'Islamic phenomenon' [is] the well known economic and demographic problems and the policy dilemmas they pose for government ... There is a withdrawal of the state ... unable to cope with the mounting burdens. This is where the Islamic economic and social sectors are moving in.[4]

Here the fact that the Islamists recognised the crisis around them and formulated an approach that facilitated their reinsertion into the public arena is apparent. The emphasis here is on the modern rather than some traditional or ancient faith system fossilised and redundant, the 'ebb and flow of Islamic fundamentalism throughout history reveals an ongoing dialectic between Islam and its social–economic–political environment'.[5]

This emphasis was reflected in the Lebanese context in the activities of Imam Musa al-Sadr. Musa al-Sadr was an Iranian-born cleric with family roots in southern Lebanon. He grew up in and around the religious seminary city of Qom. By the late 1950s Musa al-Sadr was a teacher in the seminaries and involved in religious publishing as well.

His religious training offered him opportunities to lead and inspire *Shi'a* Muslims. To this end he went to the southern Lebanese town of Tyre in 1960 and quickly rose in the ranks of the local religious clergy.

From his base in Tyre, Musa al-Sadr recognised that the system of consociational democracy that defined and shaped the political framework of Lebanon, characterising it as one of the freest Arab states in the region, in fact offered little to the country's majority *Shi'a* community. This community enjoyed little by way of the privileges of democracy. The majority formed the most impoverished elements of Lebanese society. Musa al-Sadr was quick to recognise the growing consciousness of the *Shi'a* community, its radicalisation and its vulnerability to the appeal of leftist revolutionary movements. He also knew that this community could be mobilised to effectively safeguard its interests where no other would. The charismatic al-Sadr was determined to step out of the seminary and engage in populist social action that would serve the interests of the *Shi'a* in Lebanon. By the late 1960s his doctrine of social action centred on the notion of the apparent distinction between the 'haves' and the 'have-nots' and an effective mechanism to address the dichotomy. He did this by organising an extensive social-based support system which he founded under the name of *harakat al-mahrumin* (the Movement of the Deprived). The movement was forged, in 1974, from a series of protests and demonstrations organised by al-Sadr and his followers directed at bringing the plight of the *Shi'a* to the attention of the Lebanese government. Shortly after, as Lebanon inched closer to civil war, an armed element of the movement emerged and was established as a resistance force (AMAL). Musa al-Sadr encouraged a departure from a quietist *Shi'a* presence in Lebanon to a populist social movement that would also take up arms in defence of its interests and community and serve the same community as the country descended into civil war. The social projects designed to support the community included schools, orphanages, vocational colleges, health services and literacy campaigns. Such activities aimed at building the capability of the *Shi'a* community in order to demand its share of services and power from the state. The dynamic of this new socio-economic agenda was obscured in the descent into violence that enveloped Lebanon when civil war broke out in 1975. Every community in this multi-religious state was drawn into a war that would lead to the impoverishment of the whole country. This was a war in which sectarian and confessional tensions not only engulfed opposing religious communities such as the Christians and the Muslims, but appeared within such communities as well. Musa al-Sadr meanwhile maintained his populist agenda and drew on his ecumenical approach to maintain good relations. The potential for change was altered, however, when on a visit to Libya in 1978, the leader and two of his aides were 'disappeared'.

This disappearance, however, did not limit the extent to which con-temporary Shi'ism drew inspiration and support from its populist doctrines of reform and revolution. The torchbearers of such populist doctrines within the *Shi'a* community would, however, increasingly vie with each other (as the history of AMAL and Hizb Allah rivalry attests) for the hearts and minds of this confessional constituency. They were further inspired by the fundamentalist victory in the revolution in Iran in 1979 and the ascent to power of the theocratic elite that brought Islam back to the state in such a dramatic fashion. The new regime in Tehran would back Hizb Allah over AMAL as the struggle for the hearts and minds of Lebanon's *Shi'a* continued throughout the 1980s.

Musa al-Sadr's legacy, however, remains. It is given form by the foundation established in his name and a mission to work

> towards a society free of ignorance, poverty and disease, with equal opportunities regardless of differences of faith or sex, and an environ-ment blessed by a growing dialogue between the contributions of the capable and the needs and expectations of the deprived; a dialogue built on participation and trust in one's self and in others.[6]

For others, however, the legacy has a more violent dimension associated with the prominence of *Shi'a* elements in the militia politics of war Lebanese-style. It is thus contended that the *Shi'a* 'discovery and use of terrorism [are], in a sense, the inevitable result of Sadr's radicalisation of his constituency. Radical Islam is bound to end in terrorism.'[7] Such accusations, however, fail in holding failed states, unjust regimes and authoritarian governments accountable for the part they have played in the descent to violence. There is a failure here to perceive the Islamist response in the context of wider cultures of rising social protest and agendas for change that addressed rights through reform. For in the same years that Musa al-Sadr had led the social protest movements of *Shi'a* in Lebanon, in Northern Ireland local civil rights activists took on the state in campaigns that employed direct action, civil disobedience and demonstration to highlight the distinction between the 'haves and the have-nots' and demand equal rights in respect of the state.

Where faith and politics meet on common ground

There is little doubt that the populist agenda promoted by the Islamists would secure growing support and provide an important foundation for the revivalism project, whether the project involved the establishment of a kindergarten in Tyre in southern Lebanon or a rally for youth education in Harlem. Key in distinguishing this revivalism and its socio-economic dimension from other protest movements, third world elements, leftists and socialists, however, was a repetitive attachment to the principle that Islam must not only become central to the public domain again but govern the political framework of society as well. The immutable link between faith and politics was reasserted. In this respect revivalism had a very specific religio-political character that deliberately utilised Islamic tradition in recognition of a cyclical process of reform from within. The regeneration of an authentic Muslim identity was seen as a key task for the fundamentalist project. It was one, however, that was open to a variety of interpretations.

The regeneration of Muslim identity lies in the recognition that alternative political projects – such as nationalism or socialism – in Muslim societies had failed. The failure of such projects to bring meaningful liberties – such as freedom of association, freedom of speech and the freedom to form political parties – coupled with economic crisis precipitated by a failure by secular-led regimes to generate meaningful income redistribution in society, established a credibility gap and disappointment among growing numbers of incumbent leaders of Muslim regimes. In many respects there was recognition that a crisis – of many dimensions – had emerged and Islamic fundamentalism became the most significant response. The crisis was recognised as arising from a dangerous mixture of forces, political as well as economic. This regeneration required a significant degree of re-acquaintance and discovery of Islam. But this process was not always marshalled by the traditionalists, conservatives or seminary-educated religious figures of Islam. Some undertook the process of regeneration without any formal religious training and yet they succeeded in their campaigns for the Islamisation of their neighbourhood, schools, workplaces, communities, regions and even nations. Such individuals would be assisted in a number of ways – sometimes by the very state they opposed or demanded reform from. Others found support from elements keen to promote Islam as a weapon against their enemies. They often exploited the expansion of literacy rates in Muslim domains to disseminate their ideas and arguments to a wider potential audience. Increasingly revivalism and its political dimensions in the fundamentalist guise seemed to grip a variety of countries. In part this was a backlash against the modernisation project. As such, revivalism was the enemy of modernity and of those who had an interest in the maintenance of the modernity project in Muslim domains. Throughout the 1970s the movement grew. In the Palestinian territory of the Gaza Strip the revival of Islam – as much a political as well as a social or economic force – had a profound impact on Palestinian politics, as well as on the dynamics of conflict between Israel and the Palestinians.

Palestine has always figured largely in Islam. Jerusalem has shrines that are considered to be the third most holy in Islam (after Mecca and Medina). The lands of Palestine have been endowed by Muslims for generations (*waqf*). Islam is the principal faith of the majority of Palestinians. Moreover, in the first part of the twentieth century, Islamism coloured Palestinian responses to the colonial experience through the mandate rule of the British, expanding Zionist settlement, and the imposed partition of 1947. Islamism had both an institutional and oppositional dimension and contributed to the shaping of Palestinian national identity and ideologies of resistance. The establishment of the state of Israel in 1948, the dispossession of thousands of Palestinian Arabs, and the first Arab–Israeli war left the Palestinians bereft of a state to call their own. From 1948 to 1967 Jordan and Egypt controlled the Palestinian territories of the West Bank and the Gaza Strip. Following the Six Day War in 1967 Israel occupied the West Bank, Sinai, the Gaza Strip and the Golan Heights, and annexed East Jerusalem. From this period onwards the Palestinian political vista was dominated by the secular forces of the Palestinian liberation movement, including the various factions of the PLO. And while the Muslim Brotherhood had established branches in Palestine before 1948, they were significantly absent from the Palestinian political arena. In the Gaza Strip those who had been involved in the Islamist movement and had survived Nasser's campaigns of repression found that there was little by way of organisation and strength to hold onto in the post-war period. Instead they focused their energies on a new generation of schoolchildren and young graduates who had been educated in the universities of Egypt. Here the seeds of revivalism were sown, as Hamas leader, Mahmoud Zahar, declared, 'The people returned to their religion [and] started to study Islam thoroughly and began to live Islam as a system governing their way of life'.[8] Reconstitution, however, would take almost a decade to be actualised and in part this actualisation was also down to the malign encouragement of the Islamists, by Israel, in the hope that they would oppose and bring down Palestinian secular nationalist elements. The Islamists themselves re-inserted themselves into the public arena by targeting places of learning – wrestling with the nationalists for control of local universities, setting up rival activities and projects aimed at the education of Palestinian youth and the demand for the re-Islamisation of Gazan society. The reconstituted movement was led by a charismatic lay preacher and teacher named Ahmed Yassin. By the early 1970s Sheikh Yassin had gathered a group of well-educated supporters who subscribed to the revivalist philosophies of the Muslim Brotherhood through the establishment of a welfare and charity organisation known as *Mujama*. Such a network would take an increasingly important role in integrating a Palestinian population denied rights by the Israeli occupier. The comfort of faith was apparent in the burgeoning activities of the Islamists. Sheikh Yassin had succeeded in an appeal to educated and professional people who had graduated from Arab and Western universities in sciences, medicine and engineering, only to find their aspirations for advancement stifled by the repressive polices of secular Arab states. In their frustration they turned to the traditional force of Islam for an answer.

The state bites back

The scope of the revivalist project expanded apace. Even in Muslim countries that had incorporated dimensions of Islamic government, the political potential of revivalism harnessed was recognised and incorporated by state elites. This was the case in Pakistan where, by the mid-1970s, the Bhutto regime was seen to give in to fundamentalist demands for an outward attachment by the state to certain symbols and representations of Islam. In an attempt to shore up support among the growing fundamentalist constituency, the government sought appeasement by banning the sale of alcohol, prohibiting gambling and closing down restaurants and nightclubs. This did little, however, to convince an ascendant pan-Islamic front that the government was serious about Islamisation. In response they formed their own electoral alliance and included Pakistan's largest religious parties such as *Jama'at al-Islami*. The Pakistan National Alliance (PNA) declared that it would put forward candidates for the 1977 election and that their manifesto was based on the Qur'an. They vowed that, if elected, they would enforce Islamisation and govern according to the principle of the *shari'a*. There were tensions within the PNA with respect to the Islamic vision and it was obvious that Mawdudi's *Jama'at al-Islami* aspired to a more fundamentalist application of Islamic law. The PNA campaigned against Bhutto and for Islamisation, securing a respectable poll in an election where it was widely believed that the government had rigged the ballot. In the aftermath of the election the Islamists made clear an offer of support to Pakistan's military leaders. In July 1977 the chief of army staff Zia al-Haq and other officers staged a coup and the Bhutto government was deposed. Al-Haq announced that the Constitution was suspended, martial law was imposed and within the year al-Haq had formed a government aligned with the Islamists.

Al-Haq's Islamisation programme was apparent throughout his tenure as president. Al-Haq was said to be influenced by Mawdudi and reflected a personal attachment to his faith in terms of his control of the state. Moreover, the new president recognised that Islam could serve as a means by which he could extend his authority and legitimacy over a greater number in this fractured state. Islam would serve as the motif of state unity. Often this was translated into Islamisation for show – a process that drew criticism from secular opponents and fundamentalist traditionalists alike. The latter complained that the overhaul of the state in the name of Islam was simply not being undertaken with enough sustained depth, the former that important rights cherished by the modern state were being eroded by an alliance of army officers and mullahs. The reformed structures of the state included the provision for a new Council for Islamic Ideology, which would be a forum for the Islamisation of state and society in Pakistan. Islamisation touched on all areas relating to Islam and public life, including prayer, Ramadan, social issues such as segregation, economic reform, *shari'a* and the rights of women. Al-Haq clearly wanted to transform modern Pakistan from a Muslim state to an Islamic one. This inevitably promoted the Islamic parties that had been initially marginalised in the state formation process in the late 1940s. Al-Haq was careful to co-opt *Jama'at al-Islami* into his political project, providing the important religious legitimacy to his state-shaping projects. From this platform al-Haq introduced draconian measures and punishments which he declared were a true implementation of divine Islamic law.

What proved troubling with this experiment in revivalism, however, was the intimate connection generated between Islam and the establishment of a military dictatorship in modern Pakistan. There were fears that Islam was being employed in the service of despotic ambition and that the representative ideals of the original framers of Pakistan's state were being lost in the fundamentalist flourishing that al-Haq sponsored. Islamisation provided the state with support and revenues from important Muslim players such as Saudi Arabia, but there have also been accusations that the process undermined national unity within the state, promoting, as it did, rising ethnic and sectarian tensions that undermined the stability of the state.[9] In the case of Pakistan, then, the state appeared transformed by the power of the Islamic fundamentalists during this period. This was only achieved, however, through an alliance with a dictator. Similarly, in Egypt during this period the impact of revivalism was eventually translated into power subvention with the state.

The 'believer' president: Anwar Sadat

As earlier chapters of this book have highlighted, the Islamic movement in Egypt has had a significant role throughout the twentieth century and inspired modern revivalism and fundamentalism more globally. Revivalism in Egypt, during this period, revealed a multi-dimensional character to the project. Under the rule of President Sadat (1970–81) Islamism had been encouraged as a countervailing force against other political elements that Sadat deemed as dangerous rivals to his power. Revivalism was apparent in the growing grass roots attachment to Islam and demonstrations of religiosity across society. In the capital city of Cairo the tempo of life in local neighbourhoods, schools, mosques, shops, colleges, professional associations and the university campus increasingly reflected an importance attached to the practice of Islam – through prayer, fasting, festivals such as the observance of *Eid al-Fitr* or *Eid al-Adha*, in the explosion in mosque building, and burgeoning Islamic dress codes. Street stalls and bookshops sold new books and pamphlets on Islam to increasing numbers of young men and women. New ventures and projects were funded by Islamic propagation committees from within Egypt and abroad – moreover, remittances sent by Egyptian migrant workers from the Arabian Gulf states were not only spent on consumer goods but in support of Islamic projects at home. Such remittances and other external financing boosted pilgrimage and the resurrection of summer camps and 'caravans' for Islamic learning and community that directly targeted young Muslim men. This dimension of revivalism took command of the faith away from the traditional seminaries and brought the message of the fundamentalists more directly to their audiences.

The seminaries and *waqf* institutions were shunned by a new generation of clerics who understood the potency of Islam as a vehicle for the social, economic and political transformation of Islam. They also understood that the traditional institutions of Islam and their employees did not enjoy the kind of autonomy from the state that would allow them to pursue the regime for substantive reform and change. Some preachers and clerics from within institutional Islam did, however, understand that revivalism and Sadat's policies of Islamisation presented opportunities to reach a wider audience, in the dissemination of new fundamentalist doctrines and ideologies. They used the opportunity of increased state broadcasting of Islamic programmes to air their views on a multitude of issues pertaining to modern society and Muslim identity. But it was away from the public stage that the alternative preachers increasingly held sway over public opinion. Many of these figures had an early background in the Muslim Brotherhood and they happily exploited the opportunities that Sadat's benign attitude to the organisation created. They understood that Sadat's policy of official tolerance had to be exploited in terms of regaining an important foothold within the formal structures of civil society in Egypt. This resulted in a concerted attempt to position themselves in relation to the pre-existing structures, in particular the professional associations, as well as parallel Muslim organisations that focused on service orientation to the Egyptian people. Behind such activities was the increasing aim of the total reform of the Egyptian state, to shape it according to Islamic principles.

President Sadat may have given the impression that he was taking the lead in the Islamisation project. Early in his presidency he had indicated that he would rehabilitate Islam in the Egyptian context and demonstrate its efficacy in relation to the development of the modern state in the post-Nasser era. Desperate indeed to step out from Nasser's shadow, it became apparent that Sadat would pursue a raft of policies that would repress Nasserite factions and promote a state-sanctioned revivalism. This approach had a double outcome: within the state Sadat promoted himself as a 'believer' – state media broadcast him at prayer, and undertaking other religious rites and tasks – who sought to promote government policies benefiting all Muslim citizens. Hence government policy would be a reflection of the spirit of Islam rather than the tenets of Islam. For Sadat shied away from incorporating the entire state structure into the Islamic or theocratic framework of Islam. Hence there was a facade of religiosity apparent within the Egyptian state throughout the 1970s. In addition, Sadat calculated that by allowing the Islamists back into the political arena – by releasing them from prison and letting them resume some of their activities – he could manage and co-opt them as a weapon to be deployed against his political opponents. Sadat failed to understand, however, that only complete (rather than partial) Islamisation of the Egyptian state and its policies would satisfy the demands of the fundamentalists. In this way Sadat was a victim of his own circumstance, creating the problem in his attempts to use the 'religious weapon' for his own political purposes, he went too far, failing to realise until much too late that the Islamic movement had acquired an independent life and logic of its own.[10]

On the issue of peace with Israel, as much as any other, Sadat failed to understand that the facade of Islam would not be enough to protect him from the penetrating critique of the fundamentalists. For within the Islamist fold a radical militant dimension to fundamentalism was increasingly apparent. As early as 1974 elements of the radical *takfir wal hijra* (flight and redemption) movement had attacked the state and its personnel. There is a consensus that Sadat realised the deadly force of opposition too late. It was not until late 1981 that he ordered a crackdown on the radicals and other opposition elements. A month later in October 1981 the radicals assassinated him. Although it is clear that Sadat was prepared to deploy Islam in the service of the state, he baulked at any meaningful accommodation of power between himself and the Islamists. Despite freeing the Muslim Brotherhood and allowing them to organise again, he would not permit them to form a political party or contest his power through elections. Islam's place in the state would only be accorded on Sadat's terms. These developments cannot be divorced from the other dimensions of Sadat's presidency and in particular his economic policies of liberalisation known as *infi-tah* (the open door) and his foreign policy. His economic policies did not save the country from crisis and by 1977 the country erupted into riots as prices of basic foodstuffs spiralled out of control. Thousands of Egyptians found themselves out of work and angry at the regime for failing them. Compounding the problem, Sadat, despite his decision to lead the country into war against Israel in 1973, then appeared determined to sully Arab dignity by courting the US and being the first Arab state to conclude a formal peace treaty with Israel. Sadat tried to maintain the distinction between Islam and politics and failed miserably. He roused the ire of the fundamentalists, antagonised the rest of the Arab world, and presided over the economic and political deterioration of the country. For the fundamentalists Sadat was increasingly perceived as an obstacle to the reform of the state, as fundamentalist leader Ahmad Shukri Mustafa declared: 'I reject the Egyptian regime and the Egyptian reality in all its aspects since everything in it is in contradiction to the *shari'a* and belongs to heresy … we demand a return to natural simplicity and reject the so-called modern progress'.[11] Much of the anger that the fundamentalists were able to exploit derived from growing hostility to foreign interference in the country.

Spreading the blame

The Cold War between the USA and the Soviet Union deepened in terms of vying for influence and control of Muslim countries throughout this period. The enmity between the United States and the former Soviet Union significantly altered the dynamic of politics in a number of Muslim states and also played its part in generating antipathy and hostility from the fundamentalists. The participants in this ideological war encountered a new ideological response in Islamic fundamentalism that they tried to control and contain – with largely disastrous consequences. As both parties to the conflict discovered, the taming of Muslim states would not be a simple task. Many Muslim countries became a bearpit in the extension of the Cold War emnity between the two superpowers. Both superpowers were determined to win over pliable 'client' states in Muslim domains to act as local proxies for them. By the early 1960s both sides had achieved some success in this task, but the events of the late 1960s and the 1970s caused many in Washington and Moscow to ponder the efficacy of their foreign policies. Even the achievement of détente between the two superpowers, in the early 1970s, was regarded with suspicion by the new generation of fundamentalists.

It would be fair to say that in their foreign policy considerations the Islamist dimensions of Muslim politics were largely overlooked by Soviet and American foreign policy-makers. In their attempts to contain the influence of the other superpower, policy-makers focused on Muslim states and their elites rather than the newly incipient forces of Islamism. Much of this approach may be explained in relation to the cultural antipathy that both sides exhibited towards all things Muslim. For it is contended that, 'western Christendom perceived the Muslim world as a menace long before it began to be seen as a real problem'.[12]

Soviet antagonism to all things Muslim was apparent in the ideological doctrines of communism. It appears that both sides simply underestimated the growing appeal of Islamism and the parallel growth of Muslim hostility at the result of American and Soviet interference in their own economies, political systems and cultures. The USA was perceived as wilfully ignorant in its cultural antipathy to all things Islamic. The crushing defeat of the Arab states in the war against Israel in 1967, for example, was interpreted by the radical fundamentalists as a divine sign of the price to be paid by Muslims for abandoning their faith. Such a perspective was disseminated more widely in the Muslim world with respect to the impact of Western policies on Muslim societies. In Pakistan, Muslim scholars writing in 1967, declared:

> Our deprivation from progress and our present decline are the result of our neglect of Islam, otherwise Islam and progress are inseparable ... You have acquired only immorality and evil doings from Europe. They manufacture one plane in a minute and innumerable rockets and collect billions of dollars to save the Jews, and we remain asleep in our luxuries. If we ignore our collective problems the result cannot be other than destruction.[13]

This was no simplistic assertion that modernity was bad and Islam was good. Rather, the scholars were determined to construct an argument that the oft-promised benefits of modernity and alliance with the West (and this included the Soviet Union) had failed to materialise for the majority. The cause of Muslim anger was not rooted in a theo-cultural difference, as some Western observers had contended, but in specific Western policy positions towards the Muslim world. These policy positions were perceived as revealing double standards and deep-rooted antagonism towards the Muslim people.

For Muslim secularists, democrats and socialists, the difficulty, by the early 1970s, lay in being able to give concrete and explicit expression to the material benefits of an attachment to their ideologies in such domains. For the majority of Muslims even material improvements in their lives – increased literacy, access to healthcare and other welfare provisions – were stunted and countered by a loss of political liberty and equality in their own nations. The blame for their predicament was outlined by the Islamists and translated into a searing condemnation of the ideas and ideologies associated with the modernity project and the role of the West in perpetrating the fiction of progress in the absence of faith. As one Islamist declared:

> [The] power of the West is not due to flutes and guitars, not due to dances of veilless girls, nor due to the spell of their magical beauty, nor to their naked legs ... Their supremacy is not due to their secularism ... Their power is due to science and technology ... Wisdom does not lie in how your clothes are tailored and the turban is no obstruction for science and technology.[14]

The Islamists were accused, however, of promoting anti-Americanism and anti-communism as a way to rouse popular support in pursuit of Islamic revolutionary ideals and blame everyone but themselves for the decline of Muslim states. It was argued that all the fundamentalists were doing was rousing hatred in a campaign to bring a global jihad to the rest of the world. From this perspective Islam is still viewed as something not of this modern time; it is understood as backward and anachronistic.

Revivalism to revolution?

Throughout the 1970s the revivalism project was apparent across the Muslim world. This had a significant impact on the political arena as well. Islamic fundamentalists were increasingly preoccupied not only with the recovery of the Muslim soul and Muslim society, but in articulating visions of Muslim governance through the vehicle of the state. The potential of harnessing such new thinking to popular sentiment was apparent both within the state and in those that opposed it. Sadat, for example, in taking Egypt to war against Israel in 1973, deliberately employed the symbols of Islam (rather than the Arab nationalism of his predecessor Nasser) as a rallying cry for support at home and elsewhere in the Muslim world. In the 1973 war, Egyptian soldiers again were called 'to martyrdom in the way of the honour of the motherland' (*bil-istishhad fi sabil karama al-watan*). Islam was a significant symbol employed by the Egyptian state. After Nasser's defeat of 1967, Sadat ensured that the new 'Egyptianism' would reflect an Islamic dimension; in military academies and training schools the commanders of Egypt's armed forces waved the banner of Islam. The concept of jihad was incorporated into the doctrines of war and defence established by the Egyptian military.

In the wake of a war that was perceived as going some way in recovering Egyptian pride and dignity, Islam was identified by elements of the regime as key to that success. The second element key to this issue was linked to the oil embargo organised by sympathetic Arab Muslim regimes against the West. In this period, Western dependence on the key oil-producing Arab states was at its highest and a decision to support Israel during the war would cost the USA dearly. The day after President Nixon secured emergency funds for Israel, the government of Saudi Arabia announced an embargo of oil production for the USA. It was only a matter of time before other oil-producing Muslim states joined an embargo that lasted some six months. Production slowed and prices rose to an all-time high, leaving Western economies in severe trouble. In response to the crisis the USA warned that it would consider stationing its own troops in the Gulf to protect the free flow of oil to the West. The high financial returns accrued to the Saudi state as a consequence of the embargo, along with its enhanced status within the Islamic world, resulted in more resources made available for the revivalism project. In the years that followed, Saudi-funded organisations, projects, groups and facilities promoted the flourishing of Islam in poorer areas of the Muslim world. In Thailand, Afghanistan and Pakistan, Saudi oil funds financed a flourishing network of schools (*madrassas*) which played a part in inculcating Wahabbi doctrine to its pupils. In Egypt, Saudi funds were used to promote a revived publishing industry dedicated to the dissemination of debates on dimensions of Islamic faith and society. In Gaza, Saudi funds were deployed to support students studying at the Islamic university. Revivalism was subsidised in part by such funds.

While it is true that such activities played their part in serving to radicalise Islamist sentiment, a perhaps more significant dimension to the revivalism project was the impact it had in terms of transforming most aspects of Muslim society in the late twentieth century. The campaign to re-insert Islam into the public arena succeeded in large measure. This has changed the landscape of modern Muslim states and brought Islamists and their opponents into varied forms of opposition and confrontation with each other. Little by way of an accommodation of power and influence, by either side, has been in the offing. Fundamentalist doctrines of direct social action were transformed in this period by those who literally took their message to the Muslim streets, determined to work from the bottom up to transform their societies into a more 'authentic' vision of Muslim order. In theory, no aspect of the Muslim experience was left untouched and the movement for reform would grow with each copy of the Qur'an distributed, each *hijab* donned, each nightclub closed down, and each clinic opened. A common sense of purpose grew among a new generation of Muslims in countries such as Tunisia, Indonesia, Pakistan, Iran and Malaysia. They were united in faith and in common cause over issues such as the continuing plight of the Palestinians and Western support for Israel, over the impact of materialist cultures on their own societies and the benefits that the revolution in technology and science offered.

With the force of revivalism Islam appeared to move into a mode of self-defence. Increasingly the theological connections between *tabligh wa dawa* (preach and call) have been made by street and neighbourhood preachers. This populist version of Islam has empowered thousands who have taken the demand of the Islamic call to heart. They in turn see it as their duty to bring fellow Muslims back to the 'straight path' offered by Islam. In countries such as Egypt, preachers took to the street in their quest to promote the revival of Islam. Their message was based on principles of reform and non-violence. They were not prepared to trust the state in taking the lead in bringing people back to Islam. Redemption has been offered to all, young and old, rich and poor, the socially accepted and the social rejects such as drug takers. *Dawa* members themselves, turbaned and dressed in white, now dotted the Islamic landscape – their work most apparent in slums, poor neighbourhoods and refugee camps. This was the start of the quiet revolution in mainstream Islam and it was mostly located in the poverty-stricken cities, towns and villages of the Muslim world. In places like Jerusalem and the West Bank *dawa* members worked with drug offenders in the refugee camps and impoverished villages, instilling among their number a new sense of empowerment. In some cases that empowerment was translated by others into a far more potent and militant force. Revialism also reflected those Muslims who eschewed politics, scriptural fundamentalism and found self-expression and identity with Sufi rites and practices.[15] The revival had many dimensions and not all were contained within the traditional boundaries of Islam. Revivalism contributed to a raising of Muslim consciousness. That consciousness made Muslims self-aware about their own contexts, their societies and the nature of the political rule they were to endure. Few found that they were living in an enlightened Muslim age where the principles of their faith were openly reflected in their states. Instead a sense of grievance and frustration grew at the perceived injustices apparent within their own societies. As we shall see in the next chapter, that sense of grievance found a voice in the revolutionary movement that swept the clerics to power in Iran in 1979.

Notes

1 S. Qutb, 'War, peace and Islamic jihad', in M. Moaddel and K. Talattof (eds) *Modernist and Fundamentalist Debates in Islam: A Reader*, New York: Palgrave Macmillan, 2002, p. 225.
2 C. Issawi, *An Economic History of the Middle East and North Africa*, London: Methuen, 1982, pp. 15–16.
3 Interview with Sheikh Naim al-Qassam, Beirut, May 2000.
4 S. Zubaida, *Islam, the People and the State: Political Ideas and Movements in the Middle East*, London: I.B. Tauris, 1993, p. xvi.
5 H. Dekmejian, *Islam in Revolution: Fundamentalism in the Arab World*, New York: Syracuse University Press, 1995, p. 5.
6 See www.imamsadrfoundation.org.lb
7 A. Taheri, *Holy Terror: The Inside Story of Islamic Terrorism*, London: Sphere Books, 1987, p. 75.
8 Interview with Dr Mahmoud Zahar, Gaza City, December 1989.
9 See K.A. Faruki, 'Pakistan, Islamic government and society', in J.L. Esposito (ed.) *Islam in Asia: Religion, Politics and Society*, New York: Oxford University Press, 1987.
10 N. Ayubi, *Political Islam: Religion and Politics in the Arab World*, London: Routledge, 1991, p. 74.
11 As quoted in D. Hopwood, *Egypt, Politics and Society*, London: Allen and Unwin, 1986, p. 118.
12 J. Esposito, *Unholy War: Terror in the Name of Islam*, New York: Oxford University Press, 2002, p. 67.
13 Moulana Abul Haq, cited in M.T. Usmani, *Islam and Modernism*, Karachi: Darul Ishaat, 1999, p. 38.
14 M.T. Usmani, *Islam and Modernism*, Karachi: Darul Ishaat, 1999, p. 42.
15 S. A. Arjomand, 'Fundamentalism in the context of Islamic history', in Martin E Marty and R. Scott Appleby (eds) *Fundamentalisms Comprehended*, Chicago: Chicago University Press, 1995.

4 Islam armed

Resistance in an ideological era

Who is the happy Warrior? Who is he
That every man in arms should wish to be?
(William Wordsworth, 'The Happy Warrior')

In the late 1970s, an innovative impulse to Islamic revivalism led by a new generation of Muslim leaders was becoming increasingly apparent within a variety of Muslim countries. As many post-independent Muslim states struggled to embed national secular political agendas and frameworks, Muslim clerics and young student leaders, professional people and disillusioned activists from the left, realised the potential of Islam to mobilise and possibly achieve change and new order across many societies. With this rediscovery of Muslim identity, tied to a new political agenda there was a palpable fear, that grew throughout the 1980s, that the Islamic fundamentalists were a new threat to ruling regimes. This generated, as we shall see in this chapter, a variety of responses, including attempts by state leaders and elites themselves to don the cloak of Muslim respectability and be seen to embrace Islamic mores and values to add much needed legitimacy to their rule. Such policies were often combined with an iron fist approach to the Islamic fundamentalists and their supporters and brought such elements into open confrontation with state forces. In Iran the state lost and in 1979 the revolution there appeared to signal to the rest of the world that the tidal wave of fundamentalism would sweep to other shores, not only across the Middle East but to other Muslim countries as well.

In addition, the role of Islamic fundamentalist groups in conflicts with a global dimension during the Cold War era – including the revolution in Iran, the resistance to the Soviet invasion and occupation of Afghanistan, the civil conflict in Lebanon, the activities of Libya, and the outbreak of the Palestinian Intifada, to name but a few – became increasingly apparent. The fundamentalists betrayed a militant character that in turn was so extreme that the very fabric of the modern nation-state was under revolutionary threat from their ire. The faith, as interpreted by a fundamentalist literalist corps of clerics and modern Muslim thinkers, permitted violence as a means to achieve the triumph of Islam. The emergence of this trend led to disagreements within Islam between the clerical elite with its foundation in the religious seminaries and universities of Islam, and the laypeople and jihadists. Dimensions of this disagreement were generational – between the old clerics and young educated and activist Muslims. Other dimensions related in particular to *Sunni* debates about the tradition of interpretation (*ijtihad*) and the role of individual Muslims in this task. Moreover, it became apparent that there was a growing fissure between reflective modern Muslim thinkers and those whose revolutionary activities tended to disregard doctrinal complexities in favour of what Mikhail Bakunin called 'propaganda by deed'. These elements, moreover, did indeed dream of an Islamist internationale wrought by the revolutionary overthrow of the authoritarian regimes of the Muslim world. Propaganda by deed for the former meant health clinics and kindergartens in Muslim towns and cities, and for the latter it meant terrorism of the kind carried out by *Takfir wa Hijra* when it assassinated President Sadat of Egypt in 1981. A great discrepancy in approach was revealed in the Muslim camp during this period and it was one that would continue. By the late 1990s and early twenty-first century, the propaganda by deed of terrorism had amplified to the point where other activities no longer appeared to matter to a Western audience.

The fundamentalists in general, whether Christian, Jewish or Muslim, identified secularism as the source of most of the world's economic, moral, and political problems as well as the crisis of identity that 'afflicted' individual Muslims and the wider *umma* in general. The domination of the secularists or secular political leaders, economic systems and new moral climates in a variety of Muslim countries, was recognised by the fundamentalists as a threat to Islam that had to be met through rediscovery of the faith and a fight against those who sought to relegate Islam to the margins of the political, economic and moral orders of the late twentieth century. The Muslim fundamentalist response, however, was diverse; not least because of significant sectarian differences around the issue of opposition and rebellion between *Sunni* and *Shi'a* Muslims but also because of the varied milieu from which the new fundamentalists were drawn. They were united by a powerful realisation and fear that secularists had hijacked the modernity project and that Islam would be destroyed

unless it was defended. This is not to say, however, that the fundamentalists rejected every element of the modernity project. For
example, fundamentalist thinkers and clerics regularly pronounced on
the benefits of utilising modern technological advances for their work.
The fundamentalists were also cognisant of the enormous task that lay
before them. They understood that secular influences were not merely
manifest in the types of political systems and forms of governance that
dominated their lives but also the extent to which secular cultures, even
in Muslim-ruled states, threatened the moral order that Islam demands
as a cultural expression of individual or societal identity. In this respect
the fundamentalists declared a war on 'democracy' as much as
'Disney'. Some of the fundamentalists even raged at the 'capitulating
tendencies' of the existing religious establishment for their part in
appearing to legitimise secular-dominated states. In an attempt also to
find external enemies, fundamentalist tracts identified communism and
other 'foreign' ideologies associated with the 'West' as the cause of
Muslim misery.

The agenda for change and action that accompanied discussion of
their ideas was increasingly militant, in tandem with the increasingly
wider dissemination of sermons, tapes, booklets, leaflets, newspapers,
journals, books and discussions that criss-crossed within Muslim
communities and between them. The degree of militancy that was
exposed was, however, still contingent on other factors within Islam.
This is illustrated in the significant numbers of political contexts
characterised by pre-existing conflicts that proved vulnerable to the
extreme fundamentalist tendencies of certain Muslim leaders, groups
and organisations. Where these fundamentalists were coming from
matters far more than where they were going. They were not necessarily
dedicated to forging transnational links; they were constrained by their
own internal contexts, instrumentalist agendas and other factors
including sectarian differences and rivalries. This phenomenon was
not limited merely to Islam, but was increasingly symbolic in other
ethno-national disputes that involved Christians or Hindus or other
religious groupings. Moreover, subsequent violence was then labelled as
fundamentalist or religious and, thereby, given a non-rational quality
and considered to be more potent, lethal and threatening. Violence
perpetrated by Muslims in particular would be labelled as distinctive.
In the modern era of increasingly global interconnectedness, it was also
recognised that previously 'local' disputes were able to take on a global
character or international dimensions that drew states into new
conflicts, such as the one that was to unfold in Afghanistan throughout
the 1980s.

Context is everything

Of the 42 member states of the Organisation of Islamic Conferences (OIC) in 1980, the majority, including the Republic of Indonesia, the People's Democratic Republic of Algeria, the Republic of Iraq, and the People's Republic of Bangladesh, the Federal Republic of Nigeria and the Republic of Turkey, were independent secular nation-states. In addition, for a significant number of these states independence had been achieved only in the post-war era and often with a high degree of struggle against ruling colonial powers. The framework of the modern state had often been imposed on subject populations by the European colonial powers over territories where new borders were arbitrarily drawn in the same manner. New nations and new citizens who were subject to statehood were declared, with little evidence of consultation with the leaders of pre-existing religious and other communities in these areas. It was little wonder that the legitimacy of such states and their locally appointed leaders was called into question by the fundamentalists. It was often the case that the 'hero of liberation' had a power base in one ethnic or tribal group which was subsequently favoured over others in the institutions of the state. For many of the Islamists the historical founding of the nation-state over their society with a secular outlook and foreign political, economic and social frameworks was an anathema to everything in which they believed. The fundamentalists were not alone in recognising that the authentic character and demands of pre-existing communities had either been ignored or deliberately altered through colonialism and its attachment to the nation-state in order to fulfil its political objectives. Conflict and resistance were not solely confined to the confident fundamentalist classes but had been contested by other ethnic, national and religious groups who demanded their right to self-determination and independence and freedom from the subjugation of rule by others. In some cases an uneasy accommodation had been reached, but in others the demands turned into internal conflicts that engulfed communities and became sustained by nationalist, ethnic and religious ideologies. In the case of Islam, the roots of hostility lay in the clash between its religious nature and the secular character of the state.

This difference was recognised by the leading cleric Dr Yusuf al-Qaradawi, who declares:

> the call for secularism among Muslims is atheism and a rejection of Islam. Its acceptance as a basis for rule in place of the Shari'a is downright *riddah* [apostasy]. The silence of the masses in the

Muslim world about this deviation has been a major transgression and a clear-cut instance of disobedience.[1]

This view was apparent in the variety of organisations and groups that came to the fore throughout the 1980s and will be discussed later in this chapter. Moreover, the context of change is apparent by reflecting on events in Afghanistan, Egypt, Iran and Lebanon. In all of these cases the new identity politics of Islamic fundamentalism betrayed a belief that new social and other orders would be forged through the revival and spirit of Islam.

This new spirit was translated in a number of contexts into violence, which as will be discussed in Chapter 5, was subsequently the primary means by which Islam is characterised in the post-1945 era. Violence in the name of Islam appeared to be a feature of the new fundamentalist movements and was urged by their clerics and lay leaders. Islamic countries tended to be vulnerable to conflict due to the important geo-strategic territories they occupied; this is particularly apparent in the case of Afghanistan, in relation to the former Soviet frontier and energy-rich states such as Iran. Whether this actually means that Islam is more violent than other faiths with their claims to the pacifist tradition is a moot point. As one Muslim leader was fond of pointing out,

> Was it Muslims who launched the Crusades, was it Muslims who started World War One, was it Muslims who planned the Holocaust against the Jews, was it Muslims who made the massacre in Rwanda or Srebrenica? Surely even we can't be blamed for the war in Northern Ireland where Christians are killing each other?[2]

Islam has been used to justify violence and terrorism and some fundamentalists have made it explicit that their preferred means of political change include jihad with an armed dimension. Yet elements of Muslim violence, sanctioned by the mullahs and other clerics, were a feature of fundamentalist Islam in the 1980s that also served to draw in other elements into old conflicts and contestations in new ways. In Lebanon, for example, many would assert that the United States of America was drawn into 'someone else's war' and became nothing more than another 'militia'. Yet the American presence – a symbol of international effort at peacekeeping and conflict containment – was read as a message of partisan threat and domination by some fundamentalist elements. The response to this 'threat' was a series of suicide attacks on the Americans with hundreds of lives lost and a growing sense in America of having been duped into becoming involved in 'someone else's war'. From this there also developed a sense of enmity from and towards Islam. The internationalisation of fundamentalist politics drew in other actors, including the ill-fated Soviets, and also reflected a growing ideological and intellectual struggle with the ideologies of the 'other', that would increase in contest and mutual hostility throughout the decade. The exclusivity of fundamentalist mantras appeared to make ideological accommodation from within faiths and between traditions and other ideologies increasingly impossible.

The Afghan saga

> Who, doomed to go in company with Pain
> And Fear, and Bloodshed, miserable train!
> Turns his necessity to glorious gain
> > (William Wordsworth, 'The Happy Warrior')

When a successful communist coup followed by the invasion of Soviet forces took place in the war-torn statelet of Afghanistan in 1979, few could predict that just a decade later one of the world's most important superpowers – the Soviet Union – would be defeated militarily and left on the brink of a territorial meltdown that would end the Cold War and herald in a new era where the 'End of History' and a 'New World Order' would be declared. While there were a variety of forces responsible for the spectacular collapse of communism, the *mujahideen* elements associated with the fundamentalist fringe leading the Islamic resistance in Afghanistan believed that they were primarily responsible. This led to an increased confidence and proved the logic of their Islamist doctrines and theories.

The Soviet interlude in Afghanistan was but one of many attempts by foreign forces to dominate the country. Moreover, the Muslim resistance had, in many respects, much in common with earlier resistance efforts against foreign occupiers that had coloured the Algerian struggle for independence from the French, or with the role played by Muslim militia and resistance forces in the campaign of violence against the British occupation of Egypt. Yet in Afghanistan it was the Muslim resistance which was dominant among other competing organisations and forces espousing nationalist ambitions in the Afghan milieu. Indeed, it has been contended that the Americans and the Pakistan intelligence services (ISI) consciously created the establishment, and support for *mujahideen* groups with an extreme agenda over those Islamist elements in Afghanistan that had previously prevailed. This led either to the marginalisation of more moderate nationalist groups or served to radicalise them. The ISI money pipeline encouraged extremist elements such as Osama Bin Laden and the Taliban and also acted as a useful conduit for the waging of other campaigns in Kashmir.[3] The Islamic tenor to the resistance effort was seen as successful in facing up to what had appeared to be an indomitable enemy. With the defeat of the Soviet forces, it appeared to many that Islam was the new peril. The *mujahideen* represented the potency of a new generation of adherents to the fundamentalist agenda at a time when other ideological alternatives were being declared bankrupt. Afghan society appeared to soak up the fundamentalist doctrines not only promoted by home-grown clerics but a succession of Arab *mujahideen* who espoused their own ideas and interpretations from within the fundamentalist house. As a failed state, the country was also vulnerable to competition among external elements. The war gave rise to intervention from the USA, Saudi Arabia, Iran and Pakistan, often as much in competition with each other as in support of the Afghan resistance effort. This multiethnic state would, therefore, become a focus of many contests. Images of the Afghan resistance and tracts published by its leaders and thinkers, would be disseminated by countless Muslim organisations across the globe as evidence that Islamic fundamentalism was a force to contend with. The arming of Islam by the fundamentalists would impact in countless ways.

The Afghan resistance was not always a well-coordinated effort but was instead subject to myriad pre-existing and new rivalries exposed along tribal, ethnic, sectarian, national and other lines. *Sunni* and *Shi'a* were often pitted against each other as much as the Soviet enemy. Their ethnic rivals among the Uzbeks and Hazaris regarded the Pashtuns with suspicion and an enduring common alliance was largely absent from the Afghan battlefields. Even sectarian or ethnic commonality was no guarantee of cooperation in the Islamic resistance effort. For example, a variety of '*Sunni*' Islamic resistance elements emerged, including some foreign elements. Indeed, the foreign element numbered over 25,000 during the war and most importantly many of them returned to their home countries after the war to form the nucleus of extreme armed groups responsible for acts of terrorism in countries such as Egypt, Jordan, the Philippines and Algeria. Among the *mujahideen* ranked thousands of young men who had taken advantage of the modernisation process that offered a better education. They rivalled traditionalists who had hitherto directed much of the Islamic way of life in Afghanistan. The paradox here was that those who believed that modernisation and modern education would render religion obsolete or promote secularisation in the Muslim world often witnessed the opposite effect.

The Soviet invasion prompted the growth of the resistance effort not just in Afghanistan but in neighbouring Pakistan and Iran as well. Throughout the Soviet occupation, the Islamic fundamentalists were the driving force of the resistance. Their goal was not only to end an illegal occupation by foreign forces but also to establish in their place a new Islamic state. Their vision of statehood was deeply influenced by the writings and experiences of a generation of radical thinkers who came before them, including Sayyid Qutb and Muwlana Mawdudi. Such thinkers had identified the communist menace as a real threat to Islam that had to be resisted. Until the Soviet invasion of Afghanistan, such warnings had not been taken seriously but now the time had come for action. For the fundamentalists it was now imperative that the power of the state under atheist infidel *jahilli* rule be opposed through the means of jihad. Local Islamist elements had existed in Afghanistan before the Soviet occupation, consisting of a competing variety of student-led, professional classes, and religious elites. They sought to promote an Islamic revival in Afghan society at a time when leftist secularist forces flourished, and began to call for a jihad as part of a wider programme of preaching and education among young people. In this respect they were much like other proto-fundamentalist movements of the time. As such movements grew and increased their participation in the local political scene, so fissures and tensions between local elements and their supporters were exposed. Pakistan-based fundamentalist groups such as the *Jama'at al-Islami*, led by Mawdudi, extended support to Afghan exiles and dissidents. Factions led by figures such as Gulbuddin Hekmatyar from the *Hizb al-Islami*, and Burhanuddin Rabbani from the *Jama'at al-Islami* along with many other smaller factions, often relied as much on tribal, sectarian and ethnic loyalties as Islam, and found themselves either in opposition or in delicate and short-lived alliances with each other and their sponsors or supporters. This meant that Islamic fundamentalism was tied to the grass roots of Afghan society in an intricate web of relations that centred on the nexus of tribe, patriarchy, ethnicity and faith. Later the link between tribal codes and Islam became more specific in the ideology of the Taliban, which reflected a good measure of *pashtunwali*, the Pashto tribal code.[4] Such grassroots support would prove essential in maintaining the resistance effort. In many respects this is because the resistance effort included the interests of more than one group and by some as more intimately linked with popular support for guerrilla resistance against imperialism.[5]

Sponsors and supporters of the Afghan Islamic resistance included the government of the United States of America and Saudi Arabia.

They were important in forging or foisting alliances upon the fractious Afghans. In the mid-1980s, for example, the Saudi monarchy was credited with bringing about the formation of a new alliance of groups for the Islamic resistance against the Soviets based both in Afghanistan and neighbouring Pakistan. Pakistan, under President Zia al-Haq and through the direction of Pakistani intelligence services (ISI), played a major role in Afghani affairs during this period. Peshawar in Pakistan became an important base for a number of resistance groups and their sponsors. It was here that the CIA and other intelligence agencies worked among these groups in refugee camps, *madrassas* (Islamic schools), and through front organisations to fuel the jihad against the Soviet Union. In these ways the fundamentalist resistance was nurtured and grew and attracted many Arabs and other Muslims, including Osama Bin Laden, to the Afghan arena. Foreign support for the Islamic resistance effort was significant in the sustained guerrilla effort at ousting the Russians. Indeed, by the mid-1980s there was evidence that the Afghan effort might pay off, but the human cost was high. By the end of the conflict over one million had lost their lives and over a third of the country's population were either internally displaced or had become refugees. It was only in April 1988 that President Gorbachev announced that Soviet troops would be out of the country within a year. The power vacuum that emerged in the wake of the Soviet with-drawal was mostly due to the highly factious nature of the politics that fundamentalism was wedded to in the country. This led, in the early 1990s, to the emergence of further civil unrest as various factions battled it out for ultimate power in Kabul. Such factionalism had been tacitly encouraged as a result of foreign intervention in the conflict. The policy of 'divide and rule' was apparent in the pattern of assistance by more than one external power. This policy only exacerbated tensions within and between fundamentalist organisations and alliances.

The Soviet withdrawal was, of course, proof that the fundamentalists had achieved a significant victory. A resistance effort in the name of Islam – a jihad – had succeeded in giving substance to the belief that the gun in alliance with the Qur'an not only had revolutionary potential but could actually result in the overthrow of a superpower. Where the Americans had failed, the Afghans had succeeded. Yet US complicity in supporting the fundamentalist war in Afghanistan would come back to haunt successive US administrations. American policy-makers had often set their liberal democratic principles aside in supporting leaders of organisations that espoused authoritarian, fundamentalist agendas aligned with a particular literalist interpretation of Islam in Afghanistan, while vehemently opposing such a regime in Iran. Surely there is a telling irony in the parallel souring of relations with Islamic Iran after the revolution in 1979 and the significant support for and friendly relations with the fundamentalist fighters of the Afghan resistance? Yet one response to this question is that with the loss of Iran as an ally it was only natural that the US would look to neighbouring Afghanistan as a potential replacement. The US government approved covert aid as Afghanistan was represented as the new frontline in the campaign against the 'Evil Empire' of the Soviet Union. American and British policy-makers publicly ignored the implications of supporting fundamentalists who not only opposed communism but the capitalist 'Zionist-supporting' West as well. The moral and ethical questions of such involvement were largely ignored. In a war-by-proxy the American public was not faced with the kinds of issues that they had been confronted with during the war in Vietnam. Someone else was paid to take on the communist enemy. Western intelligence agencies funded and supported the complex network of arms, training and other facilities needed to run the *muja-hideen* campaign. Moreover allegations regularly surfaced that fringe criminality, including illegal arms sales and heroin trade, were ignored or tacitly encouraged by the CIA and other foreign agencies.

The resistance, after the Soviet withdrawal, limped on and between 1990 and 1996 when the Taliban fundamentalists took Kabul, inter-factional fighting destabilised the country and made even basic reconstruction efforts almost impossible. Once the USA and the former Soviet Union reached an agreement over arms supply to the country, the Afghans were forsaken. After such intense involvement, the policy of abandonment, as we shall see in Chapter 5, left the fundamentalists free to ferment further revolutionary ambitions not just in Afghanistan but also over its borders.

Revolutionary Iran and the fundamentalist Islamic Comintern

> For wealth, or honours, or for worldly state;
> Whom they must follow; on whose head must fall,
> Like showers of manna, if they come at all
> > (William Wordsworth, 'The Happy Warrior')

In many respects the rise and growth in popular support for radical fundamentalist movements and the resort to revolutionary means to achieve their aims, were identified throughout the 1980s by assorted authors and commentators as inspired, influenced and directly encouraged by the clerics and other Muslim fundamentalists who had seized control of the Iranian state in January 1979. This identification was accompanied by a fear that an Islamic-style Comintern would lead to the infiltration of the fundamentalists throughout the Middle East and beyond, and fundamentalists now stood where once the network of revolution with Moscow at its epicentre had struck fear in the heart of the West.

It was argued that it was time to wake up to the real nature of modern Islam as expressed by fundamentalists and the threat it represented. For not only was there a threat that important energy partners would fall to the fundamentalists, but that the fundamentalists would then encourage terrorism that would threaten Western interests across the globe. There was a suspicion that if the ambitions of the fundamentalists were not contained, then the West would become especially vulnerable. The threat had to be identified and a strategy for meeting it head-on was developed.

The revolution in Iran and the openly stated ambition of Ayatollah Khomeini's new regime to 'export the revolution' would lead to an international fundamentalist Comintern. There was a fear that Khomeini's ideology and rhetoric would prove seductive to millions of ordinary Muslims; that they would transcend sectarian, historical, geographical, economic and political barriers to form a united Islamic revolutionary front. Islamic fundamentalism symbolised by the theocratic state established in the wake of the 1979 revolution represented a major threat to Western interests. The fundamentalists were also considered to pose a serious threat to the stability of pro-Western Muslim countries including Saudi Arabia, Turkey and Egypt. The new powers in post-revolutionary Tehran were perceived as masterminding and directing a Muslim plan for global domination. As one author asserted, 'Teheran administers a network akin to an Islamist Comintern, making its role today not that different from Moscow's then.'[6] Yet as events unfolded throughout the 1980s, the spectre of the global fundamentalist Comintern proved unfounded. While Khomeini and his followers may have aspired to export the theocratic model of post-revolutionary Islam, in reality, the manifestation of Islamic fundamentalism took different forms in different states. The majority of fundamentalists were concerned with local and at most regional issues. In some cases they sought to challenge state structures and urge reform, in others some elements within fundamentalism advocated a jihad to change the state elite and install a more Islamic regime. The combination of both the latter and the former was evident throughout the 1980s in Muslim countries such as Egypt or Pakistan. In Iran in 1979 and Sudan in 1985, the fundamentalists succeeded in seizing control of the state and harnessing it to a particular vision of Islamic statehood. In other countries, such as India, Islamic fundamentalist forces were allied to secessionist causes such as that in Kashmir. There was little evidence of a coherent network directed from Tehran or Khartoum that gave reason to believe in the Comintern argument. In some respects it could be argued that the establishment of the theocratic fundamentalist regime in Tehran in 1979 did as much to split fundamentalism as unite it in opposition to the West. The overtly *Shi'a* tones behind the model for revolution that was promoted out of Tehran was recognised as a threat within many *Sunni* circles, including Saudi Arabia. In a number of arenas of conflict in the Muslim world, throughout the 1980s, the contest or battle for power was as much internal to Islam as outside it. In *Sunni* circles there was widespread disquiet at the revolutionary successes of their historic rivals, and unease at the prospect that elements considered by some to be nothing more than heretics, might reshape and fashion a new Muslim agenda for the late twentieth century. In this respect it is important to detail not only the nature of the fundamentalist state under Khomeini, but to question its importance in relation to the wider phenomenon of Islamic fundamentalism during the 1980s.

Children of the revolution

The revolution that took place in Iran culminating in the exile of the Shah in January 1979 had its roots not only in fundamentalist dimensions of Islam as expressed by Ayatollah Khomeini but a variety of other factors as well, most notably from the Iranian left. In this respect I am contending that fundamentalist Islamists did not ferment the revolution alone. The growth of revolutionary agitation among ordinary Iranian people was due to the coalescence of a number of social, economic and political groupings in confrontation with an increasingly corrupt and authoritarian regime supported as an important client state of the United States of America. By the late 1970s, the writings and recordings of sermons by fundamentalist clerics like Ayatollah Khomeini and Ali Shariati were being widely circulated among the Iranian people. Such writings were not only a critique of authoritarian rule but contained an agenda for change that gave people hope. Khomeini and others identified the deep levels of discontent in Iranian society and offered Islam as the solution. As the clamour for change grew, the revolutionaries from both the left and the Islamist camp emerged to harness popular energies against the regime and its agents.

In the wake of the revolution the fundamentalists, including the clerical class of Iran (historically less tied to the state than their *Sunni* co-religionists) declared that only the establishment of a true Islamic state in Iran, guided and ruled by the clerics, could fulfil the inherent promise of the Iranian people. Despite the presence of the leftists and their counter-agenda, the fundamentalists were able to more successfully harness the revolutionary fervour of the people in the name of Islam. Protests, demonstrations and other forms of agitation broke out throughout 1978 in towns and cities in Iran that had a reputation as seats or centres of religious learning. Moreover, many of the revolutionary vanguard were drawn from the ranks of Iran's increasingly fundamentalist student body. The severity of the regime's response to such challenges only served to galvanise more and more sectors of society into further protests and demonstrations. Religious rites became an important dimension of protest and demonstration – particularly as they related to the sacrifice or martyrdom of protesters at the hands of the Iranian state. One of the most significant turning points, however, was 8 September 1978 when Iranian forces killed hundreds of protestors during a demonstration. Despite introducing a series of repressive acts, including martial law, throughout the latter part of 1978 it became clear that 'the Shah had finally lost the will and determination to hold onto power through the massive repression that would have been necessary'.[7] By early December 1978, the writing was on the wall and the Shah's days were numbered as the revolutionaries diversified their tactics and united to bring an end to the regime. In a matter of weeks, the revolutionaries had seized control of the state, the Shah and his supporters were forced to leave the country, and by early February 1979 Ayatollah Khomeini had declared the establishment of the Islamic Republic of Iran.

Two dimensions of new fundamentalism were incorporated by the clerical elite of the new republic – the agenda of anti-Westernism that the new regime declared and the notion of the 'export of revolution'. Iran then represented 'neither East nor West' and would serve as a model for the oppressed Muslim peoples of the world. Khomeini and his supporters deployed the institutions of the Iranian state to give substance to the aspiration. The idea of exporting the Iranian revolutionary model comes from the belief among many in the clerical establishment that liberation of Muslims from capitalist and communist tyranny and rule could be achieved if it were harnessed to Islam. In some respects this was very much a liberation theology. It was argued that Islamic revivalism was a vehicle by which ordinary people could achieve meaningful change in their own societies and the way they were governed. In a sense, it was an aspect of 'third worldism' representing a quest for authenticity by Muslims for Muslims. The new Iranian elite contended that if others followed in their footsteps, then a true Islamic community (*umma*) would be closer to establishment. This community would transcend the straitjacket of the modern state to create new bonds, commonalities and coalitions among and between Muslims.

Throughout the 1980s there was a variety of ways in which this aspiration was expressed by the Iranian state. For example, the Iranian government offered financial and logistical support to Islamic fundamentalist movements outside Iran, aiding both *Shi'a* and *Sunni* groups. Tehran served as a safe haven for fundamentalist dissidents from a number of arenas of conflict within the Middle East. Moreover, Tehran, in competition with Saudi Arabia, became a place within the Muslim world where Islamic conferences, workshops, dialogues and seminars, organised under the auspices of the Iranian Foreign Ministry, brought leaders, activists, thinkers and others together. In this way, it is fair to say that Iran rivalled Saudi Arabia as an epicentre of new fundamentalism and a focus for a new generation of activists and others. Elements within the new fundamentalist elite believed it was their duty to encourage other Muslim communities to seek liberation, and this viewpoint was apparent in elements of policy that emanated from the Iranian government, including the Foreign Ministry. In this regard, numerous allegations began to emerge with respect to Iran's support for terrorist organisations across the globe. In 1984, the US State Department designated Iran a supporter of terrorism and by 1987 Iran was perceived as the most significant state supporter of terrorism in the globe. Major news networks reported that the export of revolution policy had resulted in the fact that Iranian 'State institutions, notably the Revolutionary Guard Corps and the Ministry of Intelligence and Security, are thought to be involved in the planning and execution of terrorist acts and continue to support a variety of groups that use terrorism to pursue their goals'.[8] Some Western governments believed they had evidence garnered throughout the 1980s that fundamentalist Iran was exporting terrorism as part of a global effort to disrupt and bring about the downfall of pro-Western Muslim countries and Western countries themselves. The evidence of links between Iran and states such as Sudan that succumbed to fundamentalist rule in 1985 only seemed to confirm the worst fears about the new Islamic Comintern.

Islam and Africa: the tide turns in Sudan

> Where what he most doth value must be won:
> Whom neither shape or danger can dismay,
> Nor thought of tender happiness betray
> (William Wordsworth, 'The Happy Warrior')

Sudan can be represented in many different ways: it is an African country, an Arab country, a country subject to colonial power and influence. It is a country that has a significant religious division between northern-based Muslims and southern-based Christians which became manifest in the South's independence in July 2011. It is in many ways a multiethnic and tribal territory. Sudan is one of the most populous countries in Africa, and, following a coup in 1989, Islam became the formal framework of governance in the state. In Sudan civil conflict has also coloured the country. By the mid-1980s, however, it was becoming apparent that Islamic fundamentalism would define the political framework of the state more significantly. Once more the ideological power of Islam would be offered as 'the solution' and a way of providing cohesion to this deeply divided society.

The ideological impetus to the fundamentalist campaign in Sudan was provided by one individual, Hassan al-Turabi. A former member of the Muslim Brotherhood, al-Turabi, like Ayatollah Khomeini, developed a unique revolutionary ideological vision of Islam and statehood in the twentieth century. In 1989, al-Turabi's movement, the National Islamic Front, achieved power in alliance with Sudan's military led by Brigadier General Omar al-Bashir. The ensuing administration was referred to as 'an alliance between the Islamist-oriented military leadership that had brought the regime to power and the country's civilian Islamist movement that had conspired in the coup'.[9] Al-Turabi's fundamentalist formula has been articulated in a very different fashion from that of the *Shi'a*-inspired formulations of Ayatollah Khomeini and his colleagues in Iran. Al-Turabi set out to reinterpret Islam for modern-day Sudan, and in the process generated criticism from traditionalists within the *Sunni* clerical elite both at home and abroad. Unlike Khomeini, al-Turabi did not advocate theocratic rule in Sudan but rather that the Islamisation of the state be the priority. Al-Turabi declared that Islam should give the ideological character to the state: 'Sudan has only one home, which is the mosque.' In many respects al-Turabi's ideological vision is rooted historically in the diluted tenor to Islam in Sudan and a desire to enhance the Islamic character of a weak state that has been unable to easily consolidate itself in the post-independence period. In this respect, the ideological agenda offered is similar to earlier alternatives in a desire by its proponents to build a nation and a modern nation-state. As al-Turabi is quoted as declaring,

> in other countries, nationalism might be the alternative to Islam. But the only nationalism that is available to us, if we want to assert

indigenous values, originality, and independence of the West, is Islam. Islam is the only modernity. It is the only doctrine that can serve as the national doctrine of today.[10]

Al-Turabi's challenge lay also in convincing Sudan's Muslims to abandon their Sufi heritage and see Islam in more fundamentalist and political terms. In many respects al-Turabi met this challenge by advocating a formula for Islamisation that was criticised in Islamic circles for its progressive tendencies, despite being labelled fundamentalist by many in the West. Al-Turabi simply would not ignore Sudan's Islamic heritage or its influences in the late twentieth century, and this led to the emergence of a bespoke template specifically for Sudan rather than an imported pan-Islamic model. Al-Turabi attempted to achieve change from within. In the early 1980s he served as justice minister under the leadership of the secularist Nimeri but was imprisoned in the mid-1980s, as he had been in the 1970s, by the ruling authorities for his Islamist activities. Yet fundamentalist pressures had already resulted in the introduction of *shari'a* law to the country in the early 1980s, and the coup of 1989 was to be the final chapter in the ideological battle. In truth, Brigadier General al-Bashir was careful to keep the fundamentalists at arm's length in public and close to his side in private. Furthermore, in the decade that followed, an uneasy relationship developed between these elements. In the eyes of Western policy-makers and commentators, however, the ascendance of al-Turabi as a radical fundamentalist leader and the posturing of the Sudanese state eventually led the USA to suspend official assistance after the coup in 1989. Sudan was subsequently designated a state that was a supporter of terrorism in 1993, followed by a sanctions regime imposed by the United Nations in 1996 that was to last some five years.

Clearly there was a growing fear within Western policy-making circles, evident from their reading of events in Iran and Sudan, that the ascension to government of fundamentalist forces not only changed the nature of political rule in such states from secularism to Islam, but encouraged other fundamentalist groups to believe that such change could be achieved, offered spiritual and material support to such groups and organisations, and would provide a 'safe haven' to rogue elements who would otherwise not be at large in the international system. In the 1980s nowhere was this more apparent than in Lebanon, where the wide and complex repercussions of the civil conflict gave rise to a new generation of fundamentalist forces.

Lebanon: all cats look grey in the dark

Although the civil war in Lebanon broke out in 1975, by the early 1980s the conflict there had drawn in external state actors, including Syria, Israel, France and the USA. Troops from all of these countries were progressively engaged in the country. By the early 1980s the conflict reflected not only sectarian and civil dispute between and among the country's Muslim and Christian population but, as the state weakened, it was vulnerable to challenges from other non-state actors including the PLO and other militia elements. The power vacuum that emerged at state level gave rise to a flowering of other communal forces, including the newly empowered Lebanese *Shi'a*. It was from the *Shi'a* community that a number of newly armed elements would emerge. From among them, a significant corps that advocated the fundamentalist ideology espoused by Ayatollah Khomeini soon came to dominate the news headlines.

Indeed, much commentary and academic work from this period is preoccupied with the *Shi'a* militia forces in Lebanon and particular allegations of a sustained assault against Western targets. Iran was accused of waging a proxy war on Lebanese territory against the West. While there is some truth in this assertion, it belies the intense intricacies of the conflict in Lebanon and the ways in which a variety of actors were drawn into the supporting of various factions against others. Nevertheless, by the end of the decade the Iranians stood accused of supporting a terror campaign against American and other forces in Lebanon. For its part, one of the organisations most closely tied to Iran during this period, the nascent resistance movement of Hizb Allah, also stood accused by America of ordering, organising and executing a series of terrorist actions against American and other Western targets. Hizb Allah had been formed from within the *Shi'a* fold as a resistance movement following the Israeli invasion and occupation of Lebanon in 1982.

As a *Shi'a* militia movement it found itself competing for support with the *Shi'a* secularist AMAL movement led by Nabih Berri. In terms of external support AMAL was seen as more Syrian- than Iranian-aligned. Hizb Allah's leadership was mostly clerical and influenced by the spiritual figurehead, Ayatollah Fadlallah. Fadlallah, for his part, was a venerable *Shi'a* scholar trained in the holy city of Najaf but fired by his Lebanese roots to return to his ancestral homeland and its people. For Fadlallah, war, conflict and Israeli occupation demanded a dualist approach from the *Shi'a* community and its leaders: resistance and social action: 'The occupation has to end and it can only do so by resistance ... yet we have to support the community through health, educational and a social point of view, to prisoners and orphans etc.'.[11] Hizb Allah was accused of enjoying intimate links with terrorist extremists operating under the organisational banner of the 'Islamic Jihad'. It was believed that all these elements enjoyed close links in turn with the Iranians, Syrians or both variously.

For some commentators 'that *Hizbullah* owed its impact to its violence is beyond doubt ... the movement owed its reputation almost solely to its mastery of violence – a violence legitimated in the name of Islam'.[12] On the ground, however, Hizb Allah consolidated its reputation and presence among the *Shi'a* population of Lebanon not just through its armed elements (and everyone who was anyone had an armed militia at their disposal in Lebanon during the civil war), but by addressing the pressing social and welfare needs of an impoverished community that had virtually been abandoned by the state. In this way, the ideological and theological impulse behind *Shi'a* fundamentalism was also addressed and should not be overlooked. It was the attention to this dire need as much as the muscle flexing of the militias that won the support of the audience in the Lebanese theatre for the new fundamentalist doctrine of Hizb Allah. Moreover, its leaders and activities did not enrich themselves at the expense of the constituency they claimed to represent, nor were they seen to morally bankrupt themselves in the service of other people's ideologies. The link with revolutionary Iran, its attacks on Israel, and its alliance with nefarious terrorist elements such as the Islamic Jihad, however, were seen as a major stumbling block that would lead to the designation of the group as terrorist.

The difficulty for many Western governments and commentators lay in distinguishing Hizb Allah from other elements and individuals who were accused of attacks on Western targets. As the proverb goes: all cats look grey in the dark. From this perspective all fundamentalists looked the same and acted the same. In Lebanon the fundamentalist *Shi'a* were characterised by a militant revolutionary fervour and attachment to violence. Hizb Allah was established to wage resistance against Israel and bring about an Islamic state in Lebanon. The revolutionary baton was passed from Tehran to Beirut and the race was on to remake Lebanon as a *Shi'a* Islamic state.

As stated above, there was, however, nothing unusual in the Lebanese context of that time about the regular employment of military means to achieve political goals. In this way the argument that 'too much emphasis is often laid on the influence of religions on people, and not enough on the influence of peoples and their history on religions', is borne out.[13] Violence, whether *Shi'a*, Palestinian, Israeli, Phalangist or

Druze, came to define Lebanon during this period. The Armalite had replaced the ballot box in Lebanon and the engagement of fundamentalists in armed activities was necessary for basic political and physical survival. Hizb Allah's spiritual mentors insisted that armed actions were in accordance with Islamic principles, and that provoked outrage in the rest of the international community as it was subsequently perceived as condoning Hizb Allah involvement in acts of terrorism against Israeli and other Western targets. Faith legitimated violence for a variety of means, including the establishment of an Islamic Lebanon. Hizb Allah, for its part, denies that it has undertaken acts of terrorism. It represents its armed actions as popularly sanctioned legitimate steps that are taken when all others have failed. As one Hizb Allah leader declares, 'It is accepted and it is a duty to confront the enemy, to confront the aggressor and defend rights. It is rejected when violence is used as a means to attack others.'[14] For external actors, often understanding little about the specifics of the civil war – the Syrian presence, the Israeli occupiers – it was perhaps plausible that distinctions between aggressors and resistors became as blurred as the frontlines in Beirut. When the fighting was at its peak it was also even harder for outsiders to grapple with the politics of causality.

By the end of the 1980s, Hizb Allah was recognised as a permanent feature on the Lebanese political scene. They constituted a party that in 1989 backed the Taif Accords, bringing an end to civil war and a transition to peace in Lebanon. In 1992 Hizb Allah candidates stood successfully for parliamentary elections. Hizb Allah remained Lebanon's only armed militia with its forces deployed in the south of the country against Israeli-backed Lebanese forces and the Israeli army itself, which remained in occupation of south Lebanon until May 2000. Hizb Allah has always been a loyal ally of Syria and Iran. In 2005, following the assassination of pro-Western and Syrian-sceptic prime minister Rafik Hariri, pressure grew on Hizb Allah. This was further exacerbated at a popular level in 2006 when as a result of its kidnapping of Israeli soldiers the whole country was drawn into a war with its southern neighbour. Nevertheless it has remained an increasingly powerful and dominating political actor, entering government for the first time in 2011. It is now happy to accept the realities of the delicate mechanism of power-sharing in Lebanon because it believes it can exercise an important veto over other, pro-Western factions. With its deep ties to Syria and Iran, however, it continues to act as a destabilising element within the domestic arena, and threatened to embroil Lebanon in neighbouring Syria's uprising from 2011 onwards.

Resistance in an ideological age

> This is the happy Warrior; this is he
> That every man in arms should wish to be.
>
> (William Wordsworth, 'The Happy Warrior')

It is clear that throughout the 1980s a new dynamism emerged within the myriad fundamentalist movements. There were indeed many 'happy warriors' who emerged onto the fractured landscapes that defined so many Muslim Third World countries. Such warriors marched under the fundamentalist flag of Islam in the belief that revolutionary fervour and the *mujahideen* vanguard would deliver liberation from corrupt authoritarian rule and the imperial machinations of both the capitalist West and the communist East. Yet as the decade progressed, it was clear that the fundamentalist threat was manifest only in a tenuous grip of the state in Sudan and Islamic authoritarianism in Iran. As such, the new ideology in terms of regime change and Islamic governance was hardly a recipe for success. Even in war-torn Afghanistan it was clear that the multifarious *mujahideen* had succeeded against the Soviet occupiers only because of the generous level of Western backing. The ideological thrust of the fundamentalists would need to be sharpened if it were to truly succeed in mobilising the popular mass to achieve regime change in a tidal force that would alter the strategic balance of power in the Middle East, North Africa or West Asia. Moreover, too many other factors, including the rising economic forces of globalisation, would inhibit the fundamentalist impulse at an international level.

Road to enmity

By the end of the decade, alarm bells about the threat of Islamic fundamentalism were ringing in many Western capitals. As communism collapsed it was predicted that Islamic fundamentalism would emerge as the new threat. There was a notion gaining currency that the Islamic fundamentalists wanted to force Islam onto any existing non-Muslim (*kufr*) society and, in the case of Muslim societies, to impose their fundamentalist doctrines. In order to achieve their goal, the fundamentalists would use any means, increasingly violent ones, against their enemies. This view, which in many ways reflected a lesson learnt from the clash between US forces and fundamentalist fighters in Lebanon, was summed up in the following way:

Just beyond the horizon of current events lie ... [the] retribalization of large swathes of humankind by war and bloodshed: a threatened Lebanonization of national states in which culture is pitted against culture, people against people, tribe against tribe – a Jihad in the name of a hundred narrowly conceived faiths against every kind of interdependence, every kind of artificial social cooperation and civic mutuality.[15]

The stage appeared set for a new act in the ideological contest, where violence and conflict were inevitable and the room for peaceful manoeuvre limited.

The 1980s had seen the rise of a number of fundamentalist movements that were organised around the motif of Islamic resistance. Their leaders and activists claimed they had tired of waiting for international solutions to their problems or the aid of their friends and neighbours. They contended that their thinkers and spiritual guides had identified a malaise within many Islamic countries that could only be corrected by Muslim self-empowerment, resistance and self-rule. These fundamentalists believed they were a vanguard for the establishment of a better life for all Muslims. The reaction of their opponents to this new Muslim agenda was quite different. They understood themselves as being targeted by the fundamentalists. They took the attacks on the West and the East at face value. No wonder that in the West fears grew when in 1985 Hizb Allah followed up its actions with the following threats:

Let us put it truthfully: the sons of *Hizballah* know who are their major enemies in the Middle East – the Phalanges, Israel, France and the US. The sons of our *umma* are now in a state of growing confrontation with them, and will remain so until the realization of the following three objectives:

(a) to expel the Americans, the French and their allies definitely from Lebanon, putting an end to any colonialist entity on our land;
(b) to submit the Phalanges to a just power and bring them all to justice for the crimes they have perpetrated against Muslims and Christians;
(c) to permit all the sons of our people to determine their future and to choose in all the liberty the form of government they desire. We call upon all of them to pick the option of Islamic government which, alone, is capable of guaranteeing justice and liberty for all. Only an Islamic regime can stop any further tentative attempts of imperialistic infiltration into our country.[16]

In the West the fear that the fundamentalists were on the march only increased. Many of those fears appeared to be confirmed by the increasing number of terrorist actions laid at the door of Islam, discussed in the next chapter.

Notes

1 Y. al-Qaradawi, *Secularism*, www.islamawareness.net/secularism/secularism. html
2 Interview with Ismail Abu Shanab, Gaza City, August 2002.
3 A. Rashid, *Taliban: The Story of the Afghan Warlords*, London: Pan Macmillan, 2001, pp. 89–92.
4 Ibid., p. 204.
5 See G. Chaliand, *Terrorism: From Popular Struggle to Media Spectacle*, London: Saqi Books, 1987, pp. 63–64.
6 D. Pipes, 'Same difference', *National Review*, 7 November 1994.
7 P. Mansfield, *A History of the Middle East*, London: Penguin Books, 1991, p. 329.
8 See www.refworld.org/docid/4681075319.html
9 T. Niblock, *'Pariah States' and Sanctions in the Middle East*, Boulder, CO: Lynne Rienner Publishers, 2001, p. 199.
10 Quoted in M. Viorst, 'Sudan's Islamic experiment', *Foreign Affairs*, 74:3, May 1995, pp. 45–59.
11 Interview with Sayyid Mohammed Husayn Fadlallah, Beirut, May 2000.
12 M. Kramer, 'Hizbullah: the calculus of Jihad', in M.E. Marty and R.S. Appleby (eds) *Fundamentalisms and the States: Remaking Polities, Economies and Militance*, Chicago: University of Chicago Press, 1993, p. 539.
13 A. Maalouf, *In the Name of Identity: Violence and the Need to Belong*, New York: Arcade Books, 2001, p. 67.
14 Interview with Mohammed Fneish (MP), Beirut, August 2002.
15 B. Barber, 'Jihad vs. McWorld', *Atlantic Monthly*, March 1992, p. 1.
16 Hizb Allah, 'An open letter', *al-Safir*, 16 February 1985.

5 Going global

Fundamentalism and terror

> The fundamentalist seeks to bring down a great deal more than buildings. Such people are against, to offer just a brief list, freedom of speech, a multi-party political system, universal adult suffrage, accountable government, Jews, homosexuals, women's rights, pluralism, secularism, short skirts, dancing, beardlessness, evolution theory, sex. There are tyrants, not Muslims.
>
> (Salman Rushdie)

With the emergence of Islamic fundamentalism as a key dimension of Islamic politics in the twentieth century an intimate link to violence and more, specifically, terrorism has also been established. The militant political manifestation of fundamentalist groups, movements, thinkers and states based on a jihad agenda would have significant consequences for the international order. Islam and terrorism have become synonymous and part of the modern discourse on global politics. Muslim fundamentalist violence has been in evidence as part of social and political coercion within states, between states, and as part of new resistance and terrorist movements. Throughout the 1990s, Muslim fundamentalist violence was found in India, Afghanistan, Yemen, Israel, Kashmir, Pakistan, Algeria, the Philippines, Chechnya, Bosnia, Lebanon, Egypt, Kenya, Sudan and the United States of America. Muslim fundamentalist violence has been directed against Muslim women, against Muslim police officers and soldiers, against Western tourists and workers, and Western targets including Jewish institutions and individuals. Muslim violence and terrorism are blamed, in countries like India, Israel, Bali, the United States of America and Russia, for the worst ever terror attacks in contemporary history. Muslim fundamentalist violence was also increasingly perceived as the primary expression of international terrorism and terror networks in the post-Cold War era.

Such contentions underscore the argument that an intimate link exists between Islamic fundamentalism and terrorism. Evidence is drawn from a series of events in the 1990s, but before this link can be explored and analysed for validity, it is important to clarify the terms of the debate in relation to terrorism.

Warriors of terror

Terrorism is notoriously diffcult to define. Terrorism, while rooted in the vocabulary of the West since the time of the French Revolution in the 1790s, is normally conceptualised as a twentieth-century phenomenon associated with killing and violence outside the framework of the law. In essence it can be defined as an act that is politically motivated.[1] Terrorism is about threat, fear, hurt, injury, damage and destruction of state and civilian targets. The act of terrorism is understood as a symbol of an ideological agenda. Terrorism is rooted in debates about power, politics and violence as much as criminology or psychology. There is very little agreement, however, among policy-makers, diplomats, academics, journalists and others on how to define terrorism. In recent decades over a hundred definitions of terrorism have been formulated. In part, the lack of agreement relates to the power of the term 'terrorism' and the pejorative and value-laden manner in which it is employed. The application of the term has become a way in which enemies are labelled and distinctions drawn between normal or acceptable political behaviours and the deviance of the terrorists. The term lacks precision and can be used to label almost any form of political behaviour that the elites of the modern nation-state deem a threat to the status quo. By employing the label of terrorism, behaviours associated with protest against the state or the legitimacy of the state or its policies are criminalised.

Furthermore, definitions of terrorism are also tied to the debate about distinctions between force and violence, the target and the outcome of such actions. Force may even be seen as the flip side of terrorism. Force is defined as legitimate violence carried out by the state to protect its interests. Terrorism is illegitimate violence and defined as such by the state and other actors. Intention is a key dimension of debates about terrorism, particularly as it relates to the political goal or motive behind such actions. A definition of terrorism that focuses on the empirical manifestation of political violence will include a spectrum ranging from sabotage, riots, attacks on buildings and installations, hijacking and bombing to guerrilla war. Terrorism can be about fear in the eyes of the enemy, the threat of force, the race to acquire armaments of mass destruction, torture and the creation of victims.

The warriors associated with terrorism are usually non-state elements and organisations at large within nation-states or on an international scale. Nevertheless, the definition of rogue states has been designated to identify those modern states that are accused of acting as sponsors of terrorism internationally. In 2011, for example, the government of the United States of America declared that the following Muslim countries were designated as sponsors of international terrorism: Iran, Sudan and Syria. State terrorism refers to terrorism carried out by agents of the state rather than merely sponsoring or lending support to such acts. More generally, the lessons of contemporary history demonstrate that the rulers of many modern states are willing to ignore international rules and norms to engage in activities that can be described as terrorist, which by some are also labelled state terrorism. Context is also recognised as important, and the primary context is one where deep division, injustice, criminality (particularly organised and international) and conflict are already pre-existing. Conflicts, for example, are indicative of the breakdown or weakening of the state's sovereignty and state order. In conflict zones, arms proliferate and the gun, not the ballot box, becomes the primary form of political communication. Nevertheless, the moral dimension of the debate about terrorism offers a clear focus in relation to the taboo of violence against civilians. This debate, in particular, animates many in Islamic fundamentalist circles, and this theme will be explored later in the chapter.

Arenas of conflict are frequently connected to the context in which terrorist groups arise and in which terrorism is manifest. The proliferation of ethnic and national conflicts throughout the 1990s plays a large part in accounting for the rise of terrorism. The transition from traditional inter-state to internal state conflict or civil war was a significant feature of global politics in the 1990s. Some explanations of conflict stress the religio-ethnic dimension, alongside political, economic and other factors as key to the explanation for armed conflict and terrorism since 1945, asserting that, 'within histories of religious traditions ... violence has lurked as a shadowy presence. It has coloured religion's darker, more mysterious symbols.'[2] Indeed, by the 1990s, many explanations of terrorism and conflict tended to focus less on economic explanations of poverty and deprivation and more on ethnicity and in particular the religious dimension of ethnicity. If this approach is combined with the kind of theorising that asserts the equation that democracy equals peace and the absence of democracy equals conflict, then the accusation that Islam runs on a democratic deficit can only lead one to conclude that the link to terror is intrinsic. This approach has been significant in informing policy-making in the West throughout the 1990s.

Many Muslim domains today are characterised by weak or failed states, and this in turn generates instability and a propensity for conflict. Conflict, in turn, makes armed violence, of all types, increasingly inevitable. Once this is combined with the variable of economics, the likelihood of violence is further increased. Most literature on contemporary Muslim terrorism or political violence tends to ignore or underplay this variable, but it is no coincidence that the majority of Muslim countries are characterised by some of the lowest indicators for economic development in the contemporary globe. According to UNDP statistics, not one Muslim country, for example, makes it into the top thirty countries, cited in terms of life expectancy, of the UN's Human Development Indicators in 2003. When economic resources are scarce, competition for them increases and societies become increasingly vulnerable to political violence, as highlighted in Muslim countries throughout the 1990s such as Somalia, Afghanistan, Algeria and Pakistan. Such conditions expose Muslim countries to internal conflict and the intervention of other actors. Islam alone, then, is not the sole determinant of terrorism but Muslims engulfed by conflict or party to conflict are frequently defined by such a label. Terrorism is often related to conflicts that affect Muslims.

The Hydra monster

The manifestation of terrorism that occurred throughout the 1990s across the globe can be viewed from two contrasting perspectives. The first perspective is founded on the metaphor of the Hydra – the many-headed serpent-beast of ancient Greek myth. It recognises the manifestation of terrorism as a many-headed Hydra, but pins the problem of Muslim terrorism back to a single source and aligns all empirical evidence to that source: the body of the single beast. The Hydra metaphor is reflected in the argument that the virulent terrorist Islamic fundamentalism that inspired al-Qaeda in the 1990s alongside other movements including the Taliban, the Egyptian Islamic Jihad and fundamentalist states such as Sudan, are all intimately linked to one element or source: Wahabbi-dominated Saudi Arabia. Such a perspective is summed up by one writer who argues that throughout the 1990s:

> *Wahabbi*-Saudi attempts ... have led to their interference in Afghanistan ... in Israel, where the Saudi regime directly funds and guides Hamas; in Kashmir, where efforts of local moderates to resolve the status of the region have been thwarted by *Wahabbi* aggression; and in Algeria, where political tensions between the

old socialist establishment and new Islamic movements were manipulated to launch a bloody civil war ...

In addition, *Wahabbi*-Saudi agents have sought to launch entirely new fronts for their ideological war, in Somalia, in Indonesia, and in the Philippines. And finally, *Wahabbi*-influenced extremist movements continue to contest for authority in such countries as Nigeria and, of course, the all-important example of a state driven to permanent crisis by *Wahabbi* influence: Pakistan.[3]

For Schwartz, the Hydra of the Wahabbi is to be found in most manifestations of radical Muslim politics across the contemporary globe. For this author, Muslim terrorism is generated and fostered as a result of the Saudi–Wahabbi connection and its influence.

As outlined in Chapter 1, Wahabbism is epitomised as a form of scriptualist conservative fundamentalism that by the early twentieth century, through close alliance with the al-Saud family, achieved state form in the establishment of the Saudi state in 1932. Ruthven refers to the emergent state form as 'turned in on itself ... Religious zealotry was converted into the ideology of a unique political phenomenon: a quasi-totalitarian dynastic state based on the absolute supremacy of a single clan.'[4] In the 1990s it was Saudi Arabia that was accused of exporting its puritanical ideology to Afghanistan, Chechnya, Bosnia, the West Bank and the Gaza Strip, and Central Asian Muslim states such as Uzbekistan and in African countries such as Somalia and Nigeria. Individual Saudis are accused of financing the fundamentalist terror onslaught and the Wahabbi-inspired programme of the Islamisation of Muslim societies by force in countless Muslim domains. Saudi oil wealth is repeatedly cited as a principal financial pivot in the funding of fundamentalist programmes and associated terror networks. Yet, the modern Saudi state has also found itself the target of a new generation of radical Islamists, who claim that the ruling elite has abandoned the strictures of faith for the security of alliance with *kufr* (non-Muslim) elements from the West. In this way the context of Islamic terrorism is portrayed as totalitarian, tyrannical, nihilistic and deeply intolerant of those both within and outside the faith regarded as enemies.

The inference here is that it is this ideology of xenophobic intolerance that was exported to other Muslim domains and accounts for terrorism in and from those domains against local political leaders and the West. There is a sting to the tail, however, in that Western states such as the United States of America are also blamed for formulating a security and foreign policy that either turned a blind eye to such tendencies or encouraged them in the service of other ends. Moreover, the complex nature of such Islamism is further underscored by the fact that previous beneficiaries of such policies now target the West. If the logic of this argument is taken to its conclusion, then the removal of the Hydra's body should eliminate the threat posed by its heads.

The second perspective recognises that while the terrorism phenomenon executed by Muslims appeared to eclipse the 'Red Peril' of the communist era, the manifest connection between Muslims and political violence in the 1990s was more complex and diverse than the buzz-words, sound bites and images of bearded warriors or the Hydra could ever convey. No single source, I contend, explains Muslim violence in the late twentieth century. Even the most cursory glance at the first decade of the post-Cold War order betrays the true scale and picture of conflict, terrorism and the role of Muslims in it. Taken from this perspective, explanations of terrorist acts carried out by Muslims cannot be broken down into the simple dichotomy that 'they' are evil and 'we' are good. Such assumptions leave both sides unfettered in terms of moral and ethical considerations. For in as much as evil becomes a label used to identify modern Muslims by the West, the tables are increasingly turned when modern Muslims think about the way in which the West acts towards their belief system, culture and society. Moreover, if the Hydra analogy were strictly relevant, then the war on terrorism could have begun and ended with Saudi Arabia.

From resistance to terrorism

As earlier chapters of this book have outlined, the ideology of Islamic fundamentalism is rooted in the late nineteenth- and early twentieth-century project to address Muslim intellectual, cultural and political life and reassert its essential principles. For many Muslims involved in the revivalist project, modern Islam became a font of identity, empowerment, legitimate community and hope. Certain elements within the project also realised that if the project to reassert Muslim identity involved challenge and dissent, then they were not only prepared to advocate it but also to argue for the defence of Muslim lands and to assert that an offensive jihad be waged, against elements identified as existential ene-mies of the faith system. Moreover, in the context of Afghanistan, this argument was aligned with the ambitions of Western governments which were keen to use the Afghan frontline as an extension of conflict against their Soviet enemy. The question here is when, then, did jihad transform from resistance to terrorism? Former UN Secretary-General Kofi Annan defines terrorism as 'violence against civilians for political reasons'. In a context such as Afghanistan it is difficult to distinguish the terrorists from other combatants in the arena. Yet the Afghan context also highlights the ideological dimension of conflict where a potent mix of ideologies motivated the many actors, including Muslims, in that arena. But even among the Muslim actors – observant or otherwise – there were many ideological colours on display. All the actors in this arena engaged in acts of violence that were politically motivated and, it was argued, did so as part of a tactic of revolutionary warfare or counter-warfare.

Fundamentalist violence then is intimately connected to the 1990s and the changing world order. Muslim actors, of course, had perpetrated terrorism in Muslim domains in earlier decades, but it had been labelled and associated with dominant Arab nationalist ideologies and battles rather than Islam itself. Indeed, by the 1980s terrorism was a common synonym for the secular Palestinian movement or leftist elements like the Red Army Brigade. In the 1990s that common assumption and the counter-terrorism orthodoxies associated with it also changed.

Events in the 1980s, as outlined in the previous chapter, all but hinted at the revolutionary potential and violent outcomes associated with the involvement of Islamic fundamentalists. This includes the Iranian Revolution in 1979 and the programme of Islamisation and theological rule pioneered by Ayatollah Khomeini. In terms of an anti-Western dimension to the new movement for Islamic fundamentalism, this had been symbolised by Khomeini's ire at the USA – forever branded as the 'Great Satan' – and the holding of 52 American hostages for more than 400 days in the American embassy in Tehran. Furthermore, the bombing of the US Marine barracks in 1982 in Beirut by Islamic fundamentalists and the death of 241 soldiers, demonstrated to a wider audience the power of Islam aligned with violence.

By the early 1990s the catalogue of Islamic fundamentalist terror appeared limitless in scope, capacity and target as more and more movements sprang forth. Although the war against the Soviet occupier in Afghanistan was over by 1992, the mushrooming of *jihadi* fundamentalist movements was apparent and this included al-Qaeda and Taliban elements. Certainly, this phenomenon was 'facilitated' or encouraged by the following factors: the vulnerability of the state as failed and susceptible to competing and rival forces and warlords, the numbers of ex-combatants and easy access to the wealth of arms and armouries throughout the country, chronic economic underdevelopment linked to internationalisation of the opium trade, and intervention by a series of external actors and backers. For example, it is estimated that Western intelligence agencies trained and supported thousands of local Afghan and foreign Arab and other *mujahideen* forces. In Afghanistan, as one author notes, there was

> [a] state of virtual disintegration just before the Taliban emerged at the end of 1994. The country was divided into warlord fiefdoms and all the warlords had fought, switched sides and fought again in a bewildering array of alliances, betrayals and bloodshed.[5]

Many writers traced the origins of the *jihadi*, *salafi* terror campaign to this location and they were right. Who had placed the bullets in the guns and financed the explosives was open to debate, claim and counter-claim; the West was to blame, this was a classic case of biting the hand that feeds you. But it was not the USA or any other Western state that was responsible for the ideology of the *salafi* movement that figures like Osama Bin Laden spearheaded. Under successive Clinton administrations in Washington during the 1990s there was a widely held belief that terrorism had been circumscribed by 'containment'. In reality, however, the real clues were easy to discover and both Bosnia and Chechnya were illustrative of this.

Bosnia and the new jihad

The disintegration of the former Yugoslavia in the early 1990s once again demonstrated the vulnerability of Muslim populations to chaos and disorder, and the consequences of foreign intervention for the emergent political order. Before the collapse of the state the Muslim dimension of the former Yugoslavia was not an issue. The Serbian targeting of the Muslim population, however, changed this situation. An undefended Muslim population was vulnerable to the forces of outsiders, including those keen to relocate the *mujahideen* cause from the Afghan theatre. From 1992 onwards there was increasing evidence of an influx of foreign, mostly Arab, *mujahideen*, actors from Afghanistan, to Bosnia. Bosnia became the new symbol of the *jihadi* fundamentalist cause and is considered key in demonstrating the global nature of the *salafi* fundamentalist project as spearheaded by the 'new terror movements'. Moreover, there is evidence that the new terror movements were covertly supported by agencies of the US government. As foreign *mujahideen* arrived in Bosnia via Algeria, Turkey, Iran, Syria and Lebanon, the arming of Muslim insurgents was inevitable. As conflict raged, the foreign *mujahideen* played a key role in protecting the security and safety of Bosnia's Muslims against the Serb onslaught.

The Muslims of Bosnia were quite literally vulnerable to the military onslaught of their neighbours and were the weakest party in the conflict. The religious rhetoric employed by Serbian nationalism also served to radicalise and religicise one of the most secularised Muslim populations in Europe and galvanise support from fundamentalist elements across the globe. Fresh from victory against the Russians in Afghanistan, the foreign *mujahideen* foresaw an early victory in Bosnia. As Europe appeared to turn a deaf ear to Bosnian Muslim pleas for protection, the fundamentalists stepped in. The price for protection was not only the introduction of the foreign *mujahideen* but also the importation of the strict *jihadi* doctrines and ideology they espoused. This process was palpable not only within the Muslim fighting units, but in the new attempts by religious elements to alter social laws and interactions with other religious/ethnic groups.[6] The battle cry of Bosnian Muslims grew increasingly religious in tone and jihadist in tendency. The Dayton Peace Accords, that brought the war between the Muslims and Serbs to a formal end and demanded that the *mujahideen* disband and depart, came too late to alter the impact of fundamentalist demands, both within the Bosnian community and as another symbol of the rise of Islamist military power. The US government became increasingly concerned at the *mujahideen* phenomenon in Eastern Europe. Yet it encouraged, as it had in Afghanistan, the perpetuation of paramilitary elements that would serve US strategic interests as much as those of the Muslims of Bosnia, who found themselves the target of assaults and ethnic cleansing. It was apparent that containment, ironically augmented with new policies of interventionism in certain international contexts, would mire the US government in dimensions of international politics that demanded attention be paid to Muslim sensitivities. In Bosnia, an early failure to recognise the civilian dimension to the war, combined with the fact that the civilian casualties of ethnic cleansing were mostly Muslim, was read as symbolic of Western indifference in many Muslim capitals. The intervention came too late for the thousands killed and did little to dispel the myths that had already grown in radical Islamist circles. A failure to intervene early enough was interpreted as a signal from the West that Bosnian Muslim democratic impulses were to be sacrificed on the altar of Serbian nationalism.

Chechnya struggle resurgent?

> If somebody in Moscow thinks that we will only keep fighting inside Chechnya, they are totally wrong. The time of patience and hopes that the world would ever stop Putin's gang of murderers is gone … there will

no longer be peaceful life. The war will keep expanding and sooner or
later it will reach Putin's office in the Kremlin, *Inshallah* [God Willing].
(Commander of Dagestani *Mujahideen*, Chechnya, 18 December 2003)

The conflict that unfolded in Chechnya from the 1990s epitomises the
nature of contemporary ethno-national struggles and debates about
self-determination in the post-Cold War era. Conflict, between Chechen
separatists and the Russian centre, has made the region vulnerable to
instability and violence. Both sides to the dispute – the Russians and
the Chechens – have been accused of major human rights abuses
including terrorism. The religious profile of the Chechen population is
Muslim and there is a perception that since the early 1990s the Russian
state has sought to exterminate secessionist tendencies, in a new episode
of historic ethnic rivalry in this region. The Chechen capital of Grozny
came to symbolise the devastating consequences of Russian determination
to destroy the Chechen opposition. By 2000, following waves of fighting
and incursions, the centre of Grozny had been virtually destroyed.
Chechen identity is crystallised around demands for self-determination
and the rebels proclaim that their land is occupied by Russia. Their
'liberation struggle' erupted in 1994 and a full-scale war engaged Russian
forces until 1996. In 1999 conflict resumed as Chechen *mujahideen* re-
launched an offensive for independence. The government in Moscow,
however, portrayed the Chechen issue in public discourse as rooted in
terrorism encouraged by radical fundamentalist Islamic ideology. The
Chechen issue generated support within radical Islamic fundamentalist
circles and was often cited by Osama Bin Laden and other al-Qaeda
leaders, in statements regarding the demand for jihad on behalf of the
Muslim people. Furthermore, the Chechen conflict resulted in hundreds
of thousands of Chechens becoming displaced and refugees, many of
whom settled in Muslim countries in the Middle East.

Following his election in 1999, President Putin committed Russia to
solving the Chechen issue through state force rather than negotiation.
This policy had important support from the US government, which
considered the Chechen issue another front line in the 'War on Terrorism'.
Russian forces have waged successive campaigns against the Chechen
forces and played their part in enmeshing themselves, the Russian and
Chechen people, along with Chechen fighters, in a quagmire of conflict.
Russian forces have been accused by human rights organisations of
gross human rights violations including murders, disappearances, torture,
systematic abuse of human rights and sexual violence against Chechens.
Chechen *mujahideen* have in turn waged a campaign against the Russians
that has included kidnappings, suicide bombings, hijacking, assaults on

Russian military forces, and the assassination of Russian security and government personnel. In 2009 the Russian government declared that it had called a halt to its anti-terrorist operations in Chechnya, believing the republic to be stable under its pro-Kremlin President Kadyrov. The Russians, in the course of their battles, also discovered that, somewhat like their Afghan counterparts, the Chechen *mujahideen* were disparate, highly factional, subject to internal rivalries and, were allegedly, in receipt of much external support and funding from Saudi benefactors. Moderate (mostly Sufi) Chechen elements found themselves squeezed by both the Russian authorities and their radical Muslim counterparts like the Special Purpose Islamic Regiment (SPIR).

In February 2003, the Bank of England issued a notice announcing that funds held by any banks in respect of a number of 'designated' terrorist groups would henceforth be frozen. In that notice the following groups, of whom many were Chechen, were identified:

> *The Riyadus-Salikhin Reconnaissance and Sabotage Battalion of Chechen Martyrs* (a.k.a. Riyadus-Salikhin Reconnaissance and Sabotage Battalion, a.k.a. Riyadh-as-Saliheen, a.k.a. the Sabotage and Military Surveillance Group of the Riyadh al-Salikhin Martyrs, a.k.a. Riyadus-Salikhin Reconnaissance and Sabotage Battalion of Shahids (Martyrs)).
>
> *The Special Purpose Islamic Regiment* (a.k.a. the Islamic Special Purpose Regiment, a.k.a. the al-Jihad-Fisi-Sabililah Special Islamic Regiment, a.k.a. Islamic Regiment of Special Meaning).
>
> *The Islamic International Brigade* (a.k.a. the Islamic Peacekeeping Brigade, a.k.a. the Islamic Peacekeeping Army, a.k.a. the International Brigade, a.k.a. Peacekeeping Battalion, a.k.a. International Battalion, a.k.a. Islamic Peacekeeping International Brigade).
>
> *Lajnat Al Daawa Al Islamiya* (a.k.a. LDI).[7]

SPIR was also designated a terrorist group by the US government in 2002. The Chechen rebel group was accused of undertaking a range of terrorist actions. It is believed that SPIR members are radical fundamentalists deeply influenced by Saudi-inspired Wahabbi tendencies, who enjoy ideological as well as other links to the global *salafi jihadi* movement. Yet the demands of SPIR and other Chechen groups remain nationalist rather than pan-Islamic in ambition. The demand for self-determination rather than global jihad in the style of Bin Laden remains the defining feature of this movement. The radical Islamisation project did, however, become a feature of some elements in Chechen nationalism. Their agenda coincided with that of the

Afghan and Bosnian veterans who sought to Islamise the Caucasus regions. The dividing line between original nationalist demands and the jihad movement became blurred. Rebel leaders were Chechen, Turkish and even Saudi-born. Militant Afghan elements, trained in camps in Pakistan, also joined the fight for Muslim self-determination and independence in Chechnya.[8]

The Bank of England notice also mentioned two other Chechen groups with alleged *salafi* jihad connections: the Riyadus–Salikhin Reconnaissance and Sabotage Battalion of Chechen Martyrs and the Islamic International Brigade. It was alleged that the interconnections between these groups centred on their subscription to Saudi- and Afghan-inspired *salafi* doctrines and terrorist techniques. Members and fighters in these groups, as well as subscribing to Chechen nationalist demands, adhered to the *salafi* agenda promoted by the al-Qaeda leadership from the mid-1990s. In secret training grounds and *madrassas* the radical doctrine of ideologues such as Sayyid Qutb, Abdullah Azzam and Osama Bin Laden was introduced into the Chechen arena. The Chechen issue, like Palestine and Kashmir, was also employed by *salafi* elements elsewhere as a symbol of liberation that could transcend borders and Western-determined frontiers in the Muslim world. This powerful symbol generated support from across the Muslim world. Hundreds of foreign *mujahideen* began to arrive in the Chechen–Russian theatre of conflict ready for the next stage in the global jihad. By 1999, the Muslim dimension of the Chechen conflict had become 'internationalised' by the arrival of foreign fighters, foreign funding and imported radical fundamentalist ideologies. Conflict had spilled over to neighbouring Dagestan, and the rest of the Caucus region looked increasingly vulnerable. That vulnerability was soon apparent in a sharp escalation in the number of attacks launched by Chechen *mujahideen* elements, their 'martyr'-inspired tactics and an increasing belief at the international level that the Chechens represented but one dimension of the new movement for global terrorism. This made unlikely allies of Presidents Bush and Putin and was apparent in their joint statements in the wake of the 9/11 attacks on America:

> The Presidents note that terrorism threatens not only the security of the United States and Russia, but also that of the entire international community, as well as international peace and security. They believe that terrorism poses a direct threat to the rule of law and to human rights and democratic values. It has no foundation in any religion, national or cultural traditions, and it only uses them as a cover for its criminal goals.[9]

Chechen demands for self-determination appeared irrevocably lost. Such demands were interpreted by state elites in Moscow and other Western capital cities as nothing more than a front or facade for fanatic Muslim demands for a global jihad. The Chechen case demonstrated that all anti-state tactics were perceived by the authorities in Moscow as terror tactics. Moreover, international critics of the Russian government's handling of the Chechen issue focused on the complaint that by using the cover of the 'War on Terrorism', President Putin was allowed to perpetrate gross human rights abuses against ordinary Chechen people. Human Rights Watch declared:

> Russia's ongoing record of serious human rights abuse in Chechnya impugns its claim that the war there contributes to the international campaign against terrorism … The war in Chechnya mostly contributes greatly to human suffering. The international community should think seriously about whether it wants to be associated with this very abusive war.[10]

Despite the war's end the legacy of the conflict in Chechnya, including its Islamist dimensions, is not only apparent within this slowly-recovering republic's borders, but in neighbouring states and regional strategic frameworks too.

Philippines morass

As the fundamentalist phenomenon appeared to take root at a global level in diverse parts of the globe, the materialisation of Muslim fundamentalism was, however, commonly associated with the Middle East. In reality, however, as migration increased as a result of pan-Islamic aspirations, as well as the reality of the economic impulses that generate migrant labour cultures across the Muslim world, the interconnection between the Muslim Middle East and other Muslim regions or countries grew. One context where this was increasingly relevant to the manifestation of politics locally was the Philippines. Terrorism appeared to disrupt many cultures and by the late 1990s it was apparent that Manila was vulnerable not only to the manifestation of local opposition, but the apparent growth of transnational Islamic fundamentalist movements and terror networks.

Islam has been extant in South Asia for many centuries and has flourished alongside indigenous cultures and other faith systems. Indonesia has the largest Muslim population anywhere in the world; and in countries like the Philippines Muslims have remained a

minority, constituting some 5 per cent of the population and demo-
graphically concentrated in the southern regions and islands. In the past,
the Moros, as Philippine Muslims are called, possessed a degree of
autonomy through the establishment of small ruling entities. The
Moros enjoyed a separate sense of identity and did not relish enforced
national independence and territorial unity with the rest of the Philippines. This independence, achieved in 1946, was US-inspired and the
Moros resented it. From this time secessionist tendencies were apparent
as central government neglected this minority in favour of larger
demographic groupings. Like Muslim elites in other parts of Asia and
the Middle East, there was a tendency through the 1940s and 1950s for
local elements to develop nationalist ambitions. This in turn led, by the
1960s, to the emergence of a new generation of activists who demanded
independence from Manila. While some concessions were met, a sense
of disillusionment at the overall failure of nationalist secessionist
demands was apparent by the 1970s when armed elements emerged. As
the state attempted to disarm the Muslim community, a new group
came to the fore named the Moro National Liberation Front (MNLF).
The founding vision of the MNLF centred on the aspiration for independence and Islamic statehood for the Moros people. The ensuing
conflict between the state and the armed liberation groups of the
Moros resulted in the disruption and dislocation of the Moros people.
The Islamisation of the conflict was apparent in the role played by
the Organization of Islamic Conference (OIC) and Libya, between
the warring parties that led to the Tripoli ceasefire and autonomy
agreement in the mid-1970s. Factionalism, however, plagued the independence movement and by the late 1970s the rivalry had reached a
peak. Liberation leaders also now benefited from extensive contact
with and training in religious seminaries across the Muslim world and
were influenced through the revivalism phenomenon that was apparent
in other locations.

By the early 1980s the Moros movement was chiefly characterised by
that Islamic revivalism. It was also apparent by this point that President
Marcos would largely renege on his promises of autonomy. Meanwhile
the foreign-trained clerics were leading an increasingly mass-based
movement for Muslim secession. When President Marcos was deposed in
1985, the Moros organised their own demonstrations to demand
autonomy while at the same time they organised a political party to
put forward candidates in local elections. As Muslim demands were
sidelined, radicalisation seemed almost inevitable. In 1991, an MNLF
splinter group called Abu Sayyaf (Father of the Sword) issued its
demands for a free and independent state in the southern Philippines.

The group's founder was a veteran of the Afghan war and enjoyed links with other fundamentalist elements across the globe. It is contended that Abu Sayyaf was originally established in Afghanistan, funded or supported by the CIA in its task of orchestrating and providing backing to the anti-Soviet campaign.[11] Following the end of the war in Afghanistan, Abu Sayyaf elements established a new base in the Philippines. Abu Sayyaf is a jihadist fundamentalist organisation that, like the Palestinian Hamas organisation of the West Bank and the Gaza Strip, not only challenges a state authority it considers to be a usurper and infidel, but a nationalist rival with whom it competes against for popular support. Abu Sayyaf embarked on a campaign of armed violence against the authorities in Manila as well as other targets including foreigners. The ideological rhetoric of the organisation was deeply fundamentalist and rumours of links with other radical terror groups across the globe persisted.

In many respects, Abu Sayyaf represents a fringe secessionist element that acknowledges the connection with Islam as core to Moros identity. Yet whether this means that Abu Sayyaf is but one small cog in a wider transnational terror network orchestrated from Afghanistan and other 'rogue states' in the 1990s, has been subject to sustained contention. It is true that even if Abu Sayyaf is not orchestrated by al-Qaeda, it did originate from the same Afghan locale as was fostered by the CIA, in order to successfully conclude the *mujahideen* campaign against the Russians. Secession has been tied into Islamic fundamentalist doctrine with respect to this particular phenomenon. Moreover, the economic impulses that motivate armed movements and terrorists have also been considered in explaining the propensity to kidnap and ransom by Abu Sayyaf elements in more recent years. Indeed, it has been asserted that Abu Sayyaf is today 'motivated primarily by mercenary instinct, not religious sentiment'.[12]

State strategies to respond to secessionist demands have recognised the religious dimension of the Moros struggle, and the authorities in Manila represented much of their response as protection for the Christian population of the southern regions. The Moros' links to transnational fundamentalist elements surfaced in the wake of the 1993 attack on the World Trade Center and the subsequent conviction of the Egyptian Islamist, Ramzi Yousef, who had been in Manila before his arrest in Pakistan. Furthermore, authorities in Manila became convinced that Osama Bin Laden was linked to Abu Sayyaf and arms were being supplied to the group from Afghanistan. The Abu Sayyaf group remains the most combative of the anti-government organisations in the Moros secessionist movement. The majority moderates simply continue to demand independence and point to the continuing inequalities and discrimination they face from Manila. In 1996 the MNLF announced a ceasefire and has been in negotiations with the government. Another armed element, the Moros Islamic Liberation Front (MILF), also undertook a ceasefire that broke down after government raids on MILF camps and positions in 2000. Moros' demands for independence have been partly met by the concession of autonomy to the Mindanao region. In April 2010, after a series of previously failed attempts, the government reached a peace agreement with the leadership of MILF which would be monitored by an international team. This has gone some way to pacifying the demands of the majority while the extreme minority is increasingly countered as part of the global war on terrorism, supported in the Philippines through close financial and strategic alliance by the government in Manila with the government of the USA.

Can't see the wood for the trees

By the late 1990s there were very few Islamic fundamentalist groups that were not immediately allied in the Western popular imagination with the label of terrorism. Islamism more generally was cast as a terror phenomenon. Groups as diverse as the Muslim Brotherhood, Hizb Allah, Hamas, Islamic Jihad, Gama Islamiyya, FIS, the al-Nahda, AMAL, Jaama al-Islamiyya, Hizb Tahrir, GIA, GSPC, Mohammed's Army, and the Islamic Action Front were named as fundamentalists and increasingly linked with terrorism and other violence. This gave the impression of a global single-issue movement that was organising a war against the West. In addition, support for such groups was interpreted as evidence of increasing Muslim support for terrorism. The manifestation of 'rogue states' and 'fundamentalist states' that were identified as promoting or supporting Muslim terrorism was also apparent in much policy rhetoric and media coverage of Muslim countries. Countries increasingly defined by fundamentalism included Saudi Arabia, Egypt, Libya, Sudan, Algeria, Afghanistan, Pakistan, Iran, Yemen and Indonesia. Such countries were characterised by fundamentalism for a variety of reasons: sometimes state regimes themselves were considered to be coloured by the ideology of fundamentalist Islam and at other times the state was seen as locked in battle with fundamentalist activists, seeking to alter the state and even bring it down. In such circumstances, state control strategies with respect to the fundamentalist challenge were often authoritarian and repressive. Conflict became inevitable, taking the form of confrontation by fundamentalist states with their citizens or by fundamentalist citizens against the state. State coercion was palpable in a variety of contexts, including Taliban-controlled Afghanistan and the nationalist secular elite of Algeria. Moreover, the internal challenge to authority mounted by fundamentalist groups against regimes and states in Muslim domains, was also increasingly understood as representing a threat to the West or Western interests in Muslim countries. This was particularly true in Muslim states with significant oil or gas reserves. The fear expressed was that Western interests, the international capitalist economy and international stability would be significantly undermined if the Islamists were to take power of the state.

The power of Islam as translated by the ideologues of fundamentalism was perceived as a major strategic threat to the West in the post-Cold War era. Islam ascendant and characterised by angry hordes and bloody terrorism became increasingly apparent in media coverage and news reporting in particular. The notion that such a view was distorting the revival phenomenon of Islam was generally dismissed or countered with growing evidence of Muslim lawlessness and terrorism.

Muslim menace

Muslim terrorism was also increasingly linked to the concept of jihad. Indeed, not only had the term jihad entered the English language, but it was accepted as meaning holy war waged by Muslims against infidels or non-Muslims. The theological definition of jihad as a form of striving related to the soul and the individual was largely left unexplored in Western media representations. Jihad was seen as the distinguishing feature of Muslim terrorism,

> clearly conceived and conducted as a form of Holy War which can only end when total victory has been achieved ... [it] does not seek negotiations, give-and-take, the securing of specific concessions or even the mere seizure of political power with a certain number of countries.[13]

The jihad declared by Islamist leaders of fundamentalist organisations was interpreted as a declaration of war against the West. Attempts by Muslim leaders to disassociate jihad from terrorism were seen as marginal and largely ignored in Western media. Instead, terrorism as an indicator of the absence and rejection of democracy was also perceived as increasingly important. Throughout the 1990s, democratisation was seen as an important vehicle for political and economic transformation in various regions of the globe and Muslim countries in particular. The demand by the West for democratisation in a variety of Muslim contexts took for granted the absence of a culture of democratic behaviours within Islam. Democracy was viewed as a stranger to Islamist discourse and underscored the supposed preference for totalitarian and terrorist behaviours. The Islamist embrace of democratic rhetoric was primarily viewed as a ruse to deflect attention and allow the terrorists to continue with their atrocities. The repudiation of democracy and its associated principles of plurality and freedom was commonly associated with Islamic fundamentalists, who instead urged their followers to wage a holy war. The emergence of an Islamist discourse that condemned Western-inspired liberal democracy as the torment of the Muslim world, became common currency and Islam was offered as the solution. The means to the solution was understood as terrorism.

Islamic fundamentalism, understood as a manifestation of fanatic and extremist anti-democratic and totalitarian faith-based contemporary expression, coupled to a literal interpretation of Islam's holy literatures, was becoming a major threat to democratic countries. For the leaders of many Muslim countries, the threat lay in the revolutionary potential associated with the fundamentalists, and the leaders of democratic countries recognised that the revolutionary tide had to be halted, through supporting existing regimes in their campaigns against the fundamentalists. This in turn explains why so many democratic governments offer support to authoritarian states in the battle against terrorism. For terrorism became increasingly inextricable from Islamic fundamentalism. Fundamentalism is but one response to the perceived bankruptcy of Western democracy, Western state nationalism, Western development agendas and Western popular culture. Fundamentalism is a by-product of the experiences of millions of Muslims across the globe, and 'if there are in a range of Islamic countries evident barriers to democracy', one author contends,

> [this] has to do with certain other social and political features that their societies share. These would include low levels of development, entrenched traditions of state control, political cultures that inhibit diversity and tolerance, the absence of a tradition of private property, and the lack of separation of state and law.[14]

In this context fundamentalism implies a direct link to violence and terrorism in particular. The rage of Islam is manifest in the plethora of organisations and groups that emerged throughout the 1990s. These groups and organisations were led by individuals who espoused jihad and attacks against a variety of targets. Extremist fundamentalism has figured in the terrorist violence against Muslim and non-Muslim targets throughout the decade, including the increasing number of attacks on Western targets such as the World Trade Center in 1993, the embassy bombings in Kenya and Tanzania in 1998, the Taliban executions of the late 1990s, the suicide bombings in Israel, and similar violence in Kashmir, the Philippines and Yemen. In the minds of millions of consumers of the images and news reports of such incidents on radio, television, the internet and in print, a direct and intimate link between Muslim fundamentalism and terrorism was established.

The threat of Muslim holy terrorism as 'more lethal', 'more violent', 'more fanatical', lacking in rationality and driven by a quest for ultimate victory and not compromise, made this 'new wave' terrorism appear almost unbeatable. The alliance of Western states such the USA and the United Kingdom with such elements, as part of counter-terror efforts against former foes, and relations with Muslim regimes that were regularly condemned for their authoritarian treatment of their citizens, appeared initially to muddy the waters and make it difficult for intelligence experts to predict the extent to which the threat would be realised through sheer force of terror. Power remained the goal and if violence were deemed necessary, many actors would not hesitate. Force or violence would be deployed to wage the threat, to meet the threat, to counter the threat and thus alter the language of terrorism and the political landscape, as the peoples of the globe began the traverse from one millennium to another.

Fundamentalist failure?

By the mid-1990s, some authors contended that the fundamentalist movement had reached its peak and that this manifestation of political Islam was in decline. 'The failure of political Islam', lay, according to some, in the inability of fundamentalist leaders to translate their agenda at either a local, regional or global level. Despite the successes of the Iranian revolution and the rise of fundamentalist and neo-fundamentalist elements elsewhere, this did not constitute a success.[15] The Islamists seemed unable to usurp power and the revolutionary potential of fundamentalist Islam was dismissed as belonging to another age. Furthermore, it was contended that fundamentalist Islam was not a threat to the West for it did not contain the potential to truly unify Muslim believers in a global revolutionary jihad. This view was reflected in the following assertion that 'The nineties have challenged ... presumptions and expectations ... There have been no other Iranian-style

Islamic revolutions, nor have any radical groups seized power.'[16] For critics of this perspective such arguments were a denial of the major threat that Islam posed to the West in the wake of the ending of the war against communism. Yet the real portent of the argument was overlooked. For in attempting to play down alarmist assumptions about fundamentalist Islam, these authors were highlighting the context in which Muslim politics was manifest. The depth of the revivalist project at the level of society rather than politics was also made apparent: 'the resurgence of Islam in Muslim politics has been far more indigenously rooted. It has not receded but rooted itself more deeply and pervasively. Its many faces and postures have surfaced and will continue to do so.'[17]

Throughout the 1990s, Islamic fundamentalism was increasingly linked in the popular imagination and in policy-making circles in the West and other countries, with the phenomenon of holy war or holy terrorism. The inability of the radicals to expose the plight of so many Muslim populations across the globe, to expose the genuine lack of rights and injustices that dominated in so many Muslim states, was coupled to an extremist agenda for change. If they had tried to make their voices heard, had anyone listened? And if they employed violence to get attention for their cause, the violent acts succeeded in veiling the underlying grievances being brought to the attention of the world. The advocacy of political violence as jihad in the form of self-defence appealed to an increasing number within the Muslim fold. As poverty increased, unemployment rose, conflicts remained unresolved, Muslim elites enriched themselves through corruption and Western states pursued less-than-ethical foreign policies in Muslim domains, the message of Muslim empowerment through jihad that was disseminated by the radicals grew in importance.

The fundamentalists exploited a fear within many Muslim communities that the 'New World Order', defined by President Bush in 1990, was one in which the West would seek the capitulation and compliance of Muslim states and one where Muslim society would be rendered mute on the political stage. There was a fear that Muslim culture would all but disappear under the weight of Western culture promoted across the globe as the 'universal' culture of the new age. In this climate, it was argued, the majority of Muslims would remain disenfranchised and discriminated against in Muslim states, dominated by dictators who were supported by the West. Where Muslims were forced to live as migrants in non-Muslim states, they would remain discriminated against and subject to the racist agendas of the anti-immigrant and right-wing groups.

Notes

1 M. Crenshaw, 'Current research on terrorism: the academic perspective', *Studies in Conflict and Terrorism*, 15:1, 1992, p. 1.
2 M. Juergensmeyer, *Terror in the Mind of God: The Global Rise of Religious Violence*, Berkeley, CA: University of California Press, 2000, p. 6.
3 S. Schwartz, 'Defeating Wahabbism', *FrontPageMagazine*, 25 October 2002, p. 1. www.frontpagemagazine.com
4 M. Ruthven, *A Fury for God: The Islamist Attack on America*, London: Granta Books, 2002, p. 140.
5 A. Rashid, *Taliban: The Story of the Afghan Warlords*, Basingstoke: Pan, 2001, p. 21.
6 L. Cohen, *Broken Bonds: The Disintegration of Yugoslavia*, Boulder, CO: Westview Press, 1993, pp. 69–70.
7 Bank of England, 28 February 2003.
8 A. Rashid, *Taliban*, p. 92.
9 Joint Statement by President Bush and President Putin, 21 October 2001.
10 Human Rights Watch, *Into Harm's Way*, New York: Human Rights Watch, January 2003.
11 J. Cooley, *Unholy Wars: Afghanistan, American and International Terrorism*, London: Pluto Press, 2002, pp. 49–50.
12 A. Acharya, 'State–society relations: Asian and world order after September 11', in K. Booth, and T. Dunne (eds) *Worlds in Collision: Terror and the Future of Global Order*, Basingstoke: Palgrave Macmillan, 2000, p. 196.
13 A. Taheri, *Holy Terror: The Inside Story of Islamic Terrorism*, London: Sphere Books, 1987, p. 8.
14 F. Halliday, *Islam and the Myth of Confrontation: Religion and Politics in the Middle East*, London: IB Tauris, 1996, p. 116.
15 O. Roy, *The Failure of Political Islam*, Cambridge, MA: Harvard University Press, 1994.
16 J. Esposito, *The Islamic Threat: Myth or Reality?*, New York: Oxford University Press, 1992, p. 209.
17 Ibid., p. 209.

6 Ground Zero and Islamic fundamentalism

It should be no surprise that the deepest rift to have opened up since September 11th is that between America and the world's Muslims.

(*The Economist*[1])

In theory, there is a historic tension that exists between an essentially modern secular and essentially 'anti-modern' Islamic fundamentalist approach to politics since 1945. The events of 11 September 2001 appeared to confirm the existence of a great chasm between those intent on pursuing a campaign to resurrect the past and those firmly wedded to the present. Al-Qaeda, led as it was by Osama Bin Laden, represented the apogee of Islamic fundamentalism. The very scale of destruction wrought by the suicide bombers of 9/11 symbolised the assault on modernity that appeared to lie at the heart of the Islamic fundamentalism. Indeed, if we remind ourselves of the definition of fundamentalism outlined in Chapter 1 of this book, 'strict maintenance of ancient or fundamental doctrines of any religion, especially Islam', the attacks of 9/11 appeared to bear testimony to this definition as articulated by al-Qaeda's bombers.

In the wake of 9/11 and the declaration of a war on terror by the US government and others, there was a growing belief that terrorism had been made anew by Islamic fundamentalists who adhere to a belief that only by waging a war against the West could the ancient and fundamental doctrines of Islam be resurrected across the globe. While it is true that in the aftermath of 9/11 the US government signalled it was not waging war on Islam but terrorism, a widespread feeling grew nonetheless that Islam had been singled out. On the other hand, the belief that Muslims were ready to wage war against the West was also reinforced, as public authorities placed entire populations on sporadic terror alert against further al-Qaeda attacks. This has underscored the belief that since 1945 there has been a progressive return to an ancient form of context, power struggle and warfare motivated not by economic forces but religion. Furthermore, it is contended that the new religious war is not about Islam in opposition to Christianity and Judaism: 'Rather it is a war of fundamentalism against faiths of all kinds that are at peace with freedom and modernity.'[2]

This contention frames the debate in a significant way. For to reflect on Islam as a modern-day political phenomenon and its dynamic nature there was a need to ponder, in the aftermath of 9/11, on the deep polarisation and chasm between Islam and the West that appeared to have emerged. If this contention was acceptable, it then deliberately ignored the multiple forms of political expression that had been taking place within Muslim communities and between Muslim communities and others the world over. In turn, it required that the fundamentalists abandon the political goals that have motivated them for more than five decades. In order to 'become modern', anti-modern fundamentalist Muslims must, according to Salman Rushdie, restore

> religion to the sphere of the personal ... If terrorism is to be defeated, the world of Islam must take on board the secularist-humanist principles on which the modern is based, and without which Muslim countries' freedom will remain a distant dream.[3]

It became clear that a stark assumption was offered to Muslims in relation to their faith and its political expression. That assumption was that if Muslims wanted to remain part of processes of modernity that had unfolded since 1945 then they had to give up religion as a manifestation of a political identity. This assumption was reinforced in the public arena in France throughout the 1990s by the decision of the government to ban religious symbols from public workplaces and public schools. It was contended that if French Muslims wanted to remain within French society, and not be marginalised and excluded, they would be compelled to accept the strictures of secularism and abandon their religious identity in public. For the prospect of religious totalitarianism in the guise of fundamentalist Islam had generated great fear and loathing. Islam's congruence with modernity was thus called into question.

A future for Islam?

Islam's relationship with the West, with non-Muslims and with non-fundamentalist Muslims, came to dominate political discourse. 9/11 was represented by some as a wake-up call to the enormity of the threat that Islamic fundamentalists posed. Some argued that this threat was more potent than the Nazis and the Soviets since a form of warfare was being waged where the normal rules of the game were abandoned:

> As dangerous as the Soviet Union was, it was always deterred by a wall of containment and with nukes of our own. Because, at the end of the day, the Soviets loved life more than they hated us. Despite our differences, we agreed on certain bedrock rules of civilisation. With the Islamist militant groups, we face people who hate us more than they love life.[4]

Such assumptions left little room for accommodation on either side of an ever-widening divide. Islam had been increasingly perceived in Western consciousness as at odds with modern society and the values this society represented. Islam was seen as an anachronism and a monolithic house under which more than a billion Muslims were residing. The political message of Islam was perceived as dangerous and backward and its manifesto of Islam was also coloured by its condition, a condition that Lewis described as 'poor, weak and ignorant'.[5] Muslims were accused of abandoning the kind of civilised values that are believed to hold modern societies together.

The language of war now dominated the discourse. As one commentator remarked:

> If we want to win this war, we must begin by recognizing that it is a war against Islam – or to be more exact, this is Islamic funda-mentalism's war against the 'infidel' secularism of the West. Our goal in this war should be to beat down, to curtail, to drive out Islamic fundamentalism – not to replace it with our own religion, but to force Islam, like the religions of the civilized world, to lay down its arms and accept the freedom of a secular society.[6]

The clash of civilisations predicted by Huntington was being actualised through the redefinition of conflict and warfare as one in which the religious marker of civilisation did indeed establish 'battle lines of the future'. The portent of Huntington's thesis was underscored by the belief that Islam was now the civilisation that threatened the West. The threat was manifest in terms of the values that the West came to represent and that Islam was supposed to hate. Islam was defined as composed of a billion dogmatic adherents to a rigid doctrine of hate against others.

The reality, however, was that Islam is composed of millions of Muslims as much different as alike in terms of culture, nation and economy. Moreover, Muslims did not look at the rest of the world through the same prism. The diversity that revealed the true character of Islam also revealed many dimensions of ambiguity with respect to the contemporary world since 1945. In addition, other factors outside of religion accounted for the political world-view shared and disputed over within Islamic fundamentalist circles. No two Muslim societies or countries are the same. The differences, for example, between Muslim majority Bangladesh (an openly democratic state) and Saudi Arabia (an openly Islamic state) are far greater, politically, than the commonality presupposed by labelling both countries Muslim. Yet the egalitarian dimension of Islam is apparent in the realm of violence.

The suicide bomber from Gaza, the *mujahid* in Afghanistan, the Chechen Muslim fighter, the *Sunni* insurgent in Fallouja, are all united in a belief that their religion calls on them to sacrifice their life. Sacrifice is no longer purely a national effort but appears to be intimately linked to the revival of faith and a notion of sacred duty. This new force was translated into a form of terrorism that appeared to threaten the free world. Islamic fundamentalism acquired a new energy and its manifestation dominated public debates about terrorism, security, international relations and international politics. Fundamentalist rhetoric appeared to have fuelled terrorism to the point where it assumed epidemic proportions. At last it appeared that Muslims were empowered and could reclaim their identity, but only by engaging in violence and inflicting terror on others. The empowerment of Islam came at the expense of justice, freedom and humanity and continued to centre on the idea of a return to a past age. Islamic fundamentalism accounted for new forms of strengthened Muslim identity placing the political back into the picture. This kind of fundamentalism differed little from the militant purist doctrines of other fundamentalists from Judaism, Christianity and Hinduism. This, according to authors such as Marty and Appleby,[7] was what unites the fundamentalists: they are dogmatic, militant and agitate against the secular project to sideline faith. Their militancy is symptomatic of an attachment to an absolutist doctrine rather than key to any particular faith or creed. In this respect, the Islamic fundamentalists differed little from other fundamentalists or militants. This militancy was motivated by a total belief in the cause and justice of action undertaken in the name of Islam, Christianity, Judaism, love or anything else for that matter. This militancy was not necessarily altered by the prefix of Islam. Absolutist doctrines have motivated Christian fundamentalists to campaign and engage in terrorism against abortion clinics and black communities in the USA; they are visible in the hate-filled terrorist attacks by Jewish fundamentalists on the Arab population (Christian and Muslim) in the West Bank and the Gaza Strip and have led to the persecution and pogroms by Hindu-organised violence against Muslims in India.

I would contend then that in this respect Islamic terrorism was little different from other forms of terrorism motivated by other faith systems. To treat it differently was problematic. As Juergensmeyer asserted, 'religious terrorism is seldom solely a tactic in a political strategy. It is also a symbolic statement aimed at providing a sense of empowerment to desperate communities.'[8] Moreover, connotations that sacred, cosmic, millennial or absolutist battles defining religious terrorism, marking it out from other forms of terrorism, do not always withstand rigorous examination. We had in fact been here before. Whether we were reflecting on nationalist or ethnic-inspired terrorism, or other forms of religious terrorism, our abhorrence at such irrational and inhumane acts remained refreshingly similar. Nor were such manifestations of terrorism confined merely to one historic era or another. Terrorism, religious or otherwise, remained a defining feature of late twentieth- and early twenty-first-century politics. There is no Muslim monopoly in this respect. If looked at from an opposite perspective, however, Islam was the problem. The war on terrorism that was declared in the wake of the 9/11 bombings was directed at the manifestation of terrorism, rebellion and violence committed by individual or groups of Muslims. At the end of the Cold War, many Western governments, and the US government in particular, were compelled to reassess their foreign policy and security agendas. During the Cold War intelligence, security, foreign policy and economic efforts had been concentrated, decade after decade, on undermining and defeating the threat from the Soviet Union and that posed by nationalist terrorist organisations. At the end of the Cold War, Islam was the focus of new fears and policies, with national security priorities increasingly fixated on its menacing dimensions. After 9/11 the growing preoccupation with terrorism in the name of Islam was warranted, but often before this event it was not the threat of terrorism that preoccupied policy-makers but Islam itself. Unable to distinguish the wood from the trees, the actual threat was simply overlooked or confused with a sense that former allies would never turn against the West. In Afghanistãn, however, the *mujahideen* were reinterpreting the rout of the Russians with consequences for the ways in which they viewed other super-powers in the West. It was from here that the roots of al-Qaeda were sited and the threat to American national security grew. The maelstrom of conflict threw up a new terror group that claimed to speak in the name of Islam.

This virus called terrorism

In the absence of peace, justice and humanity, conflict and violence prevail. From conflict and violence, terrorism emerges. For many in the West, however,

> the threat comes because in another part of our globe there is shadow and darkness where not all the world is free; where many millions suffer under brutal dictatorship; where a third of our planet lives in poverty beyond anything even the poorest in our societies can imagine; where a fanatical strain of religious extremism has risen that is a mutation of the true and peaceful faith of Islam; and because in the combination of these afflictions a new and deadly virus has emerged. The virus is terrorism.[9]

Islam, the faith of failure, backwardness and despotic tendency, was identified as the chief culprit of global ills. Since 1945 Islamic fundamentalist doctrines, movements and organisations became a defining feature of modern Muslim states and societies. Indeed, where states had failed or were failing, where poverty gripped society and brutal dictatorship established a sense of fear, Islamists had offered aid, hope, charity and assistance. This stood in stark contrast to the images of terror associated with 9/11, the Bali bombers, the massacres at Luxor and the carnage wrought by suicide bombers in Madrid, Moscow, Mosul or Mea Shearim and the alternate manifestation of Islamic fundamentalism. How Janus-faced it appeared. Across the globe, the threat of the Islamic fundamentalism moved to the top of the agenda as dictators and democrats alike found common ground in their antipathy to Islam. By turning the spotlight on Islamic fundamentalism, others were let off the hook. In the case of Iraq and Iran, Saddam Hussein's war against the fundamentalist regime in Tehran (1980–89), recognised as one of the most futile in modern history, was actively supported by Western and other Arab governments while at the same time he went largely uncensored in his reign of tyranny on the populace of his own country.

The view that the USA and its allies embarked on a war against Islam did not diminish but grew in the wake of the US-prosecuted war on terrorism. In Afghanistan the Taliban were defeated by Western allied forces but in the wake of that war the fundamentalists remained in power. The US-supported Loya Jirga of warlords and fundamentalists holed up in Kabul held little prospect for hope in the reconstruction of a just and peaceful Afghanistan. The inclusion of states such as Iraq, Iran and Syria in an 'Axis of Evil' by the Bush administration in the spring of 2002, did little to reduce the growing perception in Muslim communities that the real target in the war on terrorism was Islam. The decision, despite significant international disquiet and vehement opposition from many Muslim states, by the Bush administration of the United States of America to go to war against Iraq confirmed Muslim fears. The overthrow of Saddam Hussein in April 2003 but the failure to discover meaningful evidence of WMD in Iraq, heightened Muslim fears that the war was a pretext for Western domination in one of the most sensitive Muslim regions of the world. The quest to establish democracy by American diktat was greeted with scepticism and less than a year later had already run into significant trouble. Within a year of the war in the spring of 2003 and the Allied occupation, Iraq had become increasingly vulnerable to *salafi jihadi* groups, who were responsible for a wave of new terrorism that subsequently has gripped the country for a decade. By May 2004 with a progressive breakdown of public order, growing *Sunni* and *Shi'a* insurgency in the central and southern provinces of the country, as well as the release of reports and pictures of Iraqi prisoners being humiliated, abused and tortured by their American and British captors, it appeared that the war for the hearts and minds of Iraqis and many millions more throughout the Muslim world had already been lost by the Western states supporting the Bush administration's war on terror. Moreover, the optic through which Muslims watched key events in the Muslim world and Western policies regarding them remained oblivious to attempts to decouple the Palestinian–Israeli conflict from others in the Muslim world. At the time, Israeli Prime Minister Ariel Sharon had successfully persuaded the Bush administration that a partial solution to the conflict with the Palestinians that denied them a voice in their own future was acceptable, if portrayed as part of the wider dimensions of the war on terrorism. Muslim commentators, along with Western diplomats and policy-makers, expressed their disquiet that such policy support set back the resolution of a conflict that remains deeply symbolic for many Muslims and offered little hope of negotiated and just resolution.

Moreover, the militants of fundamentalism – such as Mullah Omar, Osama Bin Laden and Ayman al-Zawahiri, along with many others in the al-Qaeda network – remained at large. Radical fundamentalism felt little threatened and in the Muslim world the belief that the war on terrorism was a war on innocent Muslims after all flourished.

A variety of reasons accounted, therefore, for the flourishing of fundamentalism and the concurrent growth in anti-Americanism across the globe. As a global hyperpower, the expression of American policy during this period, whether it was foreign, military or economic, was experienced by others (including Muslims) as overbearing, arbitrary and top-heavy. At the level of interstate interaction, this was frustrating. Indeed, it had been noted that in the twenty-first century,

> most of the world sees the United States as a nascent imperial power. Some nations support the United States precisely because of this, viewing it as a benign liberal empire that can protect them against ambitious regional powers. Others resent it because it stands in the way of their goals. Still others acquiesce to US imperial predominance as a fact of life that cannot be changed and must be accepted.[10]

While, in Washington, US intervention in Afghanistan, Iraq, and military support in places like Yemen and the Philippines were seen as a success, they were not viewed similarly in the Muslim world. Anti-American feeling grew among the fundamentalists who translated it back to a wider Muslim audience, as further evidence of America's imperial and religiously-inspired project to subjugate Islam. The fundamentalists, however, were not the only ones ready to beat the drum against the USA, as such sentiments were exploited by militant and activist elements across the political spectrum throughout the globe. Though the sentiments against the USA grew, there is little evidence that Bin Laden's doctrine was increasingly adhered to at a popular level. Muslims in general did not appear to see terror and violence as the vehicle for change.

The shadow and darkness

'In the shadow and darkness', then, the extreme forces of Islam appeared to hold sway in the popular imagination of the West. The connection that Islam, in conjunction with poverty and brutal dictatorship, had spawned a virus of terrorism grew ever stronger. The tentacles of terror apparent in attacks on Western capitals such as Washington, Madrid and London, on Western interests in Istanbul, Bali and Riyadh, all of which were laid at the door of the al-Qaeda network, exemplified this perception. Such visions, however, took little account of the continuing diversity and modernising tendencies of the majority of modern Islamist movements that had been established since 1945.

Plural politics, where it flourished in states where the majority of Muslims resided, established important evidence that even the fundamentalists were willing to openly contest each other for power through the ballot box and not the Armalite. Islam and democracy had been close to being reconciled with each other in Lebanon, the United Kingdom, Turkey, Bangladesh, Pakistan and Indonesia, to name but a few. Some contended that Muslims simply hid the Armalite and used the ballot box to achieve their own ends. This argument centres on an enduring suspicion of Islamist claims to power as totalitarian by design, even if the means to achieve power could be democratic in character. Establishing a casual link between Islam and the rejection of democracy in this way has been subjected to long and highly contested academic debate.

How then did such assertions stand up when measured against the participation of Islamic fundamentalist parties in electoral contests in countries like Turkey, Iraq, Pakistan, Tunisia and Egypt? The democratic pulse (decoupled from secularism), despite the sceptics, has been increasingly rooted within Islam and at myriad levels. In this respect, Islamic fundamentalists behaved in a very modern fashion, recognising that the vibrancy and relevance of Islam lie in the ability of its leaders and followers to embrace mechanisms of sovereignty that could deliver a meaningful voice to legislative processes, whether at local, national or regional levels. Increasingly, the Muslim political character was being exhibited in the open contest and peaceful compliance with the process and results of myriad electoral processes and systems. In Indonesia, the largest Muslim majority state in the world, the scheduling of open elections through the mechanism of proportional representation for members of the Indonesian legislature, is the primary feature of the political system of the state. Despite attempts by extremist radical elements to steer the accommodation between Islam and democracy off course, the majority of moderates active within the political system have begun reclaiming the political arena for their own. In Turkey the general elections of 2002, 2007 and 2011 delivered a victory at the polls for the Islamic-based Justice and Development Party: 'Turkey is a bold demonstration of how democratic development can be combined with moderate Islam. As such, the country ought to serve as a beacon to the rest of the Muslim world', contended EU Commissioner Chris Patten.[11] As a secular, European-leaning, NATO-friendly state, Turkey represents an interesting dimension of the contemporary adaptation of Islam to present politics. In the wake of the Arab Spring it has been repetitively cited by emergent Islamist elements as a model to which they aspire. The Justice and Development Party has become the mainstream political force leading the government as the country seeks to gain membership of the European Union, maintain sovereignty within a turbulent region and revitalise its economy.

While it may have been true that in the 1990s the elites of Muslim states were able to counter Muslim-led opposition, contestation at the polls and through the formation of political parties created degrees of circumvention in the twenty-first century. When, for example, the government of the United States announced its 'Greater Middle East Initiative' in early 2004 advocating reform and greater pluralism in the region, it was the Muslim Brotherhood in Egypt who also announced their support for democratic reform. Both local elites and international actors have been compelled to address other ways of acknowledging the political inroads made by fundamentalists, in respect of the hearts and minds of the Muslim public. Mainstreaming Islam with democracy through accommodation of power has been a difficult choice to make. Western governments have often struggled with the consequences.

In Iraq, the democracy project appeared within the country to be intimately tied to the 'barrel of a gun' and much rode on the ability of the American and British occupiers to turn their experiment in democratic state-building in the Middle East into a success. The occupation of Iraq radicalised fundamentalist elements, as inevitably it would, but more importantly the tussles over the transfer of power and the mechanisms for political rule devised by the Americans for Iraqi consumption had significant import, not just for Iraq, but other Muslim states in the wider Middle East. In Iraq the fundamentalists made it clear that there could be no democracy without their intrinsic involvement in devising and steering the process of state-building after Saddam Hussein. Fundamentalist leaders from the *Shi'a* community, and in particular Ayatollah al-Sistani, outlined a blueprint for a new democratic Iraq in which the end of Coalition occupation was demanded alongside elections and full democracy. In early 2004, hundreds of thousands of *Shi'a* marched in Iraq to demand elections and protest against earlier US-authored plans for designated-democracy and governance. The absence of more immediate provision for popular elections led to a rash of protests from Iraq's fundamentalist leaders and their supporters. Such moves were interpreted by mainstream fundamentalist leaders such as al-Sistani, as giving ground to the radical fundamentalists loyal to figures like the anti-occupation Islamist Moqtada al-Sadr, in Iraq's poorest urban neighbourhoods. There were fears in Washington, however, that early popular elections would benefit the fundamentalist and not the US-backed opposition exile groups, proving disastrous in respect of encouraging a stable, Israel-recognising, Western-leaning future Iraq.

Many in the US administration, remembering recent history in Iran, simply feared a *Shi'a* electoral victory because they dreaded any manifestation of Muslim power. In the end Washington was compelled to give into *Shi'a* demands for greater evidence of popular sovereignty in order to save the state reconstruction project. In 2011 when American troops finally withdrew from Iraq they left behind a fragile state vulnerable on an almost daily level to terrorist violence and the fraught political vagaries of competing *Shi'a* and *Sunni* Islamist elements. Democracy has been set back by the political deadlock with respect to government formation and controversy surrounding Prime Minister Nuri al-Maliki.

There were clearly dangers for the USA and other Western states who sought to play the game of 'divide and rule' in pursuit of democracy among Islamic fundamentalist elements. Much Islamist discourse has focussed on a perception of the complicity of the West that followed state repression of Muslim protest elements, whether following the massacre of thousands of Muslim Brotherhood supporters and members in Hama in Syria in 1982, the killing of thousands after the failure of the American-supported *Shi'a* uprising in southern Iraq in 1991, the death, torture and detention of thousands in Algeria, Egypt, Tunisia and Morocco throughout the 1990s, or the persecution of Muslims in India, Burma, the Philippines, Pakistan and Uzbekistan.

Reconciling Muslim protest against the West but in the name of democratic values proved something of a challenge. Thus while in November 2002 US secretary of state Colin Powell went some way in acknowledging this challenge when asked for a reaction following the Islamist victory in the Turkish elections, he declared that, 'The fact that the party [Justice and Development] has an Islamic base to it in and of itself does not mean that it will be anti-American in any way'. However, a contradictory view emerged when the spotlight fell on other 'frontline' states such as Afghanistan and Pakistan in the war on terrorism and the promotion of democracy.[12]

In the case of Pakistan, the USA, in particular, has found itself wrestling with something of a paradoxical context. In pursuit of the strategic and security dimensions of first the war against the Soviet occupation of Afghanistan and then the war on terror, the administration in Washington entered into a 'special relationship' with power-holders who have gained power through the barrel of a gun rather than the ballot box. In 1999 when General Musharraf took power in Pakistan, the hopes and aspirations of Pakistan's democrats were cruelly dashed. Yet in the wake of 9/11, Musharraf, despite accusations that 'Pakistan helped create and foster al-Qaeda and the Taliban [and] it has long used terror as an instrument of state policy to try to break India's hold on two-thirds of Kashmir', became a key figure in the US administration's war on terror.[13] American gratitude for Musharraf's support was manifest in a variety of ways, including a more benign attitude to the lack of democracy in this Muslim state. In the absence of democracy, Musharraf's power grew unchecked and the fundamentals of Pakistan's political system, including its Constitution, weakened by an increasing propensity to authoritarianism. Democratic tendencies in the country had already been weakened before Musharraf and his successors such as Zardari took power, but without an effective check, through external as well as internal pressure, the outlook is poor. Islamic fundamentalists in Pakistan have impacted on the country since the 1980s. The most important foundation stone of the movement, as elsewhere, have been the *madrassas* (religious schools) where millions of young Muslims have studied syllabuses that the fundamentalists determine. The graduates of these schools are the new generation of young people who will seek to reshape Pakistan according to their specific models. The state has used its funding of these schools to keep the fundamentalists on board at the expense of alienating majority, moderate, progressive opinion in Pakistan. For the millions of children (and their families) attending these schools, where they are taught, housed, fed and clothed, the *madrassa* replaces the state as the focus for loyalty and political allegiance. With democracy denied, political access closed off, representation and popular sovereignty absent, the *madrassa* and the mosque become the only public spaces where Muslim representation is legitimate. Islam's political import is thus heightened and exaggerated through a monopolistic attachment by those who feel abandoned by the state.

At the same time the state has allowed fundamentalist forces to flourish in Pakistan as part of a foreign policy strategy aimed at near neighbours and regional rivals. Moreover, Pakistan state forces have been significant actors in fostering fundamentalism both at home and in neighbouring states. Squeezed between the fundamentalists and the military lie the majority of Pakistan's democratic Muslim citizens. The absence of effective democracy giving sovereignty and representation to the majority population, means that the political ground is open to the fundamentalists who have exploited the social neglect of the state to win support. The fundamentalists in Pakistan cannot be represented simply as a monolith; they are deeply factional in terms of both sectarian and tribal divisions as well as in terms of their weight and influence in Pakistani society. They do remain a minority, but if fundamentalists increase their foothold in institutions like the military, and democracy remains absent in the country, then the state will become increasingly vulnerable to a fundamentalist takeover. In 2012 Islamic fundamentalists in Pakistan ensured that the country was rarely out of the headlines as they spearheaded protest and violence against their opponents.

All that remains

In the shadows and darkness there was a sense that the Islamic fundamentalist elements that inspired the acts of terror perpetrated by al-Qaeda throughout the 1990s and the first decade of the twenty-first century remained at large. There was a growing rather than decreasing fear at the insurmountable obstacle to freedom and democracy posed by the rhetoric of Osama Bin Laden and his supporters. In Afghanistan, where the Taliban and al-Qaeda fundamentalists founded their Islamic state, fundamentalism still remains the defining feature of the state in the post-war era. When in November 2003 a draft constitution was announced, the banner of Islam remained central to defining the country. The country remains an Islamic republic governed according to the principles of *shari'a* law and fundamentalist interpretation. Moreover, the political make-up of Afghanistan remains, despite Western aspirations for a liberal-democratic profile, deeply ingrained as Islamic and fundamentalist. The Taliban may be out of power in Kabul but they remain intrinsic to the political landscape of the country and those who have replaced them are moderate only by the meanest of degrees. The USA, by relying so heavily on fundamentalist warlords to win the war in Afghanistan against its people and the Taliban regime, were dependent on them to help construct a military-based alliance. The government led by Hamid Karzai remains populated by the old fundamentalist faces of the past rather than the new Afghan democrats of the future. The state remains as precarious as ever in Afghanistan and Islamic fundamentalism continues to flourish. Outside of Kabul, in cities like Herat, fundamentalists and pro-Taliban elements maintain the *madrassas* and form squads that maintain order. The Taliban continue to harass and harry NATO forces, with no end in sight bar an exit with no victory planned by most states for 2015. There is no quick-fix alternative to addressing the effects of a movement that is so intrinsically tied to Afghan society. Moreover, the state has to be rebuilt to a point of effectiveness rather than failure. There are fears that as the West withdraws its troops by 2015 the country will incrementally fall to the power of Taliban and other fundamentalist elements again.

In other domains the grievances that have animated fundamentalist thinking throughout the latter part of the twentieth century remained largely unaddressed. A decade after 9/11 many Islamic fundamentalists argued that the response of Western states only served to deepen their conviction that cultural antipathy and hostility continue to drive the Western attitude to Islam and its followers. Such views were explicit in statements by Hizb Allah leader Hassan Nasrallah, who declared, 'We tell the Americans that we will never be shaken in our faith under any pressure or threat, and we are not worried because the foolish American policy will only harm its own standing in the world.'[14] Fundamentalist leaders and followers remain tied to their conviction that the West represents a threat to their societies and beliefs. They fail to grasp the idea of a benign, tolerant and plural West even when Western states have intervened to protect and aid Muslim populations. A state of mutual suspicion and cynicism grows. Liberal theory is feared and interpreted by lay preachers, *madrassa* teachers and imams in the mosque as the foundation of the Western conspiracy to dominate and make subservient the Muslim people. As Muslims remain repressed in states and societies which are governed by secular nationalist elites or '*jahilli*' Muslim rulers, the protests grow and with them come extremists who preach a hatred against the West that turns Islam into a vehicle for hostility. A tension has grown in such communities and a struggle has emerged over the right to give a voice to Islam and its teachings.

Tidal wave?

The struggle for the authentic soul of Islam was taking place at the same time that the war on terrorism and the crusade for democracy in the Muslim world was stepped up by the governments of Western states. In the Middle East, North Africa, Central Asia and Southeast Asia anti-terrorist campaigns have been waged on a variety of fronts and by a variety of means. There was a preoccupation with finding a military solution to the threat posed by fundamentalist Islam in its radical manifestation. Wherever the anti-terrorism spotlight fell, the al-Qaeda 'network' appeared to be discovered. In Afghanistan thousands were captured and taken to Guantanamo Bay and incarcerated in Camp X-Ray, without rights accorded to them as prisoners of war. In the Philippines, followers of Abu-Sayyaf were accused of links with al-Qaeda and, with US support, anti-terrorist operations were launched against the network. In Yemen, US special forces trained Yemeni state forces to combat and take action against al-Qaeda supporting elements. Yet in 2012 al-Qaeda in Yemen still controlled southern territorial enclaves of this deeply unstable country and continued to threaten its enemies. In Morocco and Tunisia the government authorities have been forced to face up to the presence of al-Qaeda elements in their midst. In Iraq the infiltration of al-Qaeda and the manifestation of an unceasing wave of suicide attacks and bombings on Western and pro-Western targets have been cited as further evidence of the growing network of terror. In Syria the embattled regime of Bashar al-Assad has had to contend with popular revolt and the infiltration of al-Qaeda elements. In the Sinai peninsula al-Qaeda supporters have been responsible for a breakdown in law and order, sabotage of infrastructure and pipelines, and terror attacks.

In truth, by 2012 the existence of the global network of terror became questionable. The notion of a network implies infrastructure and, perhaps more importantly, state support. Before 9/11 Osama Bin Laden, with the exception of the Taliban regime in Afghanistan, lacked state support from Islamic states branded radical, revolutionary or otherwise. Libya, Saudi Arabia and Iran, though Islamic, had already turned their backs on Bin Laden's agenda. Even radical 'rogue' nationalist Muslim states, such as Iraq or Syria, that had supported other Islamic fundamentalist groups designated as terrorist by Western states, refused to offer backing for al-Qaeda. Despite the concerted efforts of Western intelligence agencies, no demonstrable link was proved between al-Qaeda, 9/11 and the government of Saddam Hussein. A 'network' implies an infrastructure of terrorism and support for terrorism carried out by al-Qaeda that is clearly absent among the majority of Muslim people. The assassination of Bin Laden in May 2011 by US armed forces was considered an important turning point with respect to count-terror activities and was consolidated further by the assassination of al-Qaeda leaders such as Anwar al-Awlaki and Said Ali al-Shehri. Nevertheless, many Western governments continue to support authoritarian and anti-democratic states that perpetuate abuses against their citizens because they are now new allies in the war against al-Qaeda's network of terror. The discourse on human rights and civil liberties was severely dented in Western states as governments sought to address the means by which to respond to the Islamic fundamentalist terrorist threat in their midst. Civil liberties became another casualty in the war on terrorism. In the UK, the USA, France, Australia and other states, civil liberties were eroded by the state as it pursued the war against the Islamic fundamentalists. As the ACLU declared:

> most Americans do not recognize that the USA Patriot Act ... gave the government expanded power to invade their privacy, imprison people without due process and punish dissent. Ostensibly needed for the war on terrorism, it actually put in place domestic changes so sweeping that even religious conservatives ... decided [it] had gone too far.[15]

A fuzzy boundary was drawn as Western democratic governments balanced the terrorist threat to freedom and democracy, with the rights to freedom and democracy that citizens of such states felt an entitlement to enjoy.

How the West is the best

The mutual antagonism that lay between Islam and the West continued to cast a shadow over this important global relationship. For many Muslims, fundamentalists or otherwise, in the decade after 9/11 the ways in which the West perceived and portrayed Islam generated further hostility, suspicion and fear. The ways in which Islam was covered by the media, mattered not just to drivers of opinion in Western state capitals but to Muslims themselves. Since 9/11 there has been a growing sensitivity to the negative portrayal of Muslims and the ways in which such portrayals generate hostility to Islam and its followers. Many Muslims remain concerned that a discourse of incompatibility and intolerance has come to dominate the public debate about Islam across the globe.

Furthermore in the decade since 9/11, authoritarian governments across the Muslim world also interpreted the American-led war on terrorism as a signal to unleash their own state forces against fundamentalist and other elements and to ignore past strictures from the West about human rights and democracy. All opposition was labelled fundamentalist in an attempt to characterise and conflate the whole of the Islamic movement into its extreme fringe. As a result, huge swathes of the ordinary Muslim population became further alienated and felt embattled and embittered. Western governments were quick to offer support and assistance not just to these states but to their counter-terrorism programmes as well. The boundaries of international intelligence cooperation were stretched, reinterpreted and prejudged through terrorist profiling. Increasingly, whole communities, groups and populations were regarded as part of a potential terrorist threat. The global trends towards democracy were being reversed and authoritarianism in Muslim states swung to an upward trend. In the West itself, by continuing to be perceived and labelled by media stereotypes and negative reductions, Muslims often remain feared within and outside their own societies. The *muhajiba* (woman wearing the *hijab*) have, for example, been seen as a symbol of fanatic potency, the bearded young man feared as a zealot and threat.

And in the shadows the real threat remained undiminished. The fundamentalists' exhortations to the Muslim masses were based on contemporary conditions of poverty and injustice not just past history and myths. Their rhetoric, however, failed to appeal as authentic and meaningful in terms of liberating Muslim populations from repressive governments. The threat they posed to the West, however, remained as deadly and the military response of counter-terrorism necessary.

Side-stepping secularism

Dimensions of Islamic fundamentalism are relevant to, and a challenge for, the advocates of secularism as a universal framework for political systems across the globe. Secularism is the much touted nemesis of Islam in the twenty-first century. According to this discourse, the only key that will open the door to prosperity, happiness and security is secularism and religious fundamentalism represents the dark alternative. It has been argued that in most Western states an accommodation between faith and politics has been reached as a result of historical processes of reformation and industrialisation. There is a presupposition of natural harmony and compliance at the relegation of faith from the public sphere. In reality, however, the history of late twentieth-century and early twenty-first century politics in Western states has seen a contest emerge over such assumptions. The USA has been a specific site of contest that has resulted in the reassertion of faith in the politics of the state. Faith, whether Muslim, Christian, Hindu, Jewish or otherwise, has become an increasingly public rather than a private dimension of politics. Secularism, however, has continued to symbolise the processes of modernity that have defined and shaped societies, and in Muslim countries there has been a tacit assumption that modernity or modernisation could only be achieved by jettisoning Islam. The outcome of this process of secularisation, however, has not been what modernising Muslims imagined. Instead of prosperity, happiness and security, secularised and modernising Muslim societies were characterised by poverty, inequality, insecurity, state repression and authoritarianism. Muslims found the secular reality delivered a different outcome when delivered in their own societies. In response, increasing numbers, led by young activists and lay preachers of Islam, have rejected the secular dream and turned to their faith instead.

In addressing the ills that beset their own societies Muslim lay preachers and activists called for justice, but one based on Islam rather than the secularised notions of justice outlined by thinkers such as John Rawls. Their theology, their fundamentalist interpretation, has been a challenge, not just to the secularists but to the Muslim establishment, for they interpreted Islam anew and argued that liberty lay in a return to the 'straight path'. That liberty, as earlier chapters of this book have demonstrated, was also intimately tied to the rejection of colonialism as the vehicle for the aggressive modernisation of Muslim domains. Islamic fundamentalists have offered an alternative vision of nationhood defined as Muslim and modern rather than secular and nationalist. In this respect the present, not the past, has been the focus of Muslim consternation and rhetoric. The condition of modern Muslim societies has animated Muslim thinkers. They rejected the West because the West represented their oppression, not their liberty. Modernity would be shaped, coloured and given authentic meaning through the interpretation of Muslim doctrines, not socialist tracts or theories of neoliberal economics. The secularist monopolistic tendencies towards modernity were being undermined from beneath by Muslim thinkers, activists and preachers. Moreover, by the late 1980s and early 1990s they were prepared to 'fight fire with fire' by embracing the very mechanism, democracy, that they supposedly eschewed to advance their desire for power in Muslim states.

Such fundamentalists have side-stepped secularism, turned its principled association with democracy on its head and demonstrated to Muslim popular masses that they at least symbolise a meaningful political alternative. The fundamentalists endorse democracy as the means to end the monopolistic and authoritarian tendencies of nationalist-secular elites who control the state with little sanction from the international community. The fundamentalists scorn Western fears of democratic change in Muslim states, understanding well that the fear stems from a mechanism of popular sovereignty that may put in power fundamentalists who oppose secularism. Islamic fundamentalists recognise that the popular voice, through sovereignty or grassroots vehicles, shapes and defines them in important ways. In this respect they must share the political stage rather than seek to dominate it in the same ways that their secular nationalist foes have done in the past. This is the challenge for the majority of fundamentalists who in turn may well be equipped to undermine the terrorist extremists who haunt the fringes of their faith.

Blame game

To blame Islam for terrorism, anti-secularism and all the ills of the contemporary globe was to exaggerate the issues and disguise the causes of Muslim discontent. A misplaced focus on terrorism in the name of Islam without a parallel recognition of the other dynamics of violence and terror led to a loss of perspective, and strategic insight. After 9/11, however, Westerners, and Americans in particular, could not help but focus on Islamic fundamentalism as a threat to their way of life and cherished values. They looked at Islam, and Islam was represented to them as working against their value system. Many came to believe that the tenets of Islamic fundamentalism undermined the spirit of individuality, liberty, pluralism and democracy at the heart of the American nation-building project. There is scant evidence of Islam represented in mass media as a faith system and culture or political perspective where common values could be discovered. Hence columnists opined that Islam had got it all wrong and was stuck in a time warp in need of a Reformation. Salman Rushdie declared, 'The restoration of religion to the sphere of the personal, its de-politicization, is the nettle that all Muslim societies must grasp in order to become modern.'[16] It was difficult to understand the logic of compelling Muslims to 'become modern' by asking them to undergo a process of transformation that harked back to history rather than dealing with contemporary conditions. Such logic also remained in ignorance of the modernising of Islamic thinking that, since 1945, has accompanied the major transformation of Muslim societies. Islam has been under constant scrutiny by its own thinkers and reformers. An absence of 'reformation' does not in and of itself account for the presence of Islamic fundamentalism in the twenty-first century.

Fundamentalists, in turn, nurture an irrational hatred of the West. The extremists, one writer notes, hate America

> because we appear to them spiritually lukewarm, religiously flaccid ... we cast off orthodox Christianity in the 1960s for a materialistic, liberalized, compromising approach to faith, which they despise in their own co-religionists. They hate us, most of all, for ignoring them and for underestimating the power of their faith.[17]

The revival of Islam in its fundamentalist dimension had become inextricably tied to the manifestation of violence and terrorism which appeared – through the 9/11 attacks – to have blighted the faith in its totality. The diversity and intricacies of Islam were frequently lost in this process. A decade after 9/11 the diversity and intricacies of Islam in the Middle East would be reappraised as a Jasmine revolution in Tunisia flowered into an Arab Awakening in Egypt, Libya, Yemen, Syria and beyond. This Arab Awakening would prove to be one of the biggest challenges to Islamic fundamentalists in the Arab world since 1945.

Notes

1 *The Economist*, 'The War on Terror, two years on', 11 September 2003.
2 A. Sullivan, 'This is a religious war, September 11 was only the beginning', *New York Times Magazine*, 7 October 2001.
3 S. Rushdie, 'Yes, this is about Islam', *New York Times*, 2 November 2001.
4 T.L. Friedman, 'How trust and shame became weapons of war', *The Age*, 12 January 2004, www.theage.com.au/articles/2004/01/11/1073769450437. html
5 B. Lewis, *What Went Wrong? Western Impact and Middle Eastern Response*, London: Weidenfeld and Nicolson, 2002, p. 175.
6 R. Tracinski, 'A war against Islam', *Jewish World Review*, 30 October 2001, www.newsandopinion.com/1001/tracinski.html (accessed 14 March 2013).
7 See Martin E. Marty and R. Scott Appleby (eds) *Fundamentalisms Observed*, Chicago: University of Chicago Press, 1991.
8 M. Juergensmeyer, *Terror in the Mind of God*, Berkeley, CA: University of California Press, 2000.
9 T. Blair, Address delivered to the Congress of the United States of America, Washington, DC, 17 July 2003.
10 D.K. Simes, 'America's imperial dilemma', *Foreign Affairs*, 82:6, November/December 2003, p. 91.
11 C. Patten, 'Democracy doesn't flow from the barrel of a gun', *Foreign Policy*, 138, September/October 2003, p. 40.
12 C. Powell, Remarks reported from Department of State Briefing, 5 November 2002.
13 J. Hoagland, 'Misreading Musharraf', *Washington Post*, 23 May 2002, p. A33.
14 H. Nasrallah, *Statement on America*, carried on: www.islamonline.net/English/News/2002-9/14/article30.shtml
15 ACLU, 'Civil liberties after 9/11', *ACLU Report*, 2002.
16 S. Rushdie, 'Yes, this is about Islam', *New York Times*, 2 November 2001.
17 R.S. Appleby, 'Visions of sacrifice (roots of terrorism)', *Christian Century*, 17 October 2001.

7   Islamic fundamentalism and the Arab Awakening

> An area that was a byword for political stagnation is witnessing a rapid transformation that has caught the attention of the world.
>
> (Rashid Khalidi)

Though many say the outbreak of mass protest, revolt, and revolutionary pressure in the Muslim countries of the Middle East in late 2010 was not predicted, the signs were there for all to see. It is true that from the West and in the decade since 9/11, little by way of attention had been paid to the internal political dynamics of Muslim states in the Middle East. Though the ferment of terrorism unleashed on America in September 2001 had originated in the fundamentalist designs of al-Qaeda and its Middle Eastern roots were seen as part and package of this, the West was preoccupied with the threat posed to it. True the war on terrorism led to foreign policy decisions which took major Western states into the Middle East for purposes of counter-terrorism and latterly democracy promotion. But in doing so many Western states overlooked the brewing socio-economic and political ferment and were content that authoritarian regimes such as Egypt, under Hosni Mubarak, remain within the pro-Western fold fighting the enemy in al-Qaeda and among other Islamists. Indeed, in the decade that unfolded after 9/11 the regimes of many Muslim states of the Middle East succeeded in embedding their authoritarian character by largely joining in the war on terrorism to pursue their own campaigns against opponents commonly classed as Islamist, so as to be firmly designated a terrorist/ security threat.

Such states were not restricted to the post-independent Arab one-state republics or the monarchical regimes alone but have included a mix of such types. Those that did not embark on such processes were labelled under the Axis of Evil or as rogue terrorist-supporting states which would come under Western interventionist and sanction-led pressure. All the while the Muslim populations of such states grew increasingly discontented as their own societies were beset with severe and crippling economic crises, and further state repression of forms of social or political mobilisation to highlight the absence of basic freedoms, the absence of promised political or constitutional reforms and the growing inequalities between the nepotistic cronyism and corruption of a small state elite and the rest of the increasingly impoverished population.

How do you expect me to make a living?[1]

The popular mobilisation, when it came, was certainly unexpected, as the rulers of regimes like Tunisia and Egypt were inured to the realities within their own societies and isolated from the growing socio-economic pressures that soon transformed into political demands. Within the popular movement mobilised in Bahrain, Libya, Yemen, Egypt, Tunisia, Syria and beyond, Muslims have emerged to play a pivotal role in the current trend for resisting authoritarian regimes in the Middle East. The revolt started in Tunisia in December 2010 in the wake of the self-immolation of vegetable vendor Mohammed Bouazizi in front of government offices in the provincial town of Sidi Bouzid.[2] The act of an individual Muslim in protest and its consequence unleashed a wave of popular unrest and demonstrations in Tunisia with the demand for regime change and not merely reform. Why did Bouazizi set himself on fire? Why was his death a catalyst for a region-wide revolt? The answer lies in the very ordinary dimensions of Bouazizi's life and the ability of so many citizens across the Middle East to relate to his frustration and desperation. Bouazizi sold vegetables from a cart to subsidise his family. He immolated himself on 17 December 2010 as a desperate act of protest after local officials had confiscated his cart and wares, harassing and humiliating him in the process. He existed precariously from hand-to-mouth, borrowing money to buy vegetables to sell in order to provide for a family that was unsupported by the state. Corrupt officials and local police had harassed him and deliberately prevented him from earning a living. The state – both national and local – was actively hindering a family from subsisting. The immolation led to protests against power and the corrupt elite of the Ben Ali regime. Protesters took to the street across the country and demanded democracy, freedom and an end to one-party regime rule. The president ordered his armed forces to the streets to quell the protest; their refusal sounded the death knell of a regime that ended with Ben Ali's exile on 14 January 2011.

Economic, social and political concerns motivated the populations of Arab Muslim states to take to their streets to demand reform of their leaders and even a change of power. The authoritarian resilience by which states like Tunisia, Libya and Yemen had been characterised appeared to crumble in the face of a popular rebellion.[3] The rebellion, however, appeared to have many dimensions, and pundits and experts clamoured alike to explain a series of events that appeared seismic in scale and potential for political change in the region that gave rise to Islam and its varieties of contemporary political characterisations. Hence, in part the roots of the Arab Awakening were identified as located within the milieu of socio-economic crisis that had beset the Middle East, as the deepening effects of global recession led to state imposed price rises on basic commodities and growing ranks of the young and unemployed. Such indicators of crisis had long been predicted in global development and international economic reports such as those of the World Bank, IMF, and UNDP Arab Human Development Reports. Islamic fundamentalism emerged as but one dimension of a series of explanations that were also located within discourses of secularism and its failure, globalisation, and identity politics.

The Arab Awakening has indeed led to a debate about whether the Middle East is finally transitioning from autocracy to democracy. Whether such democracy will be secular or Islamist or some kind of hybrid mixture only time will tell.[4] There has been a demand to avoid simplistic explanations such as coining events since December 2010 as a 'Facebook revolution', 'Social network rebellion' or 'Arab spring, Islamist winter' because the changes that are taking place are extremely complex – geographically, strategically, slowly unfolding and evolving, economic, ethnic, national, violent, involving a variety of local and external forces – a long transition. In sum, the Arab Awakening is a long cycle of upheaval and instability that will probably take a decade to realise. The present phenomenon has been described as part of a present-day rebellion against authoritarianism allied to demands for democracy. This demand, it is contended, puts to bed the decades old argument that Arab-Muslim culture in the Middle East explained democratic exceptionalism in the region, when the 'third wave' of democratisation was realised in Eastern Europe and Latin America in the 1990s.

Consigning Islam its place in the Arab Awakening

Consigning Islam, or specifically Islamic fundamentalism, in the Arab Awakening phenomenon has been subjected to some generalisations, suspicions and hostility. Yet such generalisations and hostilities belie a more complex and dynamic role being made apparent by a variety of actors, groups, organisations and ideologues usually residing within the Islamic fundamentalist fold. One unpredictable dimension of the Arab Awakening was the relative absence of Islam as the major organising motif behind the popular mobilisation occurring across the many countries of the Middle East region. The banner of Islam was but one of many that were raised in Tahrir Square in Cairo by the thousands of protesters who gathered to call for the ousting of President Mubarak. In Yemen's capital Sana where first hundreds and then thousands set up tents in 'Change Square', protestors represented a diverse spectrum of Yemeni society and not just an Islamic fundamentalist trope. It was suggested that qat, not Islam, was the only significant unifier among the Yemeni protestors, who first called for political reform and then for the ousting of their president, Ali Saleh. Certainly the members of the Deaf and Dumb Youth Revolution Alliance, the 'Actors' tent and 'Diplomats' tent were not calling for an Islamist theocracy to replace the Saleh regime. Islamic fundamentalists, of course, had their part in the unfolding events but were not centre stage. Indeed, the call for democracy, constitutional rule and multi-party elections heard in the demands of demonstrators – young and old alike – was and remains markedly dissimilar from radical jihadist agendas commonly associated with the politics of the Arab world. But such demands did not mean the wholesale rejection of Islamist discourses in favour of a region-wide embrace of secularism or Western democracy templates. For this approach, too, had failed to bring freedom to the majority Muslim populations of the Middle East.

Hence, Islamic fundamentalism became one part of a multi-dimensional constituency emerging to demand and agitate for change. The new generation – including Islamic fundamentalists – has expressed a new discourse based around more equalising notions of power, democracy and citizenship. Increasingly within this setting, Islamic fundamentalists who are not reconsidering their own approaches have been regarded as anachronistic. What the Arab Awakening, and its Muslim input, has also demonstrated is an iteration of the plurality within Islamic fundamentalism.[5] This is a plurality that is compelled to recognise the challenge of other discourses within the spectrum of Islamic fundamentalism, as well as the possibility or compulsion to alliance-formation with political and social elements outside it. It is epitomised by post-revolution Tunisia where, since the fall of President Ben Ali, Islamic fundamentalists in the Ennahda movement and *salafi* orders have vied with each other to establish and register new political parties under a post-revolution dispensation. Thus far the Tunisian transition has led to electoral victory in October 2011 for Ennahda when it won 89 of the 217 seats to the Tunisian Assembly, but at the price of coalition with centre-left secularists from the Congress for the Republic (CPR) and Ettakatol parties. Salafists achieved recognition in the form of registration permission from the Ennahda-led government, only for their leader Nasreddine Aloui to call for rebellion against Ennahda's declaring it unfit to rule in the name of Islam. From this example, and others such as the transition in Egypt, there is an emergent tension around interpreting Islamic fundamentalism.[6] This centres on a tradition of perceiving such elements as a threat and questioning whether transformation is capable through the politics of constitutional reform, democracy and the contestation of free, fair and plural electoral processes.

The Arab Awakening has forced Islamic fundamentalists to emerge and compete in a dynamic transitional landscape. There is evidence that, in part, there is a rejection in the current dynamics of radical jihadist fundamentalist manifestations of Islamism as epitomised by al-Qaeda, and al-Qaeda in the Islamic Maghreb (AQIM) as well as in the Arab Peninsula (AQAP). This may indicate the transition to the beginning of post-jihadi era in the Islamist politics of the Arab region. The emergence of just such an era will not be evident in every context of rebellion and awakening; it may well not be linear or internally supported. Yet there is a supposition to be made that in states such as Tunisia, where Islamist power will be ameliorated by secular centre-left and nationalist politics, that the oxygen of support drawn from alienated and marginalised constituencies will be denied to the fanatic ideologues of the radical jihadis.

The Arab Awakening has given rise to Muslim protesters who have joined with other social forces, groups and organisations to call for freedom, dignity and equality, but they have not called for a pan-Islamic transnational revolution in the Middle East. Unlike earlier eras, this is not a pan-Islamic awakening where a borderless Middle East and its Muslim *umma* emerge triumphant. The boundaries of the nation-state remain intact and Muslims and Islamists largely remain content to work within them. This has also been a form of Islamism tied to a demand for democracy. But a pall of suspicion hangs over such demands when expressed in the lexicon of Islamic fundamentalism. This has important implications in terms of debates about gender, economic development and recovery, globalisation, personal status and minority rights in those regimes where power has been wrought from the hands of the despots and placed in the hands of largely untried and untested, newly enfranchised populations and their political representatives.

The great transition

In part this transition and the role of Islamic fundamentalism within it is explicable by looking to the past. State-led top-down and social-movement bottom-up processes of Islamisation have impacted on Arab society in the region. In this respect elements of Islam have become embedded, particularly in terms of prevailing social norms of Muslim dress, the *hijab*, the beard, and the *jilbab*, or religious programming and media. But during the course of the Arab Awakening the political salience of the Islamisation project has, somewhat surprisingly, not been dominant in the wave of protest and demands being made upon ruling regimes across the region. In Jordan, for example, the Hashemite monarchy has been rocked by an enduring and unprecedented wave of non-violent peaceful protest in its capital city and provincial towns. Protestors have demanded significant political and economic reform. Islamists, the Muslim Brotherhood and its political party the Islamic Action Front, as well as *salafi* movement elements, have joined with other elements including tribal leaders and ex-servicemen, to demand such reforms.[7] In doing so the Muslim Brotherhood and salafists, as with other socio-political elements, dispossess the ruling regime of its right to monopolise the ways in which Islam is politicised. Ruling regimes in the Middle East have used Islam to claim almost divine religious status and legitimacy. Even more secularised states such as Tunisia, Iraq and the Syrian regime have conspired to employ the symbols of Islam for the purpose of regime authority and resilience. By doing so these regimes have also emptied Islam of a degree of potency – and revealed it to be no more than a marketing brand for any variety of political products or rules. This is the Islam of stability, chaos avoidance, and depleted of its politically mobilising capability. Such regimes have deemed other forms of Islamic fundamentalism a threat, a challenge to the monopoly of force and terroristic in intent. State-paid imams, mosques, schools and seminaries controlled by ministries of religious affairs have further underlined the extent to which a variety of regimes have ensured that the Islamist voice was constrained and contained and limited, in terms of acting as the mouthpiece of the regime and its power-holders. In Tunisia, before the fall of Ben Ali, the state banned Islamist preachers from the 5,000 mosques under its control. Following the Jasmine Revolution preachers such as Sheikh Mohamed al-Khelif took to the pulpit of Kairouan Grand Mosque to deliver Friday sermons attacking corruption, condemning ties with the West and demanding the implementation of *shari'a* law. But even such demands were made within the framework of constitutional rather than authoritarian dispensation.

Consigning Islam its place in the Arab Awakening means that democracy demands are introduced into the equation and the accommodation that this in turn requires of the region's Islamist movements and organisations. It is clear that Islamic fundamentalism is altered. For the jihadis and al-Qaeda it has not only been the death of their leadership, including Osama Bin Laden, that has been a blow, but that their ideological position is so dissonant to the democracy and freedom demands of those engaged in popular mobilisation. Al-Qaeda and the jihadis will attempt to take advantage if these unfolding transitions are not successful or actively supported by outside actors. Political turmoil provides al-Qaeda, AQIM, AQAP and jihadi ideologues with new opportunities to exploit, especially if socio-political and economic justices are sacrificed for continuing governance through corruption and nepotism. The threats posed by AQIM in Algeria and Libya are proof of this. Far from leading and directing the popular mobilisation now associated with the Arab world, there is already evidence to suggest that today's radical Islamists are struggling with the Muslim-led democracy movement, which has risen up within their own societies as a riposte to regimes of dictatorial rule. The legitimising value of Islam has further been diminished as a variety of regimes which have long employed the symbols and institutions of Islam struggle against popular forces which challenge this.

In conflict, Islamic fundamentalists, and in particular radical Islamist elements, attempted to break the hegemonic control of the state and its influence over the institutions of Islam. Muslim state elites acting as proxies of the West were portrayed as the near enemy in jihadi propaganda and became the target for their violent calls. Furthermore, one key defining feature of the radical as opposed to reformist Islamic fundamentalists was the call for state-overthrow and the imposition of Islamic state systems. The radicals were antagonistic to any state in the region which was tainted by the West. They were also violent, employing terrorist tactics in the name of jihad. Islamic fundamentalism, and particularly radical Islamic fundamentalism, then, has been a part of the current trend for resisting authoritarian regimes in the Muslim states of the Middle East for the last four decades. Yet even by its very taxonomy – the 'Jasmine Spring', 'the Arab Spring', the 'Arab Uprisings' – the Arab Awakening is not intrinsically an Islamist revolution as envisaged in the ideology of such fundamentalists. Islamic fundamentalism has emerged in a different guise.

The guise of Islamic fundamentalism

The present guise of Islamic fundamentalism in the Arab Awakening is different in manifestation from the past and, therefore, a different threat or challenge. By looking at Egypt, for example, since the revolution that drove President Hosni Mubarak from power on 11 February 2011, Islamic fundamentalism generally and radical Islamism particularly, was noticeable by its absence as the masses gathered in the streets and squares of cities like Cairo and Alexandria and faced-down state security forces and thugs (*baltajiyyah*). As accounts of the protestors and their non-violent tactics emerged, Islamic fundamentalist slogans and demands were rarely present as an organising motif for those who declared 'game over' and called on President Mubarak to go. Egypt's long-standing Islamic fundamentalist opponents, the Muslim Brotherhood, did not ignite or lead the Egyptian revolution. Islamic fundamentalists had a presence, its young followers and activists from the Muslim Brotherhood, *salafi* and Sufi elements joined the throngs of protesters and in so doing also defied their own leaders and the Islamist traditions they represented. Ultimately, decades as the official opposition and recognition of the Muslim Brotherhood as the most effectively organised of Egypt's political movements failed to prepare the leaders of this movement to steer the revolution, yet post-revolution they would emerge more powerfully than other political actors.[8]

Post-revolution, an array of Islamist forces emerged as an important component of the change and transition. In Tunisia, as in other parts of the region, Islamists, commonly described and understood in the West as conforming to some homogeneous radical mass, and epitomised by al-Qaeda, have in fact proved to be diverse, distinct components and currently still part of a transitional dynamic. Nevertheless, among some Western opinion there is scepticism that even if Islamists have not spearheaded an overthrow of power in the Middle East they will take power through the ballot box in order to impose Islamic states, *shari'a* law and uncompromising anti-Western foreign policy positions. Yet the current multifaceted manifestation of Islamic fundamentalism is confounding expectations, not least because the jihadi threat represented by al-Qaeda, and its networks in the region, appears to be marginal to the Arab Awakening.

Al-Qaeda and the jihadi threat

In the wake of the 9/11 era Western governments were united in identifying al-Qaeda and the global jihadi movement as one of the most significant threats of the modern age. The threat appeared to menacingly emanate from the Middle East yet its impact, as 9/11, Madrid and the London bombings demonstrated, was broad enough to also encompass the West – Europe and the US – and beyond. The Middle East appeared to be the locus of much of al-Qaeda's influence, effect and power, whether in Saudi Arabia, Iraq, Yemen or the Maghreb. In states yet untouched by al-Qaeda's presence the stated goal of such governments was to prevent – in alliance with the West – al-Qaeda from gaining any ideological or strategic foothold in their territory. Al-Qaeda's terrorist manifestation in the Middle East transformed threat perception on a regional level and globally impacted with profound consequences for the international order.

The politics of Islamic fundamentalism epitomised by al-Qaeda was represented in far wider ways. It came to be defined and under-stood as somehow representative of Islam's adherents and Islamic fundamentalism in particular. Al-Qaeda's jihadist threat preoccupied policy-makers and politicians across the globe. In the Middle East this impacted on both regional and individual states, their domestic and foreign policies, as well as their security agendas. Al-Qaeda's threat re-established the precedent for invasion and war in Afghanistan and Iraq, as well as security crises in most regimes across the region. Jihadist terrorism is regarded as the single most important terrorist threat of the twenty-first century and an outworking of the new environment created by the Arab Awakening. This was evidenced in January 2013 in the violent kidnap attack mounted by al-Qaeda in the Islamic Maghreb (AQIM) on a gas production facility in Algeria. Originally known as the Armed Islamist Group (GIA) in the wake of the military annulling elections that the Islamic Salvation Front was poised to win in Algeria in the early 1990s, the group evolved first into the Salafist Group for Preaching and Combat (GSPC), before adopting the al-Qaeda veil in 2007 to become AQIM. The GIA, in particular, had been connected to attacks in the mid-1990s on the Paris metro system, the GSPC to plots in Europe and North America prior to the attacks of 9/11. The attack in Algeria, in turn, was further linked to the Islamic fundamentalist threat in Mali, the fall-out of the collapse of the Gaddafi regime in neighbouring Libya, and Islamist militants in the Sahara. Speaking in the wake of the attack, in which Western and Algerian hostages were killed, British Prime Minister David Cameron told the House of Commons, that the battle against al-Qaeda in the Maghreb could go on for years, even decades. Western intelligence agencies have had the majority of their budgets devoted to combating such a threat. Western foreign policy formation on the

Middle East has been driven by the threat of jihadi terrorism as a number one priority.

Al-Qaeda, epitomised the new terrorism, yet al-Qaeda was all but absent from the Arab Awakening. Its leaders did not mobilise the popular Muslim masses, lead the rebel forces in Egypt, Tunisia or Libya or augment the revolutionary wave that has challenged regimes across the region. In Yemen where President Ali Saleh had turned fighting al-Qaeda into a means of regime preservation by gaining much-needed Western support and aid, the jihadists did not head the vanguard in Tent City. While there may be agreement that al-Qaeda was not Saleh's biggest threat in terms of regime consolidation, it was used in communication to the West as part of Saleh's own strategy of authoritarian hardiness. Yet the reality was all too apparent in the Yemeni factions protesting and calling for this sell-by date president to vacate his position. The internal jihadi threat, though, had little or nothing to do with the growing mass protests in Yemen, which culminated in November 2011 with Saleh's resignation and his eventual removal from power in February 2012. Only in Syria, where the popular uprising of 2011 had turned by 2013 into an armed rebellion and grinding civil war with increasingly sectarian overtones, had al-Qaeda emerged alongside other rebel fighters. The role of particular Western governments in the preservation of regimes – such as that in Yemen and Egypt, which by their own standards were undemocratic and predicated on authoritarianism and mass human rights violations – from the Islamic fundamentalist threat has, in the wake of the Arab Awakening created a form of blowback. This is because the arsenal used to support counter-terrorism efforts to disrupt this threat centred on state and elite power in the region and overlooked the disruptive effects it had on a growing and impoverished population. Both the jihadis and their enemies overlooked the potential of this constituency. This was the very constituency that mobilised to oust tyrants from power.

An alternative to Jihad

While the objective of reform or regime change may have been one that was widely shared by the people of many states in the region, the jihadi fundamentalists with their violent means for change offered a method that was rejected. Islamic fundamentalism in its representative form played a non-violent, not terrorist form in the Arab Awakening. To a certain extent this demonstrated that al-Qaeda had failed to accommodate itself to the new realities created as much by their fellow Islamists as any other emergent social and political actors in the

Middle East. It is as if al-Qaeda, ideologically tied to the greater jihad against the US and Israel, had simply overlooked the pressures, misery and constraints that millions of Arabs have lived under in the wake of 9/11. Yet in so many ways it is the general populace of the Middle East that has paid the price for al-Qaeda's fanatical rendering of Islam.

Islam and democracy, Islam and plurality, Islam and nationalism, Islam and political parties have been ascribed in al-Qaeda's ideology as wrong. Islamic fundamentalists engaged in such practices were consistently subject to attack and censure from al-Qaeda ideologues like Ayman al-Zawahiri. For these jihadis the means as much as the end appeared to matter. Addressing himself to the topic of the Arab Awakening in Egypt, jihadist ideologue Ahmed Badawi had declared,

> The state of Islam will not be established by a revolution for a loaf of bread, if that revolution was not undertaken for the sake of the *Deen* and *Shari'a* of Allah ... Mistaken are those who think that the establishment of *Shari'a* will emerge from the womb of revolutions which are calling for freedom, and mistaken are those who believe that these revolutions are an alternative to the way of the Believers ... [9]

Jihad remains central to this discourse and other forms of protest for more temporal means are rejected, as Badawi continues:

> No one should think that a revolution over unemployment will close the wine shops and nightclubs. They will not prevent women from going outside wearing make-up and unveiled and will not prevent them from showing their nakedness at pools and on the beaches. The networks of singing, dancing, prostitution and shamelessness will not be shut down by these revolutions, if they are not indeed the catalyst and motivator for these sins, when freedom and democracy become the religion and constitution of the people and are an alternative to Jihad.[10]

In some respect, then, the Arab Awakening appeared to demonstrate that jihadi ideology had reached its limits in terms of persuading the people of the region to reject powerful dictatorial rule in their favour. Previous to the Arab Awakening, jihadi propaganda had often been considered important because of the extent to which it harnessed the social media and internet to build bases of support. Western counter-terrorist discussions focussed on the ways in which to limit the viral reach of the jihadists. Yet during the course of the Arab Awakening these technologies have been successfully re-appropriated by Arab youth to promote their alternative to the jihadi rhetoric.[11]

Furthermore, as rebellion and protest ensued in Tunisia, Egypt, Libya, Yemen and elsewhere in the Middle East, in states such as Syria and Bahrain there was initial silence from the normally vociferous jihadi ideologues. The Arab Awakening appeared to take the ideologues of al-Qaeda and the jihadis by surprise. Contrary to expectation, the vanguard of the revolution in the Arab world has not been the radical, bearded *mujahids* who for decades promised to bring down *jahili* regimes, but the largely urban-based young people who have no common cause with such ideologies. Even though the same 'enemy' was being challenged the jihadis could not claim the events of the Arab Awakening as their own. Even in Syria where, as noted above, by 2013 al-Qaeda affiliate Jabhat al-Nusra had become an increasingly entrenched part of the rebellion against the regime, it was but one of the potential challenges, alongside the Syrian Kurds, the Free Syrian Army, Palestinian elements and others, to any post al-Assad dispensation and newly emergent regional security order.

Attempts to claim such revolts in the name of al-Qaeda have largely run aground within the region. So even though al-Qaeda eventually had something to say about the Arab Awakening and have become a dimension of the rebellion in Syria's revolutionary trend, they have largely remained marginal. In the wake of the revolutions in Tunisia and Egypt in 2011, al-Qaeda leader Osama Bin Laden was quoted as declaring, 'we watch with you this great historic event and share with you joy and happiness ... We are happy for what makes you happy ... Congratulations to you for your victories.'[12] But behind such bland rhetoric, jihadi ideologues such as Abu Yahya al-Libi warned their followers to limit their support or involvement. When Bin Laden's successor Ayman al-Zawahiri finally addressed himself to the Arab Awakening he drew al-Qaeda's objectives into the same universe as the protesters by identifying the same target of confrontation: the pro-Western regimes of the Middle East.

> I would like to reiterate my salute to the freeborn and noble Muslims who rose up in Tunisia, Egypt, Jordan and Yemen, who arose to confront and resist these corrupt and corruptive rulers, the Arab Zionists, who fight Islam and Hijab ... Your brother mujahideen are with you, confronting the same enemy,

declared Zawahiri.[13] Al-Zawahiri then contended that the battle against the US and associated targets would form one dimension of the protest waged by the masses on the ground in the Middle East: 'your brother Mujahideen promise that, by the Help of Allah, they will continue to strike America and its allies and damage them until they leave all Muslim lands.'[14] Al-Zawahiri then linked al-Qaeda's attack on 9/11 with the current Arab Awakening,

> Mujahideen attacked America in her homeland ... and then America was defeated in Iraq and was forced to withdraw. And then it was defeated in Tunisia, losing its agent, then was defeated in Egypt, losing its agent there and then was defeated in Afghanistan. And then it was defeated in Libya, losing its agent there, who joined its war on Islam ... [15]

Despite the absence of a leading role by al-Qaeda in the Arab Awakening, its leadership nevertheless view events through their own ideological prism, and as another link in a chain of attacks against America and the toppling of local regimes. As al-Zawahiri argues,

> The media loyal to America falsely claims that Al-Qaeda's strategy of [armed] conflict with the regimes has failed. This media is forgetting that Al-Qaeda, and most of the jihadi movement, concluded 15 years ago that conflict with the regimes should be abandoned, and that focus should be placed on attacking the leader of global villainess. Thanks to this strategy, America, especially after the 9/11 attacks, ordered the Arab regimes to increase their pressure on their peoples and on their oppositions. This helped trigger popular action and anger, leading to the eruption of a massive storm.[16]

The post-revolution phase is then 'claimed' by ideologues like al-Zawahiri as a step on the path to the establishment of Islamic states. Moreover, he warns Muslims not to let the Arab Awakening be for any other goal:

> O' freeborn and noble people in Tunisia, Egypt and all over the Islamic world! We salute you for your resolution, your steadfastness and your sacrifices! However, the path to the liberation of our nation from its prison-guards and invaders is a long one. Be extremely cautious that your sacrifices are not stolen, that your suffering is not used by others, and that outer appearances change, but injustice and servitude continues to exist.[17]

In reality such warnings are challenged by the post-revolutionary or post-revolt transition stage unfolding in Tunisia, Egypt, Libya and

Yemen where Islamists have become intrinsic parts of the unfolding constitutional and democratic process. By way of reply, jihadi ideologues have consequently developed two responses: the first to claim successful revolts as part of the same jihadist aims. Such claims are epitomised by jihadi ideologue Ahmed Bawadi, who has urged Muslims to turn their protests into a true jihad under the banner of Islam led by true *muja-hideen*: 'These revolutions and their people will not recover Palestine, nor will they take the place of jihad and the mujahideen and expel the invaders and conspirators from Afghanistan, Iraq and Somalia.'[18] The second response is to critique the 'other' Islam. Bawadi exhibits this strategy when he complains about institutional Islam and its weak role in leading the Arab Awakening and its preoccupation with official rulings and fatwas. Such revolts, he counters, must be directed to jihad and for no other purpose. The issue in terms of the jihadi response to the Arab Awakening is the non-violent, mass-based, populist route that it has taken. As such it is the antithesis of their particular interpretation of jihad as a means to transform the political structures of the Muslim world. In this respect these Islamic fundamentalists have failed to make the Arab Awakening and popular mobilisation of millions of Muslims into their own Islamist project.

Manifestation

One perhaps startling manifestation of the Arab Awakening since its outbreak in Tunisia in December 2010 is how little it initially had to do with the politics of Islamic fundamentalism and the preoccupations of the West with the Islamist threat in the years since 9/11. The Orientalist trope of a region defined by bearded fanatics and their jihadi cultures of anti-Westernism was absent in the images projected of the rebellions that unfolded in Tunisia, Egypt, Libya, Bahrain, Yemen, Syria, Jordan and elsewhere. The images on television and computer screens were in fact very ordinary, prosaic and all-too relatable; of people not like 'us' who wanted freedom and democracy. There were no mobs filmed in Arab capitals burning American flags or hoisting effigies of the American president. The Arab Awakening was taking place in the name of freedom and democracy, not jihad. Nevertheless, Islamists are playing an important part in the politics of transition. They are proving to be the electoral victors and such outcomes have caused disquiet in Western capitals. Yet the success of political parties formed by the Muslim Brotherhood in Tunisia and Egypt is explicable for reasons which have little to do with radical jihadi agendas and more to do with the politics of opposition and the resonance of their Islamic fundamentalist discourses. Hence Islamic fundamentalism is a reflection of a process of identity formation that touches on symbols which are centuries old, but lie in the broader processes of Islamic resurgence apparent in the latter part of the twentieth century. This is an acculturated identity which has been formed in the secularised context of the post-independence states of the Middle East, and reflects the impact this has had on the identity agenda. Hence the apparent appeal in favour of the Turkish accommodation between Islamic fundamentalism and secular politics rather than the theocratic dispensation of post-revolutionary Iran. In Turkey, as opposed to Iran, Islamic fundamentalists work in a democracy alongside secularists, and power-sharing has led to a government led by Islamist AKP leader Recep Tayyip Erdogan as prime minister. This approach has also led to economic and foreign policy dividends.

What is further apparent is that since December 2010 the Arab Awakening has also had different trajectories across the Middle East and with it that of Islamic fundamentalism. In North Africa, the Maghreb, transition has taken place. Revolts and revolutions have been successfully mounted and achieved. There are some superficial similarities between the outcomes in Tunisia, Egypt and Libya – tyrants have been toppled – yet even here the similarities end for one is dead, one exiled and the third tried in a Cairo courtroom. The notion of national cohesion in all three states may be strong but there are the concerns of minority groups including the Copts in Egypt and tribal groups in Libya to be taken into consideration in the newly emergent political dispensations. Islamists have enjoyed electoral success and accession to power in Tunisia and Egypt, but not unchallenged and not without the realisation that they have to hold or share power with other embedded political factions such as the military in Egypt or secular leftists in Tunisia. And in Libya, the Islamic fundamentalists in the Muslim Brotherhood, the Libyan Islamic Fighting Group (LIFG) and jihadis played their role in the revolt against Gaddafi but have yet to emerge as a major political grouping in the transition. In the first free elections in more than 40 years held in July 2012, an alliance led by secularists beat Islamist rivals, breaking the Islamist 'wave' apparently sweeping across the region in the aftermath of the Arab Spring. Closer as antecedents of al-Qaeda than the Muslim Brotherhood, Libya's Islamist political parties found that they did not resonate with the newly liberated electorate.

In the Lebanon, Syria and Jordan the Arab Awakening has yet to be fully realised in the transition from tyranny to any new political dispensation. In Syria the role of Islamists has been manifest in the many varieties of rebel forces now emergent. Furthermore, a post al-Assad Syria is bound to be characterised by the deep sectarian and ethnic divisions now emerging, and this may lead many to question whether Islamists can play a role in forging a vision of civic peace which unites the country. Syria's neighbours are not unaffected by rebellion and revolt even if it is by degrees compared to the battles taking place in Damascus, Aleppo, Homs, Deraa and Hama. The delicate sectarian balance in Lebanon, the growing political chasm in Jordan between Hashemite-ruled and ruler and the mounting crisis of credibility in the Palestinian arena, lead increasingly to predications of versions of an Arab Awakening being played out in such contexts. In each, Islamic fundamentalists can play an important role.

In the Gulf states, the portent of an Arab Awakening or popular mobilisation is not lost on this region's rulers nor on those who regard the area as of critical importance to global energy supplies. In Bahrain the risings of 2011 showed the vulnerabilities in the country's political system, and its reliance on external elements such as the Gulf Cooperation Council's (GCC) Peninsula Shield Force to quell the uprising. This may incline one to view the Bahraini monarchy as unable to remain resilient solely by using its own means. This same reliance may lead one to believe that in linking the *Shi'a* majority uprisings to events in Iran, the ruling *Sunni* elite is pandering to concerns both in the West and among the other *Sunni* ruling families in the Gulf. In Yemen, total state collapse was averted again as a result of GCC political intervention as a means of containing Yemeni instability within the country's borders. The role of Islamic fundamentalists in the majority of Gulf states has been severely curtailed in terms of the dynamics of opposition politics and responses based on the kinds of demands for freedom, democracy, an end to corruption, political and economic reform that has echoed elsewhere in the region. Yet there are predictions that sooner or later even the nominally resilient and stable regimes of Gulf monarchies in countries like Saudi Arabia, Qatar or Kuwait will succumb to the tidal demand for freedom and dignity which has epitomised the Arab Awakening. If they do, the ways in which they do so will inevitably incorporate dimensions of Islamic fundamentalism.

Direction

Thus there is a weakness that has been exposed by the people's revolt across the Middle East, and it exposes and challenges Islamism too. For decades the Islamists promised that 'Islam is the solution' and that their agendas could tackle the major socio-economic and political grievances of the people of the region. They promised also that their struggle had a transcendent quality that could unite the Muslim *umma* in jihad to obtain their objectives, whether it was for an Islamic state in Egypt or the end of Israel's occupation in Palestine. Such promises remained largely untested. When Islamists have won power through electoral contest in places like the West Bank and the Gaza Strip, so exceptional have been the circumstances and so formidable the resistance to the notion of Islamist governance that it has been difficult to discern whether this is a success or not. In Tunisia and Egypt it is still too early to judge whether Islamists will monopolise the transitional governance project, but to date resistance has been successfully mobilised when such attempts have been perceived. In Egypt in November 2012 when President Mohammed Morsi of the Muslim Brotherhood issued a decree stripping the judiciary of its right to challenge his decisions, widespread and vehement popular protest led him to quickly cancel it. In Yemen the transition is still far too tenuous to calculate the place that Islamists might occupy in the newly emergent and yet-to-be-negotiated political dispensation. By 2013, amid fears that the president could not integrate the South into a national dialogue, the political transition in Yemen was regarded as fragile. If the transition president, Abed Rabbo Mansur Hadi, fails to integrate the South into the national dialogue, the country could descend into chaos. Elements loyal to Saleh remain powerful in Yemen and the threat from radical jihadi elements such as AQAP and other elements to the overall security of the state remained viable in terms of balancing stability and transition. The power vacuum of revolution in Yemen creates an opportunity for AQAP to embed its positions in Yemen. President Hadi has remained tied to US counter-terror measures which proved deeply unpopular under President Saleh. In 2012 the US increased drone strikes on Yemen and in September that year President Hadi publicly endorsed the US measure. Yet other Islamists remained determined to contribute to what kind of Yemen will emerge from the transition. Their agendas also are altered and determined by wider issues pertinent to the Yemen transition such as the extent to which the South can be persuaded to abandon secessionist ambitions. Even though the Islamists (Islah Party) form the largest opposition party in Yemen and enjoy influence over President Hadi, they too rely on tribal, military and religious bonds to manoeuvre and implement their political agenda.

In should be noted that an important yet often overlooked dimension of the Arab Awakening is that most of the region's jihadi groups, including al-Qaeda, had actually created a disconnection with the very constituency they claimed to represent and broke the domestic link with the local political and economic struggles of the peoples of the

Middle East. The Arab Awakening demonstrated this. The impact of jihadi violence and terrorism in the region only added to the domestic tyranny and militarisation that most citizens of the region were forced to endure. This was particularly true of the post 9/11 era when the states in the Middle East employed counter-terrorism and security measures as a means of suppression and denying the rights and freedoms which subsequently motivated millions to mobilise in the rebellions that have characterised the Arab Awakening. Of course there are other factors which account for this seismic change in the region, but the point here is that jihadi violence against the citizens of the region created the excuse for the employment of hegemonic power utilised by the state to again target such citizens and deny them their rights.

In terms of an effective response to the Arab Awakening it is apparent that jihadi elements like al-Qaeda and its offshoots in AQIM, and AQAP and the nascent Syrian offshoots can only bank on the failure of the transition across the region. Where states fail, become fragile and the transition is neglected or loses momentum, such elements will be prepared to exploit the situation. The transition heralded by the Arab Awakening, however, will by necessity be a long and complicated affair and the effects will not only be domestic but clearly have strategic region-wide and international implications as well. Political elites in wealthy Gulf states will not only reflect on events (and contribute to them) in neighbouring states such as Yemen or Bahrain in determining their national security agendas, but will look at and seek to input and influence events in Jordan, Syria, Egypt, Libya, Algeria and beyond.

Islamic fundamentalists are playing a role in making new constitutions, in national dialogue processes, in tackling economic crisis and chronic social problems, in forming political parties in emerging plural polities, and in joining transitional governments, entering legislative assemblies and parliaments for the first time. They are also engaging in new alliances and power-sharing with traditional state elites such as the military as well as secularists, which has major repercussions for the political landscape of the entire region and hence for the ways in which Islamic fundamentalism more widely is understood and perceived. The assassination, in February 2013, of the well-known Tunisian politician and critic of the Islamists, Chokri Belaid, was a startling reminder that such processes of alliance and power-sharing will be punctuated by instability and even setbacks.

The durable strain between Islamic fundamentalist demands for Islamic states and the moderate aspiration to be part of plural political systems that accept Islam, is yet to be resolved in the unfolding transition in countries like Tunisia and Egypt. It is yet to be outworked in reforming states such as Jordan and Morocco, and is far from apparent in predicting the future of Syria post-al-Assad. Yet there are domestic challenges for power-holders from Riyadh to Rabat in response to this particular dimension of the Arab Awakening. Furthermore, for state actors with regional clout or ambition for influence, the ways in which they navigate the support of such demands under the new dispensation will affect their power and claims to legitimacy. Saudi Arabia, for example, in the past has supported fundamentalist *salafi* and jihadi elements across the Middle East. In a parody of that support in Radu Mihaileanu's film *The Source*, released in 2012, the battle of the sexes in a North African village pokes fun at the apparently Saudi-inspired young imam, who seeks to replace the older wiser indigenous village-based preacher who views the Islamic dimension of this 'battle of the sexes' more compassionately. The young imam, who seeks to impose a fundamentalist edict on the situation, is not only outsmarted and rejected by the villagers but also by his mother who ultimately rejects him as the son she does not recognise. The analogy may well be lost on Saudi political elites even when their regional rivals, including other Gulf states such as Qatar and Iran, manoeuvre to influence, ally and support the reformists and moderates epitomised by the Muslim Brotherhood. Although the Muslim Brotherhood and the leaders of Saudi Arabia are fellow *Sunni* co-religionists, dimensions of the emancipation agenda of the Brotherhood and decades of ideological rivalry, indirectly challenge the legitimacy of al-Saud rule and legitimacy. Egypt remains tied to Saudi aid and support yet the opportunity for power associated with the ascendance of the Muslim Brotherhood means it also emerges as a regional rival to Riyadh. Dimensions of thinking within the Muslim Brotherhood lie at odds with the Wahabbi doctrines of Islamic fundamentalism of Saudi Arabia. In part tension centres on the extent to which the elite control Islam through the institutions of the state (as they do in Saudi Arabia) or are in active opposition to elite rulers and an actor in the discourse over Islam and democracy, as the Muslim Brotherhood is.

Radical Islamic fundamentalists such as al-Qaeda remain tied to their own violence-based ideologies in a new era of what is portrayed broadly as a populist-based non-violent activism. Al-Qaeda's threat within the region is concurrently reduced but certainly is not eradicated. The threat, moreover, of al-Qaeda cells moving into zones of instability, whether in Egypt–Sinai–Gaza, Yemen, Libya or elsewhere in the Maghreb, is still signalled as a possibility. This was highlighted in January 2013 when the AQIM offshoot led by Mokhtar Belmokhtar embarked on the kidnap attack on the gas production plant in Algeria. Its threat to the West, however, conversely may yet grow. For this is a movement that signifies itself by rejection and an appeal to the disenfranchised and the disaffected.

Notes

1 J. Gonzalez, 'One man sparks changes in Tunisia', *New York Daily News*, 30 December 2011, http://articles.nydailynews.com/2011-12-30/news/30574711_1_street-protests-president-zine-anti-government-protest

2 M.A. Atassi, 'What the people want … ' in L. Al-Zubaidi (ed.) *People's Power in the Arab World*, Berlin: Heinrich Böll Stiftung, 2011, p. 28.

3 M. Lynch, *The Arab Uprising: The Unfinished Revolutions of the New Middle East*, New York: Public Affairs, 2013.

4 L.E. Miller and J. Martini, 'The regime transition in Tunisia and emerging challenges', chapter 4 in *Democratization in the Arab World*, Washington, DC: Rand Corporation (July), 2013; and A. Stepan, 'Tunisia's transition and the Twin Tolerations', *Journal of Democracy*, 23:2, 2012, pp. 89–103.

5 T. Ramadan, *The Arab Awakening: Islam and the New Middle East*, London: Allen Lane, 2013.

6 L. Noueihed and A. Warren, *The Battle for the Arab Spring: Revolution, Counter-Revolution and the Making of a New Era*, New Haven, CT and London: Yale University Press, 2012.

7 POMEPS, 'Jordan forever on the brink?', POMEPS, 9 May 2012, http://pomeps.org/2012/05/arab-uprisings-jordan-forever-on-the-brink.

8 M. Zahid, *The Muslim Brotherhood and Egypt's Succession Crisis: The Politics of Liberalisation and Reform in the Middle East*, London: IB Tauris, 2012.

9 A. Bawadi, 'Revolutions are no substitute for jihad', 17 September 2011, http://ansar1.info/showthread.php?t=36003 accessed 18 September 2011.

10 Ibid.

11 See: H.H. Khondker, 'Role of the new media in the Arab Spring', *Globalizations*, 8:5, 2011, pp. 675–79.

12 See: Scott Shane, 'In message, Bin Laden praised Arab revolt', New York Times, May 18, 2011.

13 See: www.tawhed.net/dl.php?i=1011111a accessed 25 November 2011.

14 See: www.tawhed.net/dl.php?i=1011111a accessed 25 November 2011.

15 See: www.shamikh1.info/vb/showthread.php?t=131124 accessed 28 October 2011.

16 See: http://shamikh1.info/vb/showthread.php?t=126930 accessed 28 October 2011.

17 A. Al-Zawahiri, 'Message of hope and glad tidings to our fellow Muslims in Egypt', 28 March 2011, www.tawhed.net/r.php?i=1510111j accessed 31 October 2011.

18 A. Bawadi, 'Revolutions are no substitute for jihad', 17 September 2011, http://ansar1.info/showthread.php?t=36003 accessed 18 September 2011.

8 Conclusion

> Rather than looking to an illusive future we would do better to turn
> to the past.
>
> (John Gray)

In the wake of 11 September 2001, when members of the radical
fundamentalist al-Qaeda launched their terrifying attacks on America,
many pundits in seeking to make sense of what had happened drew a
historical parallel with the Japanese attack on Pearl Harbor in 1941.
The attack brought America into the Second World War, and ultimately
a victory against the Germans and Japanese. Not since 1945, they
argued, had America been so directly targeted in a callous act of war.
In 1941 President Roosevelt spoke of 'infamy' and called the American
people to declare a state of war against those responsible for an
'unprovoked and dastardly attack'. In 2001 President Bush also called
for a war, on terrorism, and drew stark terms in a fight portrayed as one
of good against evil – 'Every nation and every region now has a decision
to make ... Either you are with us, or you are with the terrorists', he
declared shortly after the attacks.

The Islamic fundamentalists in wreaking havoc on America had
appeared, almost at a stroke, to put the whole globe out of kilter. The
attacks had 'changed everything'. The security of the entire state order
appeared to be imminently threatened by the Islamic fundamentalists
led by Osama Bin Laden. The palpable fear was that 'evil' might
triumph over 'good', 'Islam' symbolised by al-Qaeda would threaten
the established foundation of 'modern secular society'. It was feared
that intelligence failures of the grandest scale had allowed the extremist
'network' controlled by Bin Laden to attack and undermine the most
potent symbols of American (Western) power in the world. The USA
had been humiliated by 11 suicide bombers who in turn had been

despatched by their leader, who was holed up in the least developed country in the world – Afghanistan.

Challenges of the past and present

In this book I have looked at the challenges that have confronted Muslims for more than 60 years. These challenges have stemmed from the vast changes that have beset Muslim countries across the globe – often (though not always) as a result of the impact of Western ideas, projects and political domination. Most conservative explanations of the fundamentalist phenomenon in Islam, however, ignore this explanation. Muslims are blamed for their own failings and the failure of their societies. The role of the West was signified merely as 'quiet indifference' rather than the relentless expression of a foreign policy agenda designed to facilitate the national interest of Western states above all others. In some cases the challenges have been met head-on with Islamic opposition and even revolution. In all that time, however, Islamic fundamentalism – however it is defined – has remained dynamic.

Thirty years after the revolution in Iran, Islam is still perceived as a radical and militant form of threat. In the popular psyche of the West it now appears that Islam has replaced the menace of Cold War communism and 'Reds under the bed'. Yet in the 1970s and 1980s the threat of a nuclear Armageddon waged by the Soviet rulers of Moscow did give rise to the same fears, passions and policy approaches in the West. In this sense the demands of the 'here and now' and a culture of fear obscure historical depth and perspective.

This altered perspective means that the phenomenon of Islamism manifest in Muslim communities across the globe can only be understood in narrow, stark and fundamentally frightening terms. This narrow view means that the transformations that have occurred within Islamism are simply not seen as relevant. Yet, in truth, al-Qaeda is not a synonym for modern Islamism but, increasingly as the Arab Awakening also demonstrates, is its internal nemesis. The majority of Islamists in the latter part of the twentieth century and the first decade of the twenty-first century were and remain preoccupied with prosaic and mundane politics internal to their own states and societies. They do not advocate a war against or with the West, their leaders do not issue clarion calls to Muslim followers to launch a jihad against presidents or prime ministers of Western states. They do, however, advocate change within their own societies. Since December 2010 some of that change has been achieved in revolts and revolutionary movements that have swept the Middle East. These Muslims and Islamist leaders call for justice, liberty and a political order based on their interpretation of the holy scriptures of Islam as a political framework for modern society and governance.

Where these leaders and figures do threaten the West is in their ability to expose the clear double standards that have appeared to operate between Western pronouncements on freedom, justice and democracy and the actions of Western states in their dealings with the Muslim world. Muslim leaders instead are powerful social agents for change in civil society, often among a citizenry that has been abandoned by the state and left to its own devices when it comes to basic human demands for food, shelter and water. Moreover, the leadership of such states have been exposed by the Islamists for their all too cynical exploitation of Islam in order to establish their legitimacy and undermine the Islamic opposition.

Same tune, new lyrics

What is apparent from the past 60 years, however, is that Islamism has also produced new offshoots and elements that, although small in number and at the fringe of Muslim societies, represent a radical attempt to undermine the house of Islam. This radical element within Islamism adheres to dimensions of the definition of fundamentalism that centre on religious idealism, cosmic struggle, demonising the opponent, reactionary thinking, and envy of modernist hegemony. They do not so much as propose the revolutionary overthrow of power (for this implies a popular base of support) but promote an almost Islamo-nihilist destruction of the structures of established authority and order through vanguard jihadism. Such elements are anti-state because for them the modern state is nothing more than a corruption and pagan structure (*jahilli*) – even in Muslim countries. As a very modern phenomenon these elements push at the boundaries of religious revivalism and fundamentalism acting in a cult-like fashion. It may be said that they are embodied by al-Qaeda and other smaller *jihad-salafii* elements such as al-Qaeda in the Islamic Maghreb (AQIM), Boko Haram and Mujao. They do not, however, constitute a movement that is understood by Muslims themselves as representative of modern Islamism or fundamentalism. This majority of Muslims even find themselves in the cross-hairs of the jihadi elements. The strategic dimension of this phenomenon, however, as an argument that this has undermined global security, gives rise to fears in the West that these elements are in fact the torchbearers of a billion angry Muslims. A new form of international terrorism in Muslim guise has given rise to what appeared in the post 9/11 era to be an unprecedented shift in the policy of Western governments in the spheres of security and foreign policy. While there have been some shifts of gear in Western policy, including withdrawal from Iraq and Afghanistan, there are still a number of important Western European and North American governments disposed to concern over the threat that radical jihadi elements pose to their shores.

The desires by Islamic fundamentalists to bring about the establishment of Islamic governance in the modern age were convincingly equated with the goals of the Islamo-nihilists. They have been seen as one and the same thing because the end goal is assumed as being the same: an Islamic state and resurrected caliphate, achieved through the overthrow of current secular orders and systems. As we have seen in this book, however, a great many differences have emerged among fundamentalists in the past 60 years over the goals and means to Muslim governance in the modern age. Since 2010 and the Jasmine Revolution in Tunisia and the Arab Awakening these differences have been accentuated. Movements like the Muslim Brotherhood have consistently advocated a reformist approach, the Islamisation of society and demanded a role for Muslims in government. Such advocates have made clear that Islamism has to remain in tune and step with the demands made of Muslims by the modern condition and not the other way round. They do not all contend that Muslims should be dragged back to a seventh-century recreation of the divine Medinan society established by the Prophet Mohammed. What they do claim, however, is the right to autonomy and independence to interpret their own destiny. In Europe such demands have been actualised through the formation of councils and unions that work to bring religious relevance to a modern society for Muslims. Muslim scholars and religious leaders have taken charge of the debate and how it should be defined. Their views are disseminated in magazines, online services, radio programmes, newspapers and so forth. Elsewhere across the globe Muslim communities and their leaders and activists are seeking to reimpose their perspective on discourse about law, economy, politics, culture, justice, human rights and theories of governance. They do look to Islam for the answers but it is not the case that they always do this in a strictly literalist fashion based on the seventh-century model.

United in opposition

The Islamic fundamentalists have founded movements in opposition to authoritarian and repressive states. The Muslim Brotherhood in Egypt, Jordan, the West Bank and Gaza, and Syria, and the *Jama'at al-Islami* in Pakistan. These elements, and others, have paid a high price for opposition. In Egypt, for example, before the revolution of 2011 which saw the ousting of President Hosni Mubarak, the political activities of the Muslim Brotherhood were barely tolerated by the regime. They remained excluded by the state from the realm of formal politics. Their religious status was exploited as an obstacle to the political by a one-party regime intent on preservation of power. Nevertheless, the Muslim Brotherhood worked for more than 60 years to bring change within the system and not outside it. Because such movements and organisations were deemed anti-democratic, their attempts to work through democratic mechanisms to contest elections for local councils, national legislatures, professional associations and student unions have often been greeted with deep scepticism. In Muslim states their attempts to gain power through legitimate democratic means were for the most part frustrated. This denial is translated as a signal to the communities that the Islamist represents the best – the poor and politically excluded. This is the dimension of modern Islamic fundamentalism that remains the most significant in terms of its potential power as a political movement in contest with and opposition to many Muslim state structures.

The inadequacies of the modern state structure in many Muslim countries have been exposed by contemporary Islamism in relation to the citizenry and their national-based demands and concerns. This has been the case in post-revolt and post-revolutionary states in the Middle East, and in other Muslim majority states where Islamic fundamentalist parties, like the AKP in Turkey, have mobilised to work within the state system to achieve power. This has made the Islamist project a more localised and less transnational product. Islamist leaders, preachers and thinkers have turned their energies to providing a counter-culture to the message of incumbent elites. Their social, economic, welfare and education project remains the springboard of their political activities. And in this way they have demonstrated themselves to be serious rivals for power against state elites who have enriched themselves through corrupt, authoritarian and nepotistic forms of power-holding, not just within politics but over national economies as well. It is at this level of the local that we find the most consistent evidence of a formidable challenge and threat in fundamentalist Islam.

Since 2010 the resilience of such states has been brought into question, for the most part, in the Muslim majority states of the Middle East. Where once only Iran, Afghanistan and Sudan were cited as evidence of the overthrow of power achieved by forms of Islamic fundamentalist mobilisation, a question mark has been raised over the extent to which Islamist forces can overthrow power in other states. In the twenty-first century the new Islamists appear to understand that certain state structures (whether secular-inspired or otherwise) have to be accommodated within new Islamist discourse and interpretations of political power. This is not a signal of a Muslim reformation but rather an incipient recognition of an acculturation with the contemporary historic realities of state and power in the twenty-first century.

Gatekeepers of conservatism

One further reaction to this process, however, has been the emergence of a dogmatic and conservative clique in Muslim societies – the traditionalists who are the self-declared gatekeepers of the moral climate. Such elements have much in common with religious conservatives in other cultures, in their desire to hold up their faith as a social, political and economic code by which they demand society must be governed. The support of such elements for the retrogressive Islamisation of society has turned issues such as women's rights into a battle-zone between them and their enemies. As with other cases – such as the religious conservatives in Israel and the Christian fundamentalists in the United States of America – the extent to which the political leaders of modern states have employed such agendas for their own purposes has given much for secularists to worry about.

In Muslim countries the adoption by certain states of Islamisation as a means of regime maintenance may well have backfired. In 'fighting fire with fire' the leaders of Muslim states throughout the 1970s and 1980s endorsed policies of Islamisation aimed at manipulating and shaping society from above, while the Islamists pushed from below. The consequence of such policies was shown in the public arena where evidence of overt and state-sanctioned Islamism was apparent in changing dress codes, gender segregation in government offices and on public transport, social activities and public programming on the media. Pious kings and presidents were regularly portrayed as the supplicants of Islam rather than their own ambitions for power and wealth.

The public for their part took advantage of any opportunity that such policies offered but otherwise remained unconvinced at the programme of Islamisation from above. Moreover, despite state Islamisation, the state was unable to completely stifle Islamist opposition elements. Their secret presses, recording studios and accessibility to the internet allowed them to continue to produce the pamphlets, sermons and fatwa from opposition leaders that were distributed to their supporters. They understood the state to be Janus-faced, knowing that at the same time that the state endorsed the wearing of the *hijab*, the secret police (*mukhabarat*) were being despatched to imprison their leaders and activists.

Muslims and modernism

Since 1945 Islamic fundamentalism, as a political force, has become a central feature of the political arena of most modern Muslim states. Attempts by others who oppose the Islamists to repress and eradicate them have been successively thwarted. The phenomenon can no longer be simply wished away. The decision to ignore and place this force on the margins of modern political life has also given rise to extreme elements that have employed terrible violence and terrorism to highlight their cause and hasten their goals.

Instead it is better to understand, as history has demonstrated, that Islamic fundamentalism should be defined as a modern phenomenon. It is representative of the modern condition in its diversity, its terms of popular reference, its means and methods, and even its extremes. The transnational dimension is emphasised by the concurrent globalist discourse that has emerged since the end of the Cold War, but cognisant also of a past where the notion of territorial borders was always transcended by the wider Muslim community (*umma*). All this implies is that Islamic fundamentalism since 1945 should be recognised as a rapidly moving target for analysis and understanding.

Glossary

Allah The Arabic word for God that all Muslims use.
Allahu Akbar God is Great.
Ayatollah *Shi'a* religious leader.
caliph Successor to the Prophet Mohammed.
caliphate The institution of Islamic government after Mohammed.
dawla The state.
din Religion.
fatwa A religio-juridic verdict or counsel issued by a religious scholar.
hadith Commentary and report of the Prophet Mohammed.
Hajj Annual pilgrimage to Mecca, one of the five pillars of Islam.
hijab Headscarf worn by women.
hijra The emigration of Prophet Mohammed and his followers from Mecca to Medina.
ijtihad Independent reasoning, or interpretation with regard to religious issues.
ikhwan Brethren.
imam The leader of prayers in the mosque.
Islam Submission or surrender to Allah.
jahiliyya Originally total pagan ignorance during pre-Islamic era. Used in the contemporary era to characterise all societies not considered genuinely Islamic.
jihad Exertion, striving, struggle by all means, including military.
Kaba Shrine in Mecca.
kadi (Qadi, Qadhi) Muslim judge of *shari'a* law.
kufr Denotes a non-Muslim, employed as a hostile term by many Islamists.
madrassa Religious place of learning.
majlis Council.
majlis al-shura Consultative council.
mufti Muslim legislator.

mujahid   Fighter for Allah in jihad. Plural *mujahideen*.

mullah   Local religious leader.

Muslim   Follower of Islam.

salafi   Relates to the example and inspiration of the Prophet Mohammed and the four rightly guided caliphs. Fundamentalist in inspiration.

shahadah   Profession of faith.

shari'a   Islamic law.

Shi'a   Party of Ali, followers of Ali.

shura   Consultation.

Sufi   Mystical Islam.

sunna   The sayings and actions of the Prophet Mohammed.

Sunni   Majority followers within Islam.

tahwid   Muslim concept of unity or oneness.

tariqa   Path, reference to Sufi brotherhood.

ulama   Scholars or people trained in religious sciences.

umma   Community.

usulia   Fundamentalist.

Wahabbism   Puritan trend in Islam founded in seventeenth-century Arabia and the foundation stone of religious doctrine in modern Saudi Arabia.

zakat   Tax for raising dues for the poor, one of the five pillars of Islam.

Bibliography

Abu-Jabar, F. *The Shi'ite Movement in Iraq*, London: Saqi, 2003.

Abu-Rabi, I. 'Christian–Muslim relations in Indonesia: the challenges of the twenty-first century', *Middle East Affairs Journal*, 4:1–2, Winter/Spring 1998, pp. 21–37.

Abu Shaban, Hajj. Interview with author, Deir al-Balah, Gaza, September 1989.

Abu Shanab, Ismail. Interview with author, Gaza, August 2002.

Acharya, A. 'State–society relations: Asian and world order after September 11', in K. Booth and T. Dunne (eds) *Worlds in Collision: Terror and the Future of Global Order*, Basingstoke: Palgrave Macmillan, 2000.

ACLU. 'Civil liberties after 9/11', New York: ACLU Report, 2002.

Ahmad, A. *Islamic Modernism in India and Pakistan 1857–1964*, London: Oxford University Press, 1967.

Ahmed, A.S. *Jinnah, Pakistan and Islamic Identity: The Search for Saladin*, London: Routledge, 1997.

Appleby, R.S. 'Visions of sacrifice (roots of terrorism)', *Christian Century*, 17 October 2001.

Armstrong, K. *The Battle for God: Fundamentalism in Judaism, Christianity and Islam*, London: HarperCollins, 2001.

Atassi, M.A. 'What the people want … ', in L. Al-Zubaidi (ed.) *People's Power in the Arab World*, Berlin: Henrich Böll Stiftung, 2011.

Avineri, S. 'The return to Islam', in W. Spencer (ed.) *Global Studies: The Middle East*, Guildford, CT: Dushkin, 1993 (3rd edn), pp. 167–70.

Ayubi, N. *Political Islam: Religion and Politics in the Arab World*, London: Routledge, 1991.

Barber, B. 'Jihad vs. McWorld', *Atlantic Monthly*, March 1992, pp. 53–63.

Bawadi, A. 'Revolutions are no substitute for jihad', 17 September 2011, http://ansar1.info/showthread.php?t=36003 accessed 18 September 2011

Bin Laden, Osama. 'Declaration of War', 1998. See: www.pbs.org/newshour/updates/military/jan-june98/fatwa_1998.html

Blair, Tony. Address delivered to the Congress of the United States of America, Washington DC, 17 July 2003.

Brown, L. Carl. *Religion and State: The Muslim Approach to Politics*, New York: Columbia University Press, 2000.

Chaliand, G. *Terrorism: From Popular Struggle to Media Spectacle*, London: Saqi Books, 1987.

Chossudovsky, M. 'Who is Osama Bin Laden?', 9 May 2011, http://globalresearch.ca/articles/CHO109C.html

Choueiri, Y. *Islamic Fundamentalism*, London: Pinter, 1990.

——*Islamic Fundamentalism: The Story of Islamist Movements*. London: Continuum, 2010.

Cohen, L. *Broken Bonds: The Disintegration of Yugoslavia*, Boulder, CO: Westview Press, 1993.

Cole, J. *Sacred Space and Holy War: Politics, Culture and History of Shi'ite Islam*, London: I.B. Tauris, 2002.

Cooley, J. *Unholy Wars: Afghanistan, American and International Terrorism*, London: Pluto Press, 2002.

Crenshaw, M. 'Current research on terrorism: the academic perspective', *Studies in Conflict and Terrorism*, 15:1, 1992, pp. 1–11.

Dekmejian, H. *Islam in Revolution: Fundamentalism in the Arab World*, New York: Syracuse University Press, 1995.

Donner, F. *The Early Islamic Conquests*, Princeton, NJ: Princeton University Press, 1981.

The Economist. 'The War on Terror, two years on', 11 September 2003.

Enayat, H. *Modern Islamic Political Thought*, Austin, TX: University of Texas Press, 1982.

Esposito, J.L. *The Islamic Threat: Myth or Reality?*, New York: Oxford University Press, 1992.

——*Unholy War: Terror in the Name of Islam*, New York: Oxford University Press, 2002.

——*The Future of Islam*, New York: Oxford University Press, 2010.

Fadlallah, Ayatollah Mohammed. Interview with author, Beirut, May 2000.

Faruki, K.A. 'Pakistan, Islamic government and society', in J.L. Esposito (ed.) *Islam in Asia: Religion, Politics and Society*, New York: Oxford University Press, 1987.

Fneish, Mohammed (MP). Interview with author, Beirut, August 2002.

Friedman, T.L. 'How trust and shame became weapons of war', *The Age*, 12 January 2004, www.theage.com.au/articles/2004/01/11/1073769450437.html

Gibb, H.A.R. *Modern Trends in Islam*, Chicago: University of Chicago Press, 1947.

Gonzalez, J. 'One man sparks changes in Tunisia', *New York Daily News*, 30 December 2011, http://articles.nydailynews.com/2011-12-30/news/30574711_1_street-protests-president-zine-anti-government-protest

Gray, J. *Al-Qaeda and What It Means To Be Modern*, London: Faber and Faber, 2003.

Haddad, Y. *Islamists and the Challenge of Pluralism*, Washington, DC: Center for Contemporary Arab Studies and Centre for Muslim–Christian Understanding, Georgetown, 1995.

Halliday, F. *Iran, Dictatorship and Development*, Harmondsworth: Penguin Books, 1979.

——*Islam and the Myth of Confrontation: Religion and Politics in the Middle East*, London: IB Tauris, 1996.

Hizb Allah. 'An open letter', *al-Safir*, 16 February 1985.

Hoagland, J. 'Misreading Musharraf', *Washington Post*, 23 May 2002, p. A33.

Hopwood, D. *Egypt, Politics and Society*, London: Allen and Unwin, 1986.

Hourani, A. *Arabic Thought in the Liberal Age, 1789–1939*, Cambridge: Cambridge University Press, 1982.

——*A History of the Arab Peoples*, London: Faber and Faber, 1991.

Human Rights Watch, *Into Harm's Way*, New York: Human Rights Watch, January 2003.

Huntington, S. 'The clash of civilizations?', *Foreign Affairs*, 72:3, 1993, p. 31.

Issawi, C. *An Economic History of the Middle East and North Africa*, London: Methuen, 1982.

Jalal, A. 'South Asia', in *Encyclopaedia of Nationalism*, 2000. www.tufts.edu/ajalal01/Articles/encyclopedia.nationalism.pdf, p. 19.

Juergensmeyer, M. *Terror in the Mind of God: The Global Rise of Religious Violence*, Berkeley, CA: University of California Press, 2000.

Keane, J. 'Secularism', in D. Marquand and R.L. Nettler (eds) *Religion and Democracy*, Oxford: Blackwell, 2000.

Keddie, N. *Sayyid Jamal ad-Din al-Afghani: A Political Biography*, Berkeley, CA: University of California Press, 1972.

Khalidi, R. 'The Arab Spring', *The Nation*, 21 March 2011.

Khondker, H.H. 'Role of the new media in the Arab Spring', *Globalizations*, 8:5, 2011, pp. 675–79.

Kramer, M. 'Hizbullah: the calculus of Jihad', in M.E. Marty and R.S. Appleby (eds) *Fundamentalisms and the States: Remaking Politics, Economies and Militance*, Chicago: University of Chicago Press, 1993.

Kubba, Dr Laith. Interview with author, London, December 2002.

Laclau, E. *Emancipation(s)*, London: Verso, 1996.

Lapidus, I. *A History of Islamic Societies*, Cambridge: Cambridge University Press, 1988.

Lewis, B. *What Went Wrong? Western Impact and Middle Eastern Response*, London: Weidenfeld and Nicolson, 2002.

Lynch, M. *The Arab Uprising: The Unfinished Revolutions of the New Middle East*, New York: Public Affairs, 2013.

Maalouf, A. *In the Name of Identity: Violence and the Need to Belong*, New York: Arcade Books, 2001.

Mansfield, P. *A History of the Middle East*, London: Penguin Books, 1991.

Marty, Martin E. and Scott Appleby, R. (eds) *Fundamentalisms Observed*, Chicago: University of Chicago Press, 1991.

Miller, L.E. and Martini, J. 'The regime transition in Tunisia and emerging challenges', chapter 4 in *Democratization in the Arab World*, Washington DC: Rand Corporation (July), 2013.

Milton-Edwards, B. *Islam and Politics in the Contemporary World*, Cambridge: Polity Press, 2004.

Misra, A. *Afghanistan: The Labyrinth of Violence*, Cambridge: Polity Press, 2004.

Mitchell, R.P. *The Society of the Muslim Brothers*, New York: Oxford University Press, 1969.

Moussalli, A.S. *Moderate and Radical Islamic Fundamentalism*, Gainesville, FL: University Press of Florida, 1999.

Nasrallah, H. *Statement on America*, September 2002, www.islamonline.net/English/News/2002-9/14/article30.shtml

Niblock, T. *'Pariah States' and Sanctions in the Middle East*, Boulder, CO: Lynne Rienner Publishers, 2001.

Noueihed, L. and Warren, A. *The Battle for the Arab Spring: Revolution, Counter-Revolution and the Making of a New Era*, New Haven, CT and London: Yale University Press, 2012.

Patten, C. 'Democracy doesn't flow from the barrel of a gun', *Foreign Policy*, 138, September/October 2003, p. 40.

Peters, R. *Jihad in Classical and Modern Islam*, Princeton, NJ: Marcus Wiener Publishers, 1996.

Pipes, D. 'Same difference', *National Review*, 7 November 1994.

POMEPS, *Jordan Forever on the Brink?*, POMEPS, 9 May 2012, http://pomeps.org/2012/05/arab-uprisings-jordan-forever-on-the-brink

Powell, C. Remarks reported from Department of State briefing, 5 November 2002.

al-Qaradawi, Y. *Secularism*, www.islamawareness.net/Secularism/secularism.html (accessed 14 March 2013).

al-Qassam, Sheikh Naim. Interview with author, Beirut, May 2000.

Qutb, S. *Islam: The Religion of the Future*, Kuwait: IIFSO, 1971.

——*Milestones*, Beirut: Holy Koran Publishing House, 1980.

——'War, peace and Islamic jihad', in M. Moaddel and K. Talattof (eds) *Modernist and Fundamentalist Debates in Islam: A Reader*, New York: Palgrave Macmillan, 2002.

Ramadan, T. *The Arab Awakening: Islam and the New Middle East*, London: Allen Lane, 2013.

Rashid, A. *Taliban: The Story of the Afghan Warlords*, Basingstoke: Pan, 2001.

Roy, O. *The Failure of Political Islam*, Cambridge, MA: Harvard University Press, 1994.

Rushdie, S. 'Yes, this is about Islam', *New York Times*, 2 November 2001.

——*Step Across the Line: Collected Non-fiction 1992–2002*, New York: Modern Library, 2003.

Ruthven, M. *A Fury for God: The Islamist Attack on America*, London: Granta Books, 2002.

Said, E.W. *Culture and Imperialism*, New York: Vintage Books, 1994.

Schwartz, S. 'Defeating Wahabbism', *FrontPageMagazine*, 25 October 2002, p. 1. www.frontpagemagazine.com

Shane, S. 'In message, Bin Laden praised Arab revolt', New York Times, May 18, 2011.

Simes, D.K. 'America's imperial dilemma', *Foreign Affairs*, 82:6, November/December 2003, p. 91.

Simon, S. and Stevenson, J. 'Help the PA push out Hamas', *Wall Street Journal* (European edition), 16 January 2004.

Stepan, A. 'Tunisia's transition and the Twin Tolerations', *Journal of Democracy*, 23:2, 2012, pp. 89–103.

Sullivan, A. 'This is a religious war: September 11 was only the beginning', *New York Times Magazine*, 7 October 2001.

Taheri, A. *Holy Terror: The Inside Story of Islamic Terrorism*, London: Sphere Books, 1987.

Tamimi, A. 'The Origins of Arab Secularism', in J. Esposito and A. Tamimi (eds) *Islam and Secularism in the Middle East*, London: Hurst, 2000, pp. 13–28.

Tibi, B. *Islam's Predicament with Modernity, Religious Reform and Cultural Change*, London: Routledge, 2009.

Tracinski, R. 'A war against Islam', *Jewish World Review*, 30 October 2001, www.newsandopinion.com/1001/tracinski.html (accessed 14 March 2013).

Usmani, M.T. *Islam and Modernism*, Karachi: Darul Ishaat, 1999.

Vatikiotis, P.J. *Islam and the State*, London: Routledge, 1987.

Viorst, M. 'Sudan's Islamic experiment', *Foreign Affairs*, 74:3, May 1995, pp. 45–59.

Volpi, F. (ed.) *Political Islam: A Critical Reader.* London: Routledge, 2011.

Zahar, Dr Mahmoud. Interview with author, Gaza City, December 1989.

Zahid, M. *The Muslim Brotherhood and Egypt's Succession Crisis: The Politics of Liberalisation and Reform in the Middle East*, London: IB Tauris, 2012.

Al-Zawahiri, A. *Message of Hope and Glad Tidings to Our Fellow Muslims in Egypt*, 28 March 2011. www.tawhed.net/r.php?i=1510111j accessed 31 October 2011.

Zubaida, S. *Islam, the People and the State*, London: I.B. Tauris, 1993.

Index